CREATIVITY

─── and ───

MUSIC EDUCATION

CREATIVITY

—————— and ——————

MUSIC EDUCATION

Timothy Sullivan,
Lee Willingham, Editors

Foreword by **Mihalyi Csikszentmihalyi**
and
Lori Custodero

Published by the Canadian Music Educators' Association
as the first in the Biennial Series, *Research to Practice*,
Lee R. Bartel, Series Editor
2002

Canadian Music Educators' Association National Office
Department of Elementary Education,
Faculty of Education
University of Alberta
Edmonton, AB Canada, T6G 2G5

Information on ordering this book may be found at the CMEA
website. http://www.musiceducationonline.org/cmea/index.html

Printed By Britannia Printers,
138 Main Street, Toronto ON Canada M4E 2V8
416-698-7608

Sullivan, Timothy and Willingham, Lee, Editors
Creativity and music education
ISBN 0-920630-11-1

Cover Design: Mel Bartel

Printed and bound in Canada.

About the Editors

Dr. Timothy Sullivan has been at the forefront of music composition and creative music education for fifteen years. He is the recipient of many awards and commissions for his concert compositions, works for opera, ballet and dance. His music has been performed around the world by such groups as *The Dance Theater of Harlem, les Ballets de Monte Carlo* and *The Center for Contemporary Opera*. He has provided seminars and workshops in music creativity for the Canadian Music Centre, Orchestras Canada, The Ontario Arts Education Institute and the Ontario Institute for Studies in Education. He has taught at the Royal Conservatory of Music and the University of Victoria.

Dr. Sullivan lives in Toronto, working as composer, producer and writer. In 2001, his CD label, classXdiscs, released its first recording, *Golden Fire*, to positive critical reviews. In 2001, he was invited to be keynote speaker at the Asia-Pacific Orchestras Conference in Sydney, Australia.

Dr. Lee Willingham is on the faculty of the Ontario Institute for Studies in Education of the University of Toronto, where he prepares prospective music teachers for professional service. Prior to that he was Coordinator of Music for the Scarborough Board of Education. For fifteen years he taught music in Toronto Area High Schools.

He pioneered in the "composer in the classroom" programs with the Canadian Music Centre in the mid 1980's, and since that time, creative problem-solving has been part of his teaching/learning procedures, even when dealing with performing ensembles.

Dr. Willingham is the founder and music director of the Bell'Arte Singers, a Toronto based professional level adult choir. He also guest conducts and provide workshops for performing ensembles, schools, conferences, and festivals throughout North America and Europe.

Dr. Willingham is co-editor of *The Canadian Music Educator*, the professional service journal for Canadian music educators.

CREATIVITY
and
MUSIC EDUCATION

Timothy Sullivan, Lee Willingham, Editors

Contents

Research to Practice

Series Preface

Lee R. Bartel, Series Editor

Thirty years ago, in the spring of 1973, the Canadian Music Educators' Association featured the first research sessions at an annual conference and formed a Research Committee. That marked the growing recognition that there was a need in the music education profession to move from being simply practitioners to include *research* and research findings to inform its *practice*. Research seminars, journals, and books followed. In 1986 the first issue of the *Canadian Journal of Research in Music Education* appeared and was distributed to all members of the CMEA. But, despite the best hopes of the university researchers, few practicing music teachers found the journal and its research contents accessible and relevant. In 2000, the CMEA decided on a bold move – to end publication of the journal and to initiate a new publication series with the mandate of focusing on the connection between research and practice. This new biennial series, *Research to Practice,* also sets as its mission the creation of books on topics of practical relevance to music teachers internationally. Further, each book in this series will feature an international group of contributors.

The first book in this biennial series, *Creativity and Music Education,* exemplifies the goals and intent of the series. Lee Willingham and Timothy Sullivan have brought together a stellar international cast of researchers who have made their knowledge practically relevant. The topic is of great importance in music and arts education around the world. The various perspectives enliven and illuminate the multiple facets of this powerful complex construct – creativity. Welcome to *Creativity and Music Education!* Welcome to *Research to Practice: A CMEA Biennial Series.*

Lee R. Bartel
Series Editor
Chair, CMEA Research Commission

Foreword

Mihaly Csikszentmihalyi and Lori Custodero

Making music has been, all over the globe and since the dawn of time, one of the major ways human beings have expressed their emotional, cognitive, and physical skills. Thus, the making of music comes as close as any cultural activity to what we usually call "creativity." Young children express themselves through spontaneous melodies and rhythms; they improvise with their voices and with objects they turn into instruments. In the preschool years, children freely produce original musical material, and later, compose songs that incorporate both their own tunes and learned music from the culture. But after starting formal schooling, this creative impulse is often supplanted by a perception of music as expert performance, where the goal is to replicate rather than generate.

The focus on creativity as a core component of music education in this volume honours the significance and salience of our original musical experience. In order to ignite the creative potential within students, music educators often find themselves asking older children and adults to rekindle these youthful, dynamic interpretations of music as personally relevant expression, where the model is meant not only to be imitated, but to be transformed.

Creative experiences give us a sense of possibility: we experience the liberating power of someone who can make something out of nothing, whose actions have consequences. Listening to music, playing instruments, singing, and composing all demand full sensory presence, and there is a tacit awareness of our role in shaping each musical moment. In short, creative music making is compelling and enjoyable because it challenges us to define ourselves through our spontaneous actions. What attracts us to music is the chance to realize this creative potential. And realizing the potential is what keeps us engaged, and growing towards ever more difficult performances.

The challenge of creating music is twofold. In addition to making subjective decisions, the creative process requires consideration of the objective framework inherent in the formal properties of an artistic work. Described as "organized sound" by John Cage, music has implicit structure that can be interpreted simply as beginning and end, or as involving more complex patterns such as theme and variations or twelve-bar blues. Additionally, music is identified by certain harmonic, melodic, and rhythmic idioms of the culture. These formal structures and idiomatic tools provide a common ground on which individual musicians are free to play with conventional expectations; they can create a sense of comfort through accessing the familiar, or surprise by substituting the novel for the predictable.

A malleable mix of freedom and control, musical creativity allows for a personal balance between artistic freedom and perceived order – imposed by the structural characteristics of the musical content, and by conscious choices to shape that content. Because we receive aural and oftentimes kinesthetic feedback throughout the process about the outcome of our choices, because we can interpret the idioms and structure of music as guides toward perceptible goals, and because we know that what we do matters, creative music making adds up to one of the most complex and rewarding experiences open to human beings.

Teaching with creativity as a goal changes the nature of instruction in music classrooms. The editors and contributors of this important book have created a mandate for such change through their collective vision of a new musicianship. Multiple voices, spanning the roles of researcher, teacher, teacher/educator, and composer/improviser, tell convincing stories regarding how and why music education might be best practiced.

Changing the nature of instruction requires rethinking curricular design and classroom strategies. The idea of teacher

as sole purveyor of knowledge and skill is no longer adequate; instead, we need to look at teachers as facilitators
who provide tools for students to create musical challenges
for themselves. It is through the active pursuit of relevant
musical challenges – what some authors in this collection
refer to as "mindfulness" – that musicians' skills and knowledge are furthered. Designing experiences which are diverse and inclusive enough to cultivate that pursuit in each
individual requires a high level of creative thinking on the
part of all music educators, those working with children P-
12, as well as those preparing future generations for music
teaching.

Establishing a facilitating environment and empowering individuals are two pedagogical practices commensurate with
valuing the creative process in music education. A third factor emanates from the need to be open to possibilities
manifest in students' creative work and is also reflected in
the discourse presented in this publication. Rather than interpreting musical value based only on a finite, pre-deter-
mined model, teaching and evaluation that honours the
creative process must in some way embrace the unexpected.
When opportunities to pursue student-initiated and stu-
dent-defined moments of creativity occur in classrooms,
there are compelling questions teachers can ask themselves
regarding why and how students make musical decisions.
Recapitulating our musical beginnings, the creative spirit
that infuses such teaching invites a companion spirit of in-
quiry. In this way, the research-to-practice paradigm
becomes a mutually informing path toward developing a
meaningful theory of musical instruction.

Mihaly Csikszentmihalyi
Claremont Graduate University

Lori Custodero
Columbia Teachers' College

Prologue

Creativity and the Problem with Music

Lee Willingham

In teaching music students to be creative, most schools are derelict. "Good" music programs are deemed so, not because their students are excellent problem solvers or creators of new works, but primarily because of polished performing ensembles under the direction of capable and talented "directors" of music.

As arts educators, we lay claim to *creativity* as one of the pillars of our musical educative endeavours. Yet music education, so strongly rooted in performance traditions, has resulted in the virtual absence of creative problem solving processes in its teaching and learning practices.

Elliot Eisner has addressed this problem by suggesting that when taught well, experience in music refines one's qualitative judgment. "Qualitative judgment is promoted as students cope with musical problems. Musical problems are best, but not exclusively, addressed in the context of music composition. Ironically, we have little music composition going on in schools" (Keynote Address, ISME, Edmonton, Alberta, Canada,2002 Unpublished).

The educational reform that has swept the Western World in the decade of the 90's and in the early part of the new century has not helped the cause. This rapid movement of change in schooling has failed to take into account the research that at the very least, points in the direction of identifying causal relationships between music instruction and academic achievement. In fact, the business model that has been applied to education has resulted in a much too crowded learning agenda, forcing music instruction even farther to the margins. Currently, it is difficult, if not impossible, for a secondary school school student in Canada to study music for all four years of high school. In this atmosphere where music education is seriously threatened, it is even more difficult to be innovative...to depart from the comfort zone of past practices.

Music education then, is at a crossroads. Traditionally, within its rehearsal and performance dominated practices, it has provided only limited learning opportunities for creative problem solving, composition, and improvisation.

This book seeks to fill the void that we identify as *creativity in music education*. Along with the fine ensemble and solo work being done in schools, and in addition to the theory and music history being taught, this book promotes a comprehensive music education that embraces creative problem solving, as well as creating, improvising, and composing. Contributing writers who are educators, composers and scholars, have filled the pages of this volume with ideas, models, strategies, beliefs, and most importantly, their own best practices. Seventeen authors from eight countries around the world reveal that they too grapple with the challenges of making music education more than it has been.

The chapters in this book are presented within four sections: *Creative Perspectives, Creative Processes, Creative Pedagogy*, and a *Creative Postlude*. At the risk of over alliterating heading titles, we might consider that collectively, this is a representation of Creative Practice; "part of the ongoing human endeavour to fashion products or carry out projects that are considered novel or unusual" (Gardner, Howard. 1989, *Frames of Mind*). The products and projects that Gardner references are, in this case, music teaching and learning.

Obviously, there are overlaps within the sections. Those providing perspectives on creativity invariably touch on pedagogy. The pedagogues certainly provide perspective, and all of the writers in one way or another deal with process. Almost all of the writers have honoured the theme of this series, *Research to Practice*, and have provided applications that either inform the classroom teacher, or supply ready-to-go teaching strategies.

As you read the chapters, either consecutively, or selectively, you will begin to identify clusters of themes and common ground amongst the writers. My own reading of these authors is no exception. Several key issues reveal themselves in the readings and certain themes consistently recur. While a short introduction such as this is not intended to summarize chapter topics, allow me to nudge the reader in the direction of a few main threads that are woven throughout the writings presented in this book.

The first theme cluster I address is that of the **role of the teacher**. Surely, it is evident to all, that where there are good music programs, there is good teaching. Where there are creative music enterprises in the educational environment, there is a teacher who knows just how much to intervene, how to scaffold the students in a risk taking activity, and when to lay back and let the student's work unfold. This shift in power, from teacher to student, empowers the student to reach her creative potential in an atmosphere where decisions about learning are shared. The teacher's facilitating role is key, and if creativity and music education are important, then this book probes at the very foundations of our music education programs in teacher training. The axiom holds: *we teach the way we were taught.*

The role of the teacher theme segues neatly to a second main point, **the conditions for learning**. Whether it be in a traditional band or choral setting, a wilderness camp, a workshop, or regular classroom, the characteristics of the learning environment are critical. Is this a place where first attempts by young creators are encouraged and honoured? Is a place where self-correction and editing are included in the planning? Is it a safe place, where risk-taking occurs without fear of ridicule or the erosion of self-esteem? Is it a place free of judgment?

Thirdly, I glean from these writings that **teaching and learning creatively is hard work.** All music teaching and learning can be considered to be among the more rigorous of human endeavours, but the reader of these pages gets the sense of struggle, application, and perseverance required to move forward in the creative process. While for Aaron Copland it might have been that composing was as "natural as eating or sleeping", or Saint -Seans who likened the process to an apple tree producing apples, the truth of the matter is that learning to be creative in solving creative music problems, requires a generous dose of applied diligence and energy. Like any other music endeavour, the skills of creativity must be mastered in order to make the practice meaningful.

Music ensembles are frequently regarded to be effective in building **community**. Throughout these pages dealing with music creativity, a sense of communal endeavour is also evident. While composing is essentially a solitary process, so many of the corporate music practices can be and are considered to be creative. As people conceive of new ideas and move the creative process forward together, a powerful sense of *the other* surfaces. This is a community of inclusivity, receptivity, equity, and celebration.

Finally, I address the clustered theme of **diversity**. Seventeen writers have shared in seventeen different dimensions of addressing this common theme, *Creativity and Music Education*. It is most assuring to note that there is not a "right way." I wish I could teach with the magical intrigue of Doug Goodkin, or lead the "walking the tightrope" type of workshops of Peter Wiegold, or conceptualize and write like Peter Webster, or engage in the richly complex and thrilling pedagogical approaches of Veronika Cohen, or foster an interdependent community such as the one Austin Clarkson describes, but alas, I cannot. However, the beauty of this book is, that I can be all of them, to some degree, by seizing this glimpse into their thinking and doing, and enfolding it into my own personal growth and work.

Education that is creative is an education that is prepared for the unexpected. Curriculum that is based solely on achieving fixed outcomes can be guilty of excluding a magnitude of student expressive work. And lest we forget, *this entire volume is ultimately about our students*, and how they can best be served throughout their learning experience in and through music.

Timothy Sullivan admonishes us to return to the "play" in our work, to think in terms of games as a form of social pedagogy. Recently, while browsing through a cooking book, I came upon this..."creating this book has given me the opportunity to do what I love most-- play in the kitchen. I was one of those kids who made mud and snow pies on the neighbours' steps." Is our classroom a place where we can "play" in the true since of that word, or is it a place for only serious work? Do we provide time and place for our students to engage in the playful processes... the making of mud and snow pies with sound?

Since cooking is a love of mine (second only, of course, to teaching music), here is another chef's quote. "Cooking is so joyful! A a chef, I get to please people in so many ways. I want to pass my passion on to you in dishes that reflect so much pleasure."

(Aha! More alliteration!) Play, Passion, and Pleasure... words that enliven our imagination, but, perhaps, words that are infrequently applied to what we deem as "good work" in teaching and learning music. As our students engage in musical problem solving, let us contemplate what this book offers us, and invite these ideas as solutions to the problem of creativity in the music classroom.

Lee Willingham
Ontario Institute for Studies in Education
of the University of Toronto

Section 1: Creative Perspectives

Chapter 1

Creative Education

Doug Goodkin

DOUG GOODKIN is in his 28th year at The San Francisco School, where he teaches music to children between three years old and eighth grade. He is the author of four books: *A Rhyme in Time, Name Games, Sound Ideas* (Warner Bros.) and *Play, Sing and Dance: An Introduction to Orff Schulwerk* (Schott), and is the director of the Bay Area Orff Certification Course at Mills College as well as his own course on Jazz and Orff Schulwerk in San Francisco. He has taught courses in Orff Schulwerk in over fifteen countries worldwide. Doug received the distinguished *Pro Merito* Award for his contributions to Orff Schulwerk in July, 2000.

Every June, the 4th and 5th graders in my school board the bus and travel to the breathtaking coastline of Big Sur, California. For five glorious days, teachers, kids and select parents finish out the year in company with coastal redwoods, gurgling streams and a canopy of stars at night. All the problems the children had within the classroom walls— their struggles with letters and numbers, their messy binders, their unfinished homework, their squabbles with their classmates, their inability to pay attention or work in a group or listen to directions—seem to fly off with the morning breeze. We awake to the squawk of stellar jays fighting over last night's food scraps and go to bed serenaded by owls. In between, we pass long days walking through woods, playing in beaches, cooking on Coleman stoves, and singing around campfires. Life is reduced to its essentials, when watching the way flies meet and move in unison for a brief second before darting apart, observing a millipede crawling or noticing the way rattlesnake grass dances in the breeze may be the event of the day. It is a lovely way to end the school year.

The other 170 days of the year, I teach music to these children and others who range from three years old to fourteen. Most people reading that sentence will conjure up an image of someone teaching the clarinet, violin or piano, someone directing a choir, or someone passing out worksheets filled with quarter notes and major scales. They will imagine music as a subject with its own special vocabulary and set of assessable skills in which children who start off knowing nothing are taught the basics of the craft. If they're generous and had some positive experiences themselves in music, they will acknowledge that music brings enrichment to life and is a nice addition to the school curriculum. If, like so many, they passed through their music classes mouthing the words to songs they didn't like, struggling with the math of eighth notes or endlessly repeating "every good boy does fine," they may see no point in it at all and be the first to vote "cut" when the budget comes in.

My music program is based on the practice of Orff Schulwerk and begins from a startling different premise—that music is more than a subject; it is a quality of being, of doing, of thinking that is inherent in each and every one of us. My job is to release, guide, nurture and cultivate that innate musicality through a wide variety of means—speech, song, movement, folk dance, body percussion, drama, percussion instruments, recorders and specially designed xylophones known as Orff instruments. Though passing on the special vocabulary, specific techniques, assessable skills, key concepts, and traditional repertoires of music will be a necessary part of the program, the core idea is to bring the child's deep need to create out into the world through the vehicle of music.

The dictionary defines education as a twofold process— the first is "the act of imparting knowledge" and the second, "developing the faculty of reasoning and judgment". In the Western musical canon, the composer is at the top of the food chain, for composition (and its companion, improvisation) is the finest way to develop and display musical reasoning and judgment. Carl Orff brought this idea into music education when he summarized his approach with his pithy phrase "Let the children be their own composers". What is true in music is equally true in every subject. In language, the writer is at a higher level than the reader, in math, the problem-maker over the problem-solver, in science, the experimenter who investigates over the student who merely acquires knowledge.

I've titled this article *Creative Education* to attract the reader's attention, but from the start we must see how the two words are redundant. To create is to cause something new to come into being, be it a scientific principle, a poem, a new kind of sushi, an insight into a story or a child. Though a significant part of education is instruction—passing down the useful thinking that has been previously done— the deeper aim is to stimulate further thinking. That requires a creative response to all given material, making something new from what's given. Creativity is not a frill, but the very core of the educational process.

Creative education begins from the premise that creativity is our natural state of being, our primary strategy of adaptation given as a gift to our species. "Fish gotta swim and birds gotta fly" says the old song, but the human strategy is not fins or wings—it is the capacity to invent boats and planes. Rats can learn mazes, dogs can learn to respond to bells, chimps can use tools, but humans, aided by language, thumbs, and a developed neocortex, have the widest range of behaviours. Simply put, the higher up the evolutionary scale, the more plasticity of response. We are blessed with minds that can swing through ideas with as much agility as monkeys through trees. Yet though a monkey's agility is guaranteed by instinct, humans have the capacity to over-ride their natural instincts, neglect, inhibit or repress their creative inheritance. Education is the strategy by which we can ensure that our creative promise is nurtured and cultivated.

Why begin this article with a short description of our camping trip? It struck me that living five days out in nature helped reveal our *nature* as shown in children left to follow their instincts. I noted that some of the faces of creativity that appeared spontaneously in the camp were the same as those I plan consciously in the music class. In the section that follows, I hope to cross-reference camp with class to demonstrate that it is not only possible to formally adapt what we think of as vacation to the school experience, but indeed, it is necessary if we are to take creative education seriously. Though I, like my students, still give a whoop of joy when school ends and summer vacation begins, the difference between the two is increasingly negligible—there is much of the feeling of summer in my schooling and much of

4

the feeling of schooling in my summer. What ties them together is the constant exercise of the creative faculties.

A Day at Camp

So let us wake up with the children, eat a hearty breakfast
and go to morning meeting to discuss the day's activities.
Today is beach day and we gleefully gather our towels and
bathing suits in anticipation of a glorious morning with sun
and surf. Today, however, we are reminded that it is late
Spring in California. When we arrive, the wind is whipping
up the sand and where we imagined ourselves lying about
in baking sun and scurrying into the surf for refreshment,
we now find ourselves huddled against the wind.

The old cliché springs to life — "Necessity is the mother of invention." How do the kids adapt? Some immediately start
digging a big hole to hunker down in. Others discover a
felled tree stump and build a little shelter using their towels. Still others go further down the beach until they find an
outlet that is somewhat protected from the wind. Some
make up a frisbee contest, throwing it with the wind and
pacing off their record, wind-assisted throw. While the
adults complain about their plans being thwarted, the kids
adapt quickly with their fresh creative responses.

When it's time to go, we hike back to camp on paths bor-
dered by poison oak. A group of us begin to sing the old
song "Poison Ivy" (by the Coasters) and immediately set to
work on the California version. Before long, a new chorus
has been invented:
"Poison O- -o-o-o-o-o-oak, It ain't no
jo- -o-o-o-o-o-oke.
Every day when you're walkin',
poison oak will come a stalkin' you
Dow-ow-ow-ow-own."

Once set in motion, the creative process picks up momentum and the first verse emerges.

"Panoramic view (doo-doo-doo-doo-doo)
Wildflowers, too (doo- doo-doo-doo-doo)
You'll start scratchin' like a hound (doo-doo-doo-doo-
doo)
The minute your hiking group has found..."

(CHORUS)

After another verse, we move on to the bridge:

> "The sun it is a-shinin', the kids have stopped their whinin'
> The weather is as perfect as can be.
> No mosquitoes are a-buzzin', we've got cookies by the dozen,
> But poison oak is waitin' there for me."

And so it goes until we have a full-blown song. We will sing the song at the nighttime campfire and it will become a school classic, passed down from one year to the next by the kids themselves. If we hadn't known the *Poison Ivy* song, we might have made up something new, but being given the form, our creative impulses were focused. We took something known and changed into something else that spoke directly to our experience.

Back at camp, we go down to the wind-sheltered stream. Within minutes, the air is filled with shrieks of delight as the kids splash in the icy waters. They revel in the clear running water under tan oak and alder trees, dig their toes into the sandy beach or pick their way over round river stones (perfect for skipping). They emerge from the water seeking bone-warming sun or refreshing dappled shade. The stellar jays and crows squawk overhead, crawdads lurk in the shallows and squirrels skitter up and down the trees. The children are unequivocally happy and doing what children have always done and love to do. They need no instruction in *Stream Appreciation*, no curriculum in *Water Play*, no program in *Being Happy in Nature*. They take to it all like...well, like fish in water. It is their nature to take pleasure in nature and this, too, is part of their creative legacy. As the poet Wendell Berry so eloquently describes it:

> "To be creative is ...to keep oneself fully alive in the Creation, to keep the Creation fully alive in oneself, to see the Creation anew, to welcome one's part in it anew."
> (Berry, Wendell; What Are People For?; Northpoint Press, SF; p. 91)

The children's unabashed delight in the miracles of creation is evident—but there is more. They are not passively appreciating the scene—they are actively engaged in it. Once bodies and minds are set in motion, creativity is not far behind. After a few minutes of simply tossing the ball in the water, they soon invent a game—Stumpball. Two teams and one point for every time the ball hit the side of the tree stump in the middle of the stream, two points for hitting the top. Other kids sit at the edge of the water making sandcastles. Downstream, others are making a little dam with rocks. Some are huddled on the beach making up a poem about the crawdad they saw. Whether working with sand, rocks, balls or language, the children are instinctively creating, this time not for problem solving, but for the sheer pleasure of creation.

Before going to the beach in the morning, we take a silent morning hike. Walking single file up a path through woods that open into a meadow, a teacher at the end of the line comes up the line tapping each child in turn. When tapped, the child sits on the path until the whole line is seated, each child about ten feet from the nearest neighbour. We sit in silence, listening, observing, feeling, dreaming. After ten minutes or so, the teacher comes back down the line to gather the children for the return walk, still in silence. At night, we do it all again, but without flashlights and with a sky of stars visible overhead.

Now it's afternoon and after enough time at the stream, we have a 45 minute "quiet time." The children can read, write, draw, rest or simply sit around in silence. Many begin with their nose in the book and then start to watch the squirrel with the wounded leg or notice the way the leaves swirl when the stellar jays make their landing.

These times to be still and quiet are delicious and contrary to some people's image of children's need for constant movement and stimulation, the children love it. In speaking of zazen meditation, a formal practice of stillness, Zen master Suzuki Roshi makes a profound link with creativity. He speaks of three kinds of creation, as follows:

"The first is to be aware of ourselves after we finish zazen...When we emerge from nothing, when everything emerges from nothing, we see it all as a fresh new creation. The second kind of creation is when you act, or produce or prepare something like food or tea. The third kind is to create something within yourself, such as education, or culture, or art, or some system for our society. So there are three kinds of creation. But if you forget the first, the most important one, the other two will be like children who have lost their parents; their creation will mean nothing." (Suzuki, Shunryu; Zen Mind, Beginner's Mind; Weatherhill, NY/ Tokyo p. 67)

By the end of the day, we will have had three such periods of silence and stillness out in the woods and each one has something different to offer. The poet William Stafford affirms this practice with three pithy statements:

"For a real writer, there are three main ways: morning, afternoon, night."

"Always do your writing in a wilderness."

"Look around, listen. Feel the air." (Stafford, William: Crossing Unmarked Snow; The University of Michigan Press, pp 4/7)

After quiet time, we hike to the ball field and play a game of softball while the adults cook at the barbecue pit. The kids know the rules, take pride in their abilities to bat and field and take pleasure in the team effort. Though the rules are set and the procedures straightforward, there are many spontaneous decisions that must be made—throw to first or second? Run for home or stay on third? Bunt or swing hard? And today, the rules themselves are flexible. Because some kids have not played much, there are no strike-outs. Each batter can choose underhand or overhand pitching. Every one gets a chance to play and every one gets a chance to bat. We keep score and that gives an exciting edge to the game, but no one comes to the barbecue upset because they "lost".

After the barbecue, it's time for that camping favourite, *s'mores* (toasted marshmallows with a chocolate square on top sandwiched between two graham crackers). Kids look for the stick to roast their marshmallow, but like so many moments in the day, this too becomes a ritual.

Twelve kids at a time come up with their sticks and get into two lines facing each other, with six kids in each. To live accordion music, they dance four steps towards each other and tap their sticks three times, return four steps to their place and tap the ground three times, go back into the middle once more and stay there while tapping their partner's stick "tap tap tap tap tap." Standing with the sticks in an arch, the last couple comes through the line where two adults wait poised with marshmallows to put on their sticks. That couple proceeds to the fire to roast them while the dance is repeated.

After s'mores, it's back to camp for the evening campfire. There we share the news of the day, have a a contest for the ugliest flashlight-lit face, watch skits the kids have created and sing songs. Throughout the week, we have sung songs about birds (*Whippoorwill*), local critters (*The Crawdad Song*), forest legends (*The Frozen Logger*), habitat (*The Rattlin' Bog*), water (*The Water Is Wide*) stars (*When You Wish Upon a Star*) and more. Now it's our last night, so we sing a repertoire of songs about going home—*Day Oh, Jamaica Farewell, Sloop John B.* and *Swing Low Sweet Chariot.* When it's dark, it's story time and accompanied by drum, dulcimer and flute, I tell the ancient Greek myth of *Pysche and Eros.* When the story's done, we set off on our nightwalk. After we return to the campfire, the kids go to bed while the adults wander around the campfire singing a good night song. (That tradition of Wandering Minstrels has a new name now thanks to a child's creative mis-hearing—"The Wandering Nostrils.")

The next morning, it's time to break down camp and when all the gear is packed. We make a shoulder-to-shoulder line and walk slowly in step picking up garbage, led by live Bulgarian bagpipe music. When the camp is spotless, we gather one final time for a closing circle of appreciation, thanking the trees, flowers, bugs and birds for their hospitality, the parents for their time, the kids and the teachers for their good work. Another moment of silence, a hand-squeeze passed around the circle, a final group squeeze with raised arms and back to school we go.

Creativity in the School

How do these camp experiences translate to the music class in the school? What do both the camp and the music class have to offer to the greater school experience? In this section, we'll make some connections that hope to reveal how our creative instincts can be nurtured into lifelong creative habits. Our point of reference will be our experience of the day in camp.

• The Windy Beach: The wind at the beach called forth the inventive mind for our own comfort—a low-level survival strategy. The equivalent in music class is the non-negotiable givens of our situation—a schedule, a space, a time frame, a class size and a class chemistry. For more mornings than I care to admit, the sheer fact of kids about to arrive in my room when I hadn't time to plan threw my brain into survival mode—and indeed, some of my most creative classes have come from the spontaneous ideas that erupt 30 seconds before the bell! The Orff arrangements I make are always tailored to a specific class size, a specific class chemistry and a specific class level of musicality. Like Duke Ellington writing for his band, I often write settings with specific children in mind as well. These kind of variables keep the Orff teacher's wheels greased—we can never simply turn to page 33 on Tuesday as we did last year. It is a structure imposed from without that stimulates our creative response.

• The "Poison Oak" song: When my friend Polo Vallejo brought a group of Wagogo musicians from Tanzania to Europe, he noted that they began to sing some new songs he had never heard while living with them in Africa. When he asked about them, they explained that they were making up songs to tell the people back home about their travels. Our instinct to share our stories and tell the news is another powerful stimulant of creativity. (And conversely, I can't help but think that our obsessive documentation via cameras and videocameras contributes to the atrophy of our own creativity!) Our song about poison oak was the same process at work.

In the music class, we will often change the words of games and songs to fit our experience more closely. We may sing the original version of a song like "Head and Shoulders"—"Milk the cow, baby" and then ask the students to make up their own verses based on what they do every day—"Go to soccer, baby," etc..

The *S'more Stick Dance* is a close cousin of this process, re-creating a dance to fit the functional needs of an activity. A close look at traditional dances around the world will show stylized versions of motions present in the daily work or evocative of native animals. Indeed, most cultures don't view creativity as a special talent reserved for artists or self-conscious works of art—it is a practice that prepares, cele-brates and ritualizes the work of survival. By echoing these practices in the camp and music class, we are teaching child-ren that art is not decoration, but a functional way to acti-vate community and mark the events of the day—from toasting marshmallows to singing kids to sleep to cleaning the camp with bagpipe accompaniment.

• Stream time: One day after school, my fellow music teach-er and I were trying out an arrangement on the instru-ments when some kids wandered in from Daycare. They spontaneously chose instruments and started playing with us. The music attracted more kids and for 30 minutes straight, we had a wonderful jam session!

Time to just hang out and jam free from time pressures or worry about the result seems essential to creativity. (Indeed, the revolutionary new languages formed by Charlie Parker and Dizzy Gillespie or Jerry Garcia and the *Grateful Dead* came from such extended "stream time"). Artists in all fields need unstructured time left alone to follow their Muse. They need time to get to the edge—and sometimes, the depths—of boredom until something emerges—which it always will. (Indeed, one of my biggest concerns about today's child is the arsenal of instant stimulation that short-circuits this process).

My ideal school would have several soundproof rooms filled with instruments for kids to just play on without adult guidance. Instead, I offer opportunities inside of the class to create with minimal guidance—setting out drums or scarves or paper plates with some general guidelines for play and exploration, watching the ideas, highlighting some, developing others. Sometimes I simply send kids off to dif-ferent corners of the room with a group of instruments and say, "Make up a little piece." There is a quality of creativity that demands to be left free to see what comes up—and when we trust that something will, it invariably does!

• Quiet time: There is a lovely little children's book called *The Listening Walk*. A little girl tells about all the sounds she hears when she walks with her father around the neigh-bourhood. After reading the book, I often take a listening walk with the children around the school and then we share what we heard at the end. In a similar vein, I sometimes sing a fast song with the kids in which we all stop suddenly at the end—the silence that follows is intensified by the sudden ending and we are often rewarded by delightful surprises. (The one rule is that we ourselves can't make any of the sounds). When we play this game around the campfire, the results are especially magical as we hear the hoot of an owl, the croak of a frog or the drone of the stream.

The musician's job—and joy—is to listen and that is a faculty like any other that can be cultivated and nurtured. We must take time to listen to the music always around us (an idea formalized by John Cage's composition *4:33*) and "quiet time" is a good discipline to that end.

Likewise, we have many listening experiences in class enjoying the classics of jazz and the European art music canon. Sometimes I have the children lie down in a relaxed position—so much of our musical listening is background that the mere act of stopping to listen is a delight.

• The baseball game: If music is an opportunity for individual creative expression, it is equally a vehicle for group expression. Individual voices must blend and create a whole greater than the sum of its parts. That requires teamwork and a sense of collective purpose. In baseball, the team works together to win the game. In music, the team strives to fully express the piece. Both require training, coaching, and much practice, alone and as a group. Both sport and art also require rules. Carl Orff stated clearly that "the imagination must be stimulated," but he also wrote that "opportunities for emotional development, which contain experience of the ability to feel, and the power to control the expression of that feeling, must also be provided." (Orff, Carl; *The Schulwerk*; Schott, NY p. 245) Controlling that expression requires specific techniques and much practice within the boundaries of given rules and this is equally the task of the music program.

If one hand of creativity likes being left alone, the other thrives on limitations and guiding structure. "Make a melody with this rhythm and four notes" might yield more musical results than "play whatever you want and however you feel." Music class is filled with many such structures and the imagination thrives on them, especially as the children get older. Often, the tighter the focus, the more satisfying the result.

Though art and sports both require rules, art needs something a bit different. Break the rules in sport and there will be a fine or penalty. Break the rules in fugue-writing or figurative painting or metered poetry and there may be a breakthrough to a higher level of expression. The rules in art are flexible guiding structures and part of creativity's mandate is to know precisely when to break them. I once invited the children to create a B section to a melody in a given scale. One child asked if he could use Bb, a note not in the scale. I replied that he should stick with the given task. When it came time to play their solutions, he looked at me with a gleam in his eye and played the Bb. During evaluations, I commented, "You really wanted that Bb, didn't you?" He heard something outside of the box and as an artist, trusted his intuition. He got an A in that assignment.

During our camping baseball game, we consciously switched the rules to accommodate beginning players. So too in the music class. Our concern is not winning the competition or grooming the next generation of musical super-stars—we are there to serve the musical promise of every child at their highest level of capability. By removing the fear and anxiety of striking out, the children grow more confident in their ability to hit the ball and get on base. Every child in the school participates in the music program for their entire 11 years there and in all my 27 years there, I have never seen a child graduate who hasn't felt some degree of confidence in their ability to play, sing, dance and improvise.

• The campfire. Finally, we come to the campfire and that's the part of the music program concerned with repertoire. Deciding which songs fit the occasion for each night of camping is the task, but without a large repertoire to choose from, there is little possibility of making a creative choice. By the time they graduate, the kids at my school will have sung well over 100 songs, played at least 50 pieces on the instruments, danced at least 25 folk dances, and acted in eight plays.

The number of students who continue in the performing arts in high school may be slightly higher than those who come from a school with no arts programs, but the comment we receive most often from alumni and alumni parents is how their arts experiences carried over in other ways—giving them confidence to speak in a group, encouraging them to think about things from a different angle, offering them skills to make a rap about Othello in English class or a collage for their history project. Creativity is by no means confined to the arts—indeed, our times require creativity in every endeavor—but the arts are essential to its full blossoming.

Tomorrow's Story

We have already noted that creativity is a vital survival mechanism for human beings. Lacking the speed of the cheetah, the camouflage of the lizard, the agility of the monkey, the strength of the lion, we depend on the imaginative mind to survive. We adapt on the spot to each problem thrown our way—getting food and water, escaping from predators, protecting ourselves from weather—with inventive and creative solutions.

Since the problems keep shifting—from the Ice Age to Global Warming, from Mongol hordes to the McDonald's invasion—we must continue to be creative to adapt and survive. Today's problems are unique as the global village struggles with diminishing resources, global warming, inequitable distribution and the clashing of diverse viewpoints. All of yesterday's solutions—economic growth, military build-up, religious and national loyalty, logging and mining—are now counter-evolutionary. New problems need new solutions and new perspectives. The people best equipped to offer that is the next generation of children— but only if we resist passing on our old prejudices and train them to be creatively facile.

If the children at my school were in charge of the world, Bush and Gore would be co-Presidents and have to work together. The leaders at the Palestine-Israel peace talks would spend some time each day dancing, singing and making up music together. The people cutting down the rainforest would have a quiet time each day where they wrote poetry about the plants and animals around them. These make perfect sense to the children. But the adults stuck in yesterday's patterns can't even dream these possibilities, never mind agree to try them out.

At a time when we need the full range of our creativity, we simply can't afford business as usual, in schools and outside of them. Creative education is not a luxury reserved for the privileged aesthetes, but a necessity for us all. Yet neither schools as they stand nor our present culture are friendly to our creative needs. Knowing that creativity demands time left alone and a certain degree of boredom, we should beware of the remote, the video library, the Nintendo game, the Internet chat room. We should be careful of the five-year old soccer team with uniforms coached by adults, the harried schedule of piano, aikido and PSAT lessons. We should spend less time shopping and more time picnicking in the park. We should call into question both things and practices made merely for efficiency and profit, steer away from fundamentalist and dogmatic ideas, step back from the excessive consumerism, all practices that freeze the creative spirit. Conversely, we should welcome and celebrate anything that unthaws it.

"A good book should be an axe for the frozen sea within us" wrote Kafka and reading good literature and poetry, listening to good music, watching good dance, viewing good art and eating good food is not a bad way to start. But don't stop there—write poetry, make music,cook meals sing songs, paint pictures and dance! And don't worry if it's good or saleable or aesthetic. Sometimes the mere act of creating is enough.

I came home from camping with my spirit refreshed and my hope for humanity restored. For a brief moment, I could read the newspaper and see every story as yesterday's news. The real story, tomorrow's story, took place by a little stream in Big Sur, California, where the creative spirit ran as clear as the running water, fanned by a fragrant breeze and sung by the voices of birds and children at play.

Chapter 2

Creative Thinking in Music: Advancing a Model

Peter R. Webster

PETER WEBSTER is the John Beattie Professor of Music Education and Music Technology at Northwestern University. He holds degrees in music education from the University of Southern Maine (BS) and the Eastman School of Music at the University of Rochester (MM, PhD). Prior to Northwestern, Webster taught in the public schools of Maine, Massachusetts and New York and was on the faculty at Case Western Reserve in Cleveland, Ohio for 14 years. His published work includes articles on technology, perception, preference, and creative thinking in music. His writings have appeared in Psychomusicology, Journal of Research in Music Education, Contributions to Music Education, Council for Research in Music Education Bulletin , Arts Education and Policy Review, and in journals outside the field of music. Webster is co-author with David Williams of Experiencing Music Technology, 2nd edition, the standard textbook and CD used in introductory college courses in music technology. He is writing a new book on music composition in the schools with the music education doctoral students and faculty at Northwestern.

When the history of music education in North America is written many years from now, the time period represented by the end of the 20th century and the beginning of the new millennium might well be remembered as a critical point in the profession's history. It will be noted that practical, theoretical, and research-based writings focused attention on *both* product and process in the teaching and learning of music. In addition to the nurturing of fine solo and ensemble performances, a more comprehensive approach to music education is now emerging which embraces the study of composition, improvisation, music listening, cultural context, and relationships to other arts. In the United States, this trend began in the sixties with the Comprehensive Musicianship Project and the Manhattanville curriculum project and continued with the Yale, Tangle-wood, and Ann Arbor symposia in following years .

In more recent times, the National Voluntary Standards in the Arts (1994) have come to mark a more comprehensive approach. In other countries such as the United Kingdom and Australia, attention to music composition and improvisation as curricula foci have been long established. It is clearly the case that no longer can a music teacher expect to be successful by only teaching children how to perform the music of others, paying little attention to the development of aesthetic decision-making and musical independence of students.

Within the scope of educational philosophy, constructionist views of teaching and learning prevail. Although not really new to educational theory with roots that can be traced to Piaget and Dewey, constructionistic thinking has been given focus in writings on school reform (Gardner, 1991, 1999). The basic goal of constructionism is to place emphasis on creativity and to motivate learning through activity. Learning is seen as more effective when approached as *situated in activity* rather than received passively (Kafai and Resnick, 1996). At the heart of these ideas is the shift away from thinking about education as being centred solely in the mind of the teacher and more as partnership between teaching and student with the teacher as the major architect of learning. Project-centred learning is celebrated with students working to solve problems. Affect is seen as part of and as an aide in the learning experience. The teacher assumes more the role of a "guide on the side" as opposed to a "sage on the stage."

Another critical contextual issue in music education is the powerful presence of music technology as an aid to instruction and the support given to music teaching by Internet resources (Williams and Webster, 1999). Notation, sequencing, and digital audio software running on powerful, affordable personal computers provide important resources for music education practice and research. Specially written software packages designed to encourage composition and improvisation are now readily available for use in schools and at all levels of instruction. Internet resources serve as an increasing rich reservoir for teachers to challenge students to solve musical problems and to distribute and gather examples of creative products in music.

Chapter Overview

It is in this context that I offer the ideas in this chapter.[1]
The work here is based on my analysis of recent research on
the topic of creative thinking in music for students in
primary, secondary, and tertiary education since my review
of this literature earlier (Webster, 1992). A central mission
of this chapter will be to present a more advanced model of
creative thinking in music based on this and the contextual
issues noted above. I will begin with why the understanding of creative thinking is so important for music and
specifically for music education. I will do this by listing
certain basic tenants about music, relating them to the
educational climate today.

Next I will move to the research base with a short account
of the study of "creativity" in the general psychology
literature, focusing on the last five decades.[2] This is a rich
and complex literature and I have space only to summarize
the major categories of research in order to demonstrate its
importance for the conceptual model. I will follow this with
a review of some of the most important music research in
the last five years.

In the concluding sections, I will summarize traditional
aspects of a definition of "creativity" and suggest one of my
own that is drawn from theoretical and empirical work. I
will present my revised model here and offer comment on
its newer features. The chapter ends with some speculation
about future studies.

Importance of Musical Creativity for Music Education

It is necessary to remind ourselves of why this whole topic is
so important for our field. "Music education" in its broadest
sense is a sub-field of music ultimately concerned with the
most effective teaching and learning of music as art. Most
musicians today teach; and, as a result, are music educators.
However, the term "music education" has come to mean the
application of teaching and learning techniques to primary
and secondary school children. I want to make it clear,
however, that concepts developed here about creativeness

and music education are applicable to the wider context than just the teaching of music to the young. The musicologist, theorist, studio teacher, conductor—these professionals are all in this together.

At the risk of stating the obvious, there are three fundamental ways that humans engage in musical behaviour: (1) listening (by far the most common of behaviours and the absolutely least studied as a creative experience), (2) composition (perhaps the least common, but most studied), and (3) performance. Listening exists as a focused experience with repeated listenings, often resulting in a formal analysis that might be represented in some symbol system; or, more often, listening is a single-time, "in the moment" experience in which the listener forms a sense of the music without the goal of a formal analysis.

Performance is also of two types. One type is the reproduction of music written by others and the other is the creation of music "in the moment" within a context—often referred to as "improvisation." Although there are settings where teaching and learning is focused primarily on one or the other, each behaviour is mutually supportive of the other in our quest as music educators to teach about music. Good music teaching usually involves all these types of behaviours.

Music teachers design environments that help learners construct their personal understanding of music. There are thousands of ways to do this and our authentic assessment of learning is the gauge of our success. One obvious gauge of how successful we are as teachers is the extent to which our students can make aesthetic decisions about music as listeners, composers, and performer/improvisers and to develop a sense of musical independence. Such independent thinking does not happen if each decision is dictated. Teachers must teach for independent thought. The best music teachers are the ones that are not needed by the student when formal education has ended.

Most music teachers agree that student decision-making (perhaps all of "musicianship") is predicated on the ability to hear musical possibilities without the actual presence of the sound—being able to "think in sound." Active listeners need to hold musical structures in memory as a work unfolds. Composers need to imagine sound combinations.

Performers/improvisers must have a target performance in mind. Music teachers must help students gain this ability to hear music in their heads and manipulate these sounds in increasingly more abstract ways.

All of this is possible only if students are encouraged to "create" music through all the available behaviours. Some will be more successful with one type of behaviour over another, but each is critical for the development of music cognition in the grandest sense. For all these reasons, it makes sense to think of creative experience in music as a central focus of music education.

General Literature

J. Paul Guildford's 1950 keynote address to the American Psychological Association (Guilford, 1950) is a marker for the commencement of the modern-day study of this topic. In the address, he noted the lack of attention paid to divergent thinking[3] and called for more systematic study. His work would evolve into the formation of a factor-of-intellect model of human intelligence that celebrated the intersection of product, operations and content (Guilford, 1967). His subsequent factor analytic studies brought attention in psychology to a multiple intelligence theory that was meaningful. The specific model proposed came under fire by the research community due to the problems inherent in factor analysis as an empirical methodology (Sternberg, 1999), but the spirit and logic behind Guildford's work lives on in many guises.

Since that time, the growth of formal study of creativity has been slow, at least until most recently. There are two edited volumes published in the last few years that are excellent compilations on the subject of creativity. The first is by Finke, Ward, and Smith (1996), published by MIT Press. The book has fourteen chapters aimed at offering a contemporary view of creativity in a cognition context. Topics such as insight, problem-solving, memory, and incubation are included, as well as an interesting opening chapter by the editors on cognitive processes in creative contexts. There is also attention paid to machine intelligence and on connectionism and neural nets.

A more recent collection of writings was published by

Cambridge University Press, edited by Sternberg (1999). This volume is perhaps the most comprehensive and definitive, single volume in the field of creativity and contains 22 chapters written by many notable scholars in the field today. Authors include Gardner, Csikszentmihalyi, Feldman, Weisberg, Amabile, Runco, Simonton, and Gruber, among others. The book is important because it documents the recent upturn in interest among cognitive psychologists in the study of this difficult topic.

There are now two major journals devoted to the topic, *Journal of Creative behaviour* and the *Creativity Research Journal*. Two books on adult creativity, designed for the trade press, have been written—one by Gardner (1997) and the other by Csikszentmihalyi (1997)—and each applies recent work to the explanation of genius.

Despite these developments, creativity as a construct (or as a set of complicated constructs) has been avoided in modern psychology. Sternberg and Lubart (Sternberg, 1999) offer six possible reasons:

• mystic and spiritual roots of this topic which tends to put off the more scientific community

• its pragmatic, commercial nature exploited by those who offer popular accounts of the creative thinking process which are not based on theory and research

• early work on the subject that was not theoretically or methodologically central to the field of psychology, and, as such, not respected

• problems with definition and criteria that "put off" the research who is looking for easier and perhaps more conceptually understood topics for tenure and promotion committees to understand

•approaches that have view creativity as an extraordinary part of an ordinary thing so as not to really need separate study, and

• unidisciplinary approaches to creativity that have tended to view a part of creativity as the whole phenomenon, trivializing or marginalizing the study. (p. 4)

As a musician, I would add a seventh reason and that is the sheer nature of the music experience seems to defy analysis.

The study of creativity in music involves a complex combination of cognitive and affective variables, often executed at the highest levels of human thinking and feeling. It is further complicated by our inability to clarify from where the inspiration for creative ideas comes. Then, on top of that, there is little evidence about the development of these ideas to form a finished whole. This is such a complicated set of either long-term engagements (composition, repeated music listening, or decisions about previously composed music in performance) or "in the moment" engagements (improvisation and one-time listening), that only those professionals in the creative field with deep understanding of music have any hope of untangling the complexity.

Those researchers in general psychology that have been brave or inspired enough to deconstruct the general creative experience through empirical study have taken the following approaches (Mayer, 1999)[+]:

• *Psychometric.* Assessment work aimed at the creation of tools to measure specific traits or evaluate overall creative ability (Guilford, Torrance, McKinnon)

• *Experimental.* Traditional empirical paradigms designed to seek cause and effect relationships (Sternberg & Davidson, Collins & Amabile)

• *Biographical.* Studies that use historical data to understand the creative process and creative thinking (Wallace and Gruber, Gardner, Simonton)

• *Psychodynamic.* Writings based on clinical evidence and philosophical/psychological speculation about creativeness (Freud, Kris, Kubie)

• *Biological.* Data derived from physiological data (Martindale & Hines, Hudspith)

• *Computational.* Conceptual work based on mathematical and computer-based models and simulations (Boden, Shank)

• *Contextual.* More qualitative work based on the realities of social context (Csikszentmihalyi)

Each approach has strengths and inherent weakness. Selected reading of studies in each approach is highly recommended to gain a sense of the contemporary scene in the general literature. In designing a model of creative thinking in music, this literature helps to bolster the aspects of enabling conditions (both personal and culturally-based) and enabling skills (personal competence) that are so critical for creative thought. Much of this literature, too, underscores the vital importance of divergency of thought and imagination in context with the more convergent thinking that often involves just plain hard work.

Promising New Research in Music Teaching and Learning

When comparing the approaches in the general literature to music on this topic, the psychometric, experimental, and contextual approaches are noticeable. A more "descriptive" approach is emerging in music, too, which places emphasis on the content analyses of the creative music experiences themselves. Ten years ago, I published a review of the literature on creative thinking in music education (Webster, 1992). I have continued to maintain an annotated bibliography that attempts to cover the field of music teaching and learning.[5] The latest organizational model for this literature is provided in Figure 1 and includes studies organized in three major categories: (1) *theoretical*, works based on philosophical or psychological arguments as well as review, standards and historical writings; (2) *practical application*, literature designed to inform praxis but not derived fundamentally from empirical evidence; and (3) *empirical*, work from numerical or observational data. This empirical category is the most complex, with studies that examine teaching strategies, assessment design, technology, relationship between variables in and outside music, and the actual creative experience. The Conditions category within Relationship is a major recent trend, with work on collaboration and social context as most important. Work with technology and teaching strategies is growing quickly as well.

The early literature model (1992) was based on less than 200 writings. The current review of this literature is based on an annotated bibliography over twice the size with much of the newly published sources coming from the empirical and practical categories.

Figure 1. Overall Literature Model

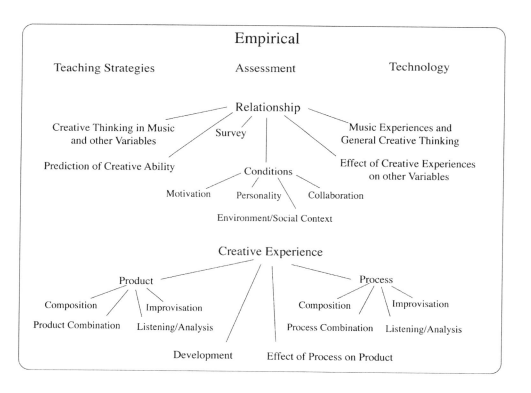

There are a number of trends that can be seen in the literature in the last 10 years. Here is a summary of the major developments noted in this new literature:

• Far wider array of methodologies, especially qualitative approaches

• Adoption of the post-modern tendency to question the assumptions made by previous generations and to be concerned more completely with social context. Many scholars have questioned older theories and models. (Barrett, Hargreaves, Burnard)[6]

• Heighten interest in the young child's work with invented music notation and the child's discussion of the notation as a window to understanding knowledge (Barrett, Gromko, MacGregor)

• New approaches to assessment, including (1) consensual techniques (Hickey), (2) peer assessment (Freed-Garrod), and (3) novice evaluation (Mellor)

• Attention to the role of collaboration (Kashub, Wiggins, MacDonald/Miell)

• New speculation and experimentation on the role of music technology (Hickey, Stauffer, Ellis)

• Emergent thinking on the pedagogy of composition teaching (Odam)

• New work on cause/effect and relationship (Auh, Hagen, Fung)

• New work on compositional strategies (Auh, Folkestad)

• Thought processes, using protocol analysis, while composing (Younker/Smith, Kennedy)

• New studies on how various musical behaviours (composition/improvisation/listening) relate to one another (Swanwick/Franca, Savage/Challis)

• Study of developmental patterns of creative thinking (Marsh, Barrett, Younker, Swanwick)

• Creative thinking in performance, aided by technology (Dalgarno)

• Study of improvisation and composition as connected experiences (Burnard, Hamilton, Wiggins)

What is Creative Thinking in Music and What is its Process?

The recent study of creative thinking and the whole notion of creativeness, both in and outside of music, have developed strong momentum in education circles and much new information is now available. In this section, I draw from this and earlier work in order to help define what we really mean by creativity and its process in music.

For many years I have maintained that "creative thinking" is really a term that has its base in what most of us understand to be "creativity." "Creativity" is not a useful term because it is so misused. For example, Mom and Dad may marvel at the "creativity" or their five-year-old daughter Maria because she can "read" music. Uncle John might think Maria has "creativity" for music because she can draw perfectly proportioned quarter notes on a drawing pad. Maria's piano teacher might conclude (perhaps mistakenly) that Maria exhibits "creativity" for music because of the flawless performance of her recital piece on Sunday afternoon. Each of these achievements may be impressive and of great importance to the musical development of Maria, but **none** of them inherently has anything to do with what creativity in music really is: *the engagement of the mind in the active, structured process of thinking in sound for the purpose of producing some product that is new for the creator.* This is clearly a thought process and we are challenged, as educators, to better understand how the mind works in such matters—hence the term "creative thinking." (Webster, 1990)

Based on this working definition, I continue to believe that creative thinking is a dynamic process of alternation between convergent and divergent thinking, moving in stages over time, enabled by certain skills (both innate and learned), and by certain conditions, all resulting in a final product. Nothing in the newest literature has suggested to me anything different. I believe that creative thinking is not a mysterious process that is based on divine inspiration or reserved only for those who are labeled as "gifted" or "genius." It can be defined and identified in us all. Creative thinking also occurs at various levels, from the spontaneous songs of the very young child to the products of the greatest minds in music.

Over the years, I have tried to maintain a model of creative thinking process that has anchored my assessment work and my conceptual writing. The early model was first published in 1987 (Webster, 1987). Figure 2 presents a new version of this model based on newer literature both in and outside of music.

Figure 2. Model of Creative Thinking Process in Music

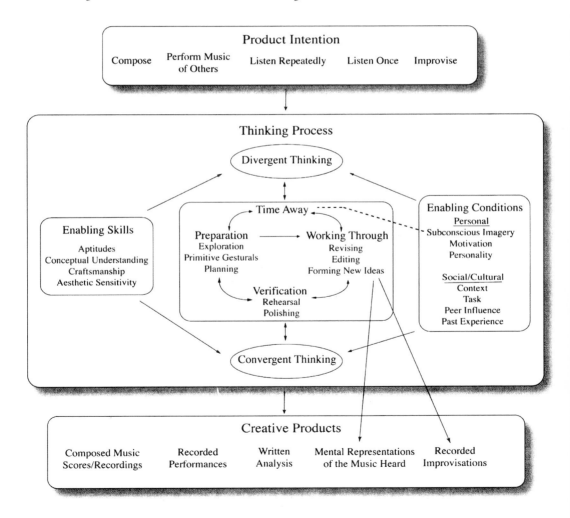

What Remains

The basic design of the model remains the same. Continued review of definitions of creativeness in both the general and music literature reveals five common elements: (1) a problem-solving context, (2) convergent and divergent thinking skills, (3) stages in the thinking process, (4) some aspect of novelty, and (5) usefulness of the resulting product. Regardless of the discipline, most experts agree that creative thinking is driven by a problem and a need for its solution. In the arts, the problem is more a "force" in the creator that inspires or drives the creative spirit. In music, the response to this force is embodied in (a) composition, (b) performance/improvisation and (c) listening and analysis. These are the product intentions that drive the process itself and are the resulting products that come from creative thinking.

In moving from the product intention to the result, the thinking process is a constant interplay between two qualitatively different ways of thinking. Divergent thinking on the part of the music creator involves imaginative thought. Here the creator is exploring the many possibilities of music expression, always cataloging, sifting through, rejecting, accepting only to change yet again. Small kernels of musical thought, which might be a melodic or rhythmic phrase, a harmony, a timbre, or even longer and more complex patterns of music, are all imagined and possibly realized on some musical instrument. These primitive gesturals (PGs) are all part of the exploration process that often characterizes the opening periods of creative thought. Such thinking is largely divergent in nature. Of course, such thinking occurs all through the creative experience as ideas are refined, then rejected, and new periods of divergency occur.

All of this is cast against convergent thinking that is more linear and more analytical. Here, the aesthetic decisions are made and the gesturals are turned into entities that are far from primitive. The thinking in this case is more discriminatory and driven by an emerging plan that many be conscious or subconscious. Musical material is rejected or celebrated, manipulated and fine-tuned. This kind of thinking might logically occur closer to the end of the creative process, but not always. The interplay between divergent and convergent thinking is almost magical in scope and is at the centre of creative thinking.

This movement between divergent and convergent thinking is aided by enabling conditions that are largely outside of the influence of formal education. Equally important are sets of enabling skills that are more likely influenced by formal education. Conditions and skills work to enable both the convergent and divergent thoughts and help to drive each.

Finally, I have continued to maintain that the results of the creative thinking process must always be represented by some form of product. This separates real creative thinking from day-dreaming or fantasy. Musical products take the form of written compositions, performances of music both pre-composed and improvised and analyses both written and mentally represented during listening.

What is New

"In the moment" vs. Reflective Thought. One new aspect of the model is my attempt to account for the "in the moment" creativeness that occurs in improvisation and single-time, music listening. Composition, performance of previously written music, and music analysis resulting from repeated listening are all time-independent. The creative processes have the benefit of "time away." Improvisation and single-time listening unfolds in fixed time and the creative thinking is part of a flow of musical behaviour that does not benefit from reflection to the extent that the others do. For this reason, I have tried to be specific about the differences between the two types of listening and between composition and improvisation in terms of their representation as intentions and products.

This unfolds more completely in the centre of the model and the depiction of stages. Here, I have added a line of movement from *Preparation* to *Working Through* and then lines that move from *Working Through* directly to the products. What I mean by this is that creators, during improvisation and single-time listening, form explorative ideas, work through them, and then move directly to product.

Model Centre. The reader familiar with my last model

might be startled to see that I no longer use the traditional notion of "preparation, incubation, illumination, verification" that grew from my endorsement of the Wallas model created some years ago (Wallas, 1926). I still am quite sure that stages operate in the creative process and have retained the notions of preparation, verification, and incubation (though I have renamed this "Time Away" which seems to make more conceptual sense to me). I have come to believe that illumination is not as much a stage as a qualitative event that occurs many times in the creative process. I also feel that the notion of verification is best reserved for the final polishing stage of the creative processes that are more reflective in nature. The idea of "Working Through" is attractive because it functions both in terms of reflective thinking and "in the moment" thinking. It is this stage, too, that likely occupies the greatest percentage of creative time and is the most indicative of convergent/divergent thinking in combination. This idea awaits further data analysis, as do many of the aspects of the model.

Note too, the use of a circular motion in terms of these stages and the indication with double-headed arrows that the movement is often clockwise and counter-clockwise as the creator progresses in a non-linear way through the process. I have retained a link from the "Time Away" stage to the *Subconscious Imagery* personal, enabling condition. This awaits more scientific verification as we learn more about brain function.

Expanded Enabling Conditions. Because of the mounting evidence on the role of social context, I felt it was necessary to stress this effect set. The kind of task and the context in which the task is set can have a strong effect on creative thinking. The roles of peer interaction in collaborative settings and in past experience all play a role as well. As we learn more about creativeness in and outside of school settings, I feel certain that this list will grow and become more specific.

Product Clarity. Finally, I have tried to be more specific about the kinds of products that result from creative thinking. This may seem trivial to some, but my intent was to be more clear on just what objects are the focus of study when we decide to pursue the study of creative thinking from a product perspective.

Future Issues

This is such an exciting field of research. It remains full of tremendous difficulties and raises the ire or many scholars whose work is perhaps rooted in a more focused and controllable world. Be that as it may, we have never known more about this critical aspect of music teaching and learning and the future looks bright. I end with just a few of the future directions for music teaching that we should consider:

• We need more work on social context, particularly the role of popular music to frame compositional and improvisational work. Clearly certain popular idioms that are easy to grasp play a dominant role as entry points for compositional and improvisational thinking, but what is less clear is the path toward more sophisticated skills.

• We need to study the revision process and how it functions in the teaching context. We need to learn how to go beyond the primitive gesturals to encourage kids to think in sound at a more sophisticated level.

• Related to this are the issues of teacher control: when do we step in to change something or suggest a new path?

• Experimentation with open-ended vs. more closed-ended tasks for creative teaching and research deserves more study.

• Experimental validity is an issue. How can we make the actual collection of data more realistic and deal more directly with the time constraints and contexts of "school" vs. out of school?

• When do children start composing music with "meaning"? After age 9, or long before? What does it mean to compose with "meaning?"

• When we ask children to compose or improvise or listen or perform "in school," is the result different than if these behaviours were done out of school?

• When children compose, are they working from a holistic perspective or are then working locally without a plan?

• Is it fair or correct to evaluate the quality of children's creative work with the eyes of adults?

• Are there stages of creative development in children?

• Is it really possible to study and define creative listening?

These and hundreds of other questions remain.

Notes

1. Portions of this chapter were presented at the European Society for the Cognitive Sciences of Music (ESCOM), 10th Anniversary Conference on "Musical Creativity, "Universite de Liege, Belgium, April 5, 2002

2. For a summary of these events, see Mark (1996).

3. The concepts of "divergent" and "convergent" thinking are at the heart of much of my writing and thinking about creativeness. Divergent thinking is simply that kind of thinking for which the result has no single goal and a number of products may result—a kind of personal brainstorming. Convergent thinking is work that focuses on a final result. Creative work involves both kinds of thinking many times and in many complex ways.

4. See the Mayer source for a more detailed description of each approach and for references to the scholar's work whose names appear in this listing.

5. For an overview of the literature in music and the most recent annotated bibliography, consult the following website resource: **http://pubweb.northwestern.edu/~webster/creatthink.html**

6. For reference to this literature, see the annotated bibliography noted earlier.

References

Csikszentmihalyi, M. (1997). *Creativity: Flow and the Psychology of Discovery and Invention* . New York: Harper Collins.

Finke, R., Ward, T., & Smith, S. (1996). *Creative Cognition: Theory, Research, and Applications.* Cambridge, MA: MIT Press.

Gardner, H. (1991). *The Unschooled Mind: How Children Think and how Schools Should Teach.* New York: Basic Books.

Gardner, H. (1997). *Extraordinary Minds: Portraits of Exceptional Individuals and an Examination of our Extraordinariness.* New York: Basic Books.

Gardner, H. (1999). *The Disciplined Mind : What All Students Should Understand.* New York: Simon & Schuster.

Guilford, J. (1950). Creativity. *American Psychologist. 5,* 444-454.

Guilford, J. (1967). *The Nature of Human Intelligence.* New York: McGraw-Hill.

Kafai, Y., & Resnick, M. (Eds.). (1996). *Constructionism in Practice: Designing, Thinking, and Learning in a Digital World.* Mahwah, NJ: Lawrence Erlbaum.

Mark, M. (1996). *Contemporary Music Education,* (3rd ed.) New York: Schirmer Books.

Mayer, R. (1999). Fifty Years of Creativity Research. In: Sternberg, R. (ed.). *Handbook of Creativity.* New York: Cambridge University Press., 449-460.

National Standards for Arts Education, (1994) Reston, VA: Music Educators National Conference.

Sternberg, R. (1999). *Handbook of Creativity.* New York: Cambridge University Press.

Sternberg, R. & Lubart, T. (1999) The Concept of Creativity: Prospects and paradigms. In: Sternberg, R. (ed.). *Handbook of creativity.* New York: Cambridge University Press., 3-15.

Wallas, G. (1926). *The Art of Thought.* New York: Harcourt, Brace.

Webster, P. (1990). Creativity as Creative Thinking. *Music Educators Journal, 76 (9),* 22-28.

Webster, P. (1987). Conceptual Bases for Creative Thinking in Music. In Peery, J., Peery, I. & Draper, T. (Eds). *Music and Child Development,* (pp. 158-174). New York: Springer-Verlag.

Webster, P. (1992). Research on Creative Thinking in Music: The Assessment Literature. in R. Colwell (ed.), *Handbook of Research on Music Teaching and Learning*, 266-279. New York, Schirmer Books.

Williams, D., & Webster, P. (1999). *Experiencing Music Technology*. (2nd ed.). New York: Schirmer Books.

Chapter 3

Defining Musical Creativity: A Critical Examination of Concept and Measurement

Sean McLennon

SEAN MCLENNON has been teaching classroom, choral, and instrumental music at St. Michael's School in Happy Valley-Goose Bay, Labrador since 1990. He received his B. Mus. and B. Mus. Ed. degrees from Memorial University of Newfoundland. He also holds a Master of Music degree (music education) from the University of Western Ontario. He is currently the president of the Newfoundland and Labrador Music Educators Association as well as a board member of the Canadian Music Educators Association.

Musical Creativity . . . What is it and how do we measure it?

Or, is it possible to define and measure it? The literature on the nature of creativity is diverse considering its lack of research tradition, and from it arise many different definitions of the concept. Although studies in the assessment of general creativity occurred as early as the beginning of the twentieth century, research on creativity in music education is a fairly recent phenomenon (Richardson, 1983). As Peter Webster (1992) points out, the relative lack of research tradition in musical creativity is not due to a lack of interest, but with the problems associated with the definition and assessment of the concept. However, because the concept of creativity is difficult to pin down should not result in it being avoided. The contrary should be true—that more extensive research into a definition and a means of assessment be carried out. To this end, a few brave philosophers and psychologists have endeavoured to lift the shroud of mystery surrounding creativity (and its implications for music education) by focusing on building models and developing means for its assessment.

The goal of this chapter is to examine two existing models of musical creativity and to consider them in light of other researchers' views and findings. It will also consider the possibility of measuring musical creativity and identify some of the pitfalls associated with this effort. A number of tests of musical creativity will be compared with special emphasis placed on Peter Webster's (1994) *Measure of Creative Thinking in Music* (MCTM). The validity of this and other tests will be questioned.

Definitions are important because they, in part, form one's underlying assumptions of the nature of a phenomenon and guide research into that phenomenon. As is explained later, the various definitions of creativity identified in the literature may be organized around various themes, namely, (1) the creative product, (2) the mental process (creative thinking) during creative activity, (3) the personality and cognitive traits of the creator, (4) the environmental conditions surrounding creative thinking, or (5) some combination of the previous four. This broad conceptual base makes it difficult to define and even more difficult to assess musical creativity. All of these factors, or variables, need to be considered, and each variable is connected to the others.

Compounding the problems of the assessment of *musical* creativity is the notion of applying assessment techniques of general creativity to musical creativity. This assumes that creative ability can be generalized across domains—a questionable and controversial issue in the creativity research literature. For example, Howard Gardner argues that while creativity is context-specific, there may be certain generic mental processes common to creative thinking in all domains (Gardner, 1988, pg.300). David Perkins speculates that there may not be any specifically creative abilities that cut across domains. Instead, creative abilities may be understood as exceptional versions of familiar mental operations such as remembering, understanding, and recognising (Perkins, 1981, pg. 274).

Now, let's consider the first model of musical creativity, that of Peter Webster.

Webster's (1987) Conceptual Model of Creative Thinking in Music

Webster's model is based on the premise that there are three principal ways that people involve themselves with music as art: composition, performance/improvisation, and analysis. Because these are considered as goals to creative thinking, they are referred to as "product intentions" (Webster, 1987, pg. 158). At the same time, they represent the final product of creating. For this reason they are also termed the "creative products." What comes between the intentions and the products is the creative "thinking process." Here is a depiction of Webster's Model:

Product Intentions——>Thinking Process——>Creative Products
1. Composition   ___   1. Composition
2. Performance/Improvisation ___   2. Performance/Improvisation
3. Analysis   ___   3. Analysis

Enabling Skills   Enabling Conditions
1. Musical Aptitudes   1. Motivation
2. Conceptual Understanding   2. Divergent/Convergent Thinking
3. Craftsmanship   3. Environment
4. Aesthetic Sensitivity   4. Personality

Below the "thinking process" you see four groups of "enabling skills" and four groups of "enabling conditions". Once an intention is established, the creator must rely on certain skills which enable and promote the thinking process. Webster terms these "enabling skills" and identifies them as (1) musical aptitudes–these include skills of tonal and rhythmic imagery, musical syntax, musical extensiveness, flexibility, and originality, (2) conceptual understanding–single, cognitive facts that comprise the substance of musical understanding, (3) craftsmanship–the ability to apply factual knowledge in the service of a complex musical task, and (4) aesthetic sensitivity–the shaping of sound structures to capture the deepest levels of feelingful response. These enabling skills are used in different ways, depending on the intention of the creator.

The enabling skills can be thought of as personal skills. However, according to Webster, there are other influences on the thinking process that are not musical. These influences vary from person to person and mingle with the enabling skills. These influences are termed "enabling conditions", and can be described as: (1) motivation–internal and external "drives" that keep the creator on task; (2) subconscious imagery–mental activity that is separate from conscious thought that may help to inform the creative process when the creator is occupied consciously with other concerns; (3) environment–a multitude of characteristics of the creator's working conditions that contribute to the creative process (examples given by Webster are financial support, family conditions, acoustics, media, societal expectations), and (4) personality–some personal traits or attributes of creative persons that may hold some significance for enabling the creative process (e.g., risk taking, spontaneity, openness, preference for complexity).

These four conditions are not to be taken lightly. In fact, there has been a great deal of research done on these conditions individually. Beth Hennessey and Teresa Amabile provide a good overview of the conditions of creativity in their chapter of *The Nature of Creativity* (Hennessey & Amabile, 1988). For example, in their discussion they outline studies that have been carried out on the effects of intrinsic and extrinsic motivation on creativity (e.g., Crutchfield, 1961, 1962; McGraw, 1978; Lepper and Greene, 1978; Deci and Ryan, 1985). The results of all of these studies indicated that creativity is adversely affected by increases in extrinsic motivation. One possible explanation for this finding is that when people are intrinsically motivated, they seek situations that interest them and that require the use of their creativity and resourcefulness.

In addition to the "creative" person displaying certain personality traits as mentioned by Webster, it has been shown that certain cognitive traits are often associated with creative individuals (Tardif & Sternberg, 1988). Among these traits are relatively high intelligence, originality, articulateness and verbal fluency, and a good imagination. However, the presence of these traits in an individual does not guarantee creativity.

Environmental conditions receive considerable attention in the recent research literature on creativity, and will be expounded upon in the examination of Elliott's model at a later point in this chapter. Research indicates that a creator's environment, particularly social conditions, plays an essential role in the process of creativity as well as in the interpretation and measurement of creativeness (more on this later). Webster's model hints at this relationship, but does not explore it to its full potential or take it to its necessary conclusion. This "oversight" is one of the pitfalls of his MCTM (i.e., the need for more attention to environment and social conditions).

Subconscious imagery is connected with a particular stage of operation in the thinking process in Webster's conceptual model, so at this point it is necessary to outline the thinking process in detail. According to Webster (1987), creative thought moves from one type of thinking—divergent thinking—to a second type of thinking—convergent thinking—and is facilitated by four stages of operation (i.e., preparation, incubation, illumination, and verification).

These four stages are the same stages proposed by Graham Wallas in 1926, except that he called them *stages of control* (Wallas, 1926). Webster describes the four stages in the following manner: (1) Preparation–one becomes aware of the problems at hand and of the dimensions of the work that lies ahead, (2) Incubation–"informal" or "part-time" thinking of the problem at hand (usually associated with subconscious thought or subconscious imagery). As Webster points out, "It is during this phase that divergent thinking may play a crucial role, for it is here that a number of musical solutions are considered" (pg. 166). (3) Illumination–this stage is referred to as the "Eureka!" or "Aha" stage where the solutions become clear. More realistically, this stage comes in controlled segments; perhaps a number of smaller solutions that point the way to the final version. Some writers on the topic of creativity consider this stage to be an over-romanticization or even a myth (e.g., Weisberg, 1986). (4) Verification–this is the final stage in which the solution is worked out and tested.

Divergent thinking, which is analogous to personal brainstorming, involves the generation of many possible solutions to a given problem. Convergent thinking involves the weighing all of the possibilities and converging on the best possible answer.

The creative thinking process then, according to Webster,

can best be described as that process whereby one sets out to solve some problem (in this case a musical problem–product intention) by employing divergent thinking skills in the beginning, progressing through the stages of operation, and eventually converging upon a solution (i.e., a creative product). The whole process is continually influenced by the enabling skills and the enabling conditions.

According to Tardif and Sternberg (1988), "one of the characteristics of creative individuals is the way in which they approach problems" (pg. 435). They do not always approach different problems in the same way, or, they may approach the same problem in different ways. In suggesting a model of creative thinking, one has to be careful not to limit the thinking style or approaches available to simple problem solving.

Webster's model, with its stage-like movement from divergent to convergent thinking, seems somewhat rigid, even though the stages of operation are not *meant* to be rigid. Does this model allow one to start problem solving from a convergent thinking perspective, for example? Is it possible to skip a stage in the actual thinking process? In fact, some writers such as Weisberg (1986) and Perkins (1981) do not agree with the inclusion of some of the stages. Hopefully, the answer to these questions is "yes" if the model is to be a realistic one. It would be impossible to build a model of creative thinking if one depends on an unreasonably idealistic concept of what a model is, or on an unreasonably idealistic concept of what creativity is. If one's concepts of either are too idealistic, failure is inevitable. For example, based on the notion of an idealistic definition of creativity (e.g., breaking boundaries in unpredictable ways) and of a model of something (i.e., a model contains rules that predetermine the behaviour of that something), the quest for building a model of creativity would contain a logical paradox—predetermination and unpredictability are inconsistent (Perkins, 1988).

Moreover, while divergent thinking (i.e., brainstorming and flexibility) is important to Webster's model, it has been argued by some that creative thinking does not necessarily depend on divergent thinking. Indeed, according to one researcher (Weisberg, 1986), there is much evidence to indicate that divergent thinking is not crucial to creativity, and creative solutions to problems come about by means of thought processes that are no different from those involved in other sorts of thinking. This is in agreement with what Perkins was alluding to earlier (see above)—creative abilities may be thought of as exceptional versions of common thought processes such as remembering, understanding, and recognizing. Seen from this perspective, personal brainstorming, based on the assumption that creativity depends on divergent thinking loses some of its power in this context, as does the concept of flexibility (the ability to generate many different ideas).

By now one can begin to recognise some of the inherent dangers of trying to construct a model of creativity. By their very nature, creativity and creative thinking are elusive and "free" in nature. It is still important, however, to theorize about and try to build models of this concept. It is through theorizing and model building that more understanding can be acquired and better theories and models developed. The development of theories, concepts, and models is essential to music education in order to know what we are teaching *for*. It is with this in mind that we will now consider the need to include Elliott's model of creativity which places more emphasis on cultural and social contexts with regard to creativity.

Elliott's (1990) "Head and Shoulders" Model of Creativity

First of all, Elliott considers the concept of creativity to involve three dimensions: a producer, the product produced, and the activity whereby the product is produced (Elliott, 1990). So far, this is in line with Webster's concept. But, as Elliott then states, "this is obviously incomplete since in any instance of human creativity it is also possible to consider the context in which the doer does what s/he does" (pg. 15). Webster does say that a creator's environment has an effect on the process of creative thinking, but one needs to take a much broader look at the person, process, and product in a social context. Elliott's point finds a good deal of support in the literature, as many writers feel that the inclusion of culture and society is essential for a complete definition of creativity (e.g., Gardner, 1989; Csikszentmihalyi, 1988). For example, according to Howard Gardner (1989):

41

> A creative person is one who can regularly solve prob-
> lems or fashion products or carry out projects in a *do-*
> *main* which are initially considered novel or unusual
> but ultimately come to be accepted in one or more
> cultural setting. The creative achievements...occur
> only at the hands (or in the minds) of individuals who
> have worked for years within a domain and are cap-
> able of fashioning—often over significant periods of
> time—products or projects that actually change the
> ways in which other individuals apprehend the world.
> (pg. 113)

Gardner has combined the concepts of creative person and
product and has added a cultural dimension to his definition
of creativity.

Similarly, Mihaly Csikszentmihalyi (1988) points out

> We cannot study creativity by isolating individuals and
> their work from the social and historical milieu in
> which their actions are carried out. This is because
> what we call creative is never the result of individual
> action alone; it is the product of three main shaping
> forces; a set of social institutions, or *field*, that selects
> from the variations produced by individuals those that
> are worth preserving; a stable cultural *domain* that
> will preserve and transmit the selected new ideas or
> forms to the following generations; and finally the *in-*
> *dividual*, who brings about some change in the do-
> main, a change that the field will consider to be crea-
> tive. (pg. 325)

In this definition, creativity is a phenomenon that results
from interaction among the three systems—field, domain,
and individual. Furthermore, Csikszentmihalyi observes
that "without a culturally defined domain of action in which
innovation is possible, the person cannot even get started"
(pg. 326).

The whole process of creativity in a social context is Darwi-
nian in nature. First of all, there is the process of the creator selecting ideas or solutions (if divergent thinking is
employed). He starts with a number of potential solutions
and narrows them down to a few viable ones. And, in a
broader social context, as Csikszentmihalyi explains in his
definition, it is society that selects from the variations produced by individuals those that are worth preserving, and it
is culture that will preserve and transmit the new ideas or
forms to the following generations (variation, selection, and

transmission are the main phases of every evolutionary sequence). Every new idea that is added to the domain will become an input for the next generation of persons. Thus, a spiral model of creativity can be inferred from this description. One cycle of the spiral represents a cycle in the process of cultural evolution. This is analogous to Darwin's theory of biological evolution in which natural selection and survival of the fittest are key. Indeed, Csikzentmihalyi (1988) argues that it is responsible to conclude "that creativity is one of the aspects of evolution" (pg. 333).

Richard Dawkins (1976) coined the word "meme" to refer to a "unit of imitation" that was transferred from one generation to the next. A meme could be any structured information that was worth passing on through time. Csikszentmihalyi concludes his discussion of evolution by pointing out that a domain can be thought of as a system of related memes that change through time, and what changes them is the process of creativity.

This brings us back to Elliott's "head and shoulders" model of creativity which also relies on society and evolution in order for creativity to be completely understandable. Elliott claims that to be able to decide the merit of an achievement—to decide whether something is creative or not—one usually looks for aspects that are "extraordinary", "unusual", or "unfamiliar". Moreover, to be able to decide if something is "extraordinary" one must depend on what one already knows through experience. One has to take into account the product's background (its familiar features, including its links with past productions) as well as its foreground (its new or unusual features). For example, in the *Eroica* Symphony, Beethoven did not invent "music", nor did he invent "symphonic music". The *Eroica* combines both the familiar and the unfamiliar; "it stands on the shoulders of other achievements" (Elliott, 1990, pg.20). Therefore, creative musical achievements depend upon a network of relationships among specific musical practices and prior musical achievements, as well as audiences, standards, and the social conditions pertaining to each and all of these. Therefore, it would be hard to conceive of anything that was truly unique in the sense of being completely unrelated to anything we know (unless it came from another planet).

The "head and shoulders" model of creativity can now be

thought of as a system of building on past experience in order to comprehend the creativeness of something new. Past experience includes social and musical context. This model is basically more of an assessment model rather than a procedural model. Elliott does offer some further insight into process, but he takes a very praxial (performance-based) approach, the model being rather specific to the performance of music.

Measuring Creativity

While there are various tests and measures of general creative thinking (e.g., Torrance, 1966, 1973, 1981; Guilford, 1967 cited in Hargreaves, 1986), there have been very few attempts to measure creative thinking in music. The reasons, again, have to do with the youthfulness of the field and the many problems associated with measurement. Some aspects assessed in the general creativity tests include divergent thinking abilities (i.e., fluency, flexibility, originality, and elaboration), while other tests focus on personality traits (e.g., Tardif and Sternberg, 1988). The best known measure of general creative ability is the *Torrance Tests of Creative Thinking* (TTCT). The TTCT measures the traits of fluency, flexibility, and originality. As will be seen, researchers in music have been greatly influenced by these tests. There are other approaches to measuring creative behaviour involving ethnographic research, case studies, cognition research, and environmental research. This discussion will focus mainly on the psychometric approach (tests of divergent and convergent thinking) since that is the approach taken by the researchers in the area of musical creative thinking outlined herein.

Margery Vaughan (1977) made the first significant attempt to measure creative thinking in music. Subjects were asked to improvise (1) rhythm patterns as a response to a given stimulus, (2) melody patterns in a similar manner, and (3) a piece showing how the subject feels during a thunderstorm. A panel of judges used a scoring scheme to evaluate factors of musical fluency, rhythmic security, and ideation. Although considered incomplete by modern standards, Vaughan's work is significant in that it represents the first attempt to construct musical tasks to evaluate creative thinking in music (Webster, 1992).

One may ask, "How valid is a scoring scheme that uses a panel of judges or "experts"? Amabile (1982) has gone to great lengths to investigate this procedure and has shown that it is possible to utilize a number of judges in order to establish acceptable interjudge reliability. She also claims that the only requirement of a good judge is familiarity with the domain of endeavour in which the product was made. This begs the question, "Shouldn't a judge also be experienced in making judgments?" It is one thing to be experienced in a particular field, but it is something completely different to be experienced at making judgment calls within that field. Does an experienced performer, for example, automatically make a good adjudicator?

Wayne Gorder's *Measures of Musical Divergent Production* (MMDP) (1980) was also based on the models of Torrance and Guilford. His subjects responded to stimuli by singing, whistling, or by playing a familiar instrument while being rated according to fluency, flexibility, originality, and quality. The tasks themselves were represented as skeletal music notation, and the subjects were asked to improvise using the motives, note heads, or contour markings as guides. According to Webster (1992, pg. 271), Gorder's studies are important in the literature because of their success in defining the qualities of creative thinking assessment in music, both theoretically and statistically.

The most recent test of creativity in music is Peter Webster's *Measure of Creative Thinking in Music* (MCTM) (Webster, 1994). Like the others, it is also a test of divergent thinking skills, namely (1) musical extensiveness, or the amount of clock-time involved in the creative tasks, (2) musical flexibility, or the extent to which the musical parameters of "high/low" (pitch); "fast/slow" (tempo); and "loud/soft" (dynamics) are manipulated, (3) musical originality, or the extent to which the response is unusual or unique in musical terms and in the manner of performance, and (4) musical syntax, or the extent to which the response is inherently logical and makes "musical sense".

The factors of musical extensiveness and musical flexibility are measured objectively by either counting the actual seconds of time a child is involved in a task in the case of musical extensiveness, or by observing the manipulation of musical parameters in the case of musical flexibility. Musical originality and musical syntax are to be evaluated by a panel of judges for best results, although Webster states that one observer is permissible. Rating scales based on developed criteria are used to assess these factors (i.e., originality and syntax). This is where the measurement techniques become "slippery". Webster suggests that the evaluators practice by viewing a random sample of children's performances in order to achieve an overall sense of the evaluation procedure. The test takes approximately twenty to twenty-five minutes to administer, and the scoring time is about forty to forty-five minutes.

The first question that comes to mind with the MCTM is "What exactly is the test measuring by assessing the four factors outlined above?" It is easy to get caught up in the statistics of test results, criterion validity, factor analysis, etc., but what exactly do these four factors translate into in the end? Are the right questions being asked? (i.e., are flexibility, extensiveness, originality, and syntax the right questions?) According to David Perkins (1988), it is possible that they are not.

Perkins (1988) outlines three levels of mechanisms that help explain creativity as a function of the human mind: (1) Potencies—computational powers of the mind. Creativity may depend on a person's performing certain mental operations very effectively, operations that do not lend themselves to a strategic approach (e.g., a powerful musical memory, the ability to "image" sounds). (2) Plans—patterns by which a person's deployment of his potencies is organized. Plans are analogous to a schema or frame (e.g., Beethoven's notebook). (3) Values—refers to the larger values that shape the direction of a person's endeavours. For example, in the plan of generating and selecting solutions, the criteria one applies to selection reflects personal values.

In particular, Perkins cites some studies which report only scattered support for the correlation between fluency/ flexibility and actual creative achievement (e.g., Wallach and Kogan, 1965; Wallach, 1976b; Perkins, 1981 in Perkins, 1988). The Torrance test reported a high correlation between fluency, flexibility, and creativity but, upon further investigation of test results, it was found that the factors

(fluency, flexibility, originality, and elaboration) correspond-
ed to the tests themselves rather than the traits scored. So,
Perkins concludes, the Torrance tests may not measure fluency, flexibility, originality, and elaboration so much as they
do performance on several tasks globally related to creativity.

Since the MCTM and other measures of musical creativity
are based closely on the Torrance test (Webster, 1979), is it
possible that these, too, have the same design flaws?

Another problem in the measurement of creativity is addressed by Csikzentmihalyi (1988). The problem occurs
when one does not take historical context into account
when trying to assess a person's creativeness. He offers a
couple of examples. One is the case of Botticelli, who was
for centuries considered to be a crass painter, and the wom-
en he painted "sickly" and "clumsy". Only in the mid-nine-
teenth century did some critics begin to reevaluate his work
and appreciate its creative qualities. Csikzentmihalyi explains, "The only way to establish whether or not something
[or someone] is creative is through comparison, evaluation,
and interpretation. Sometimes, as we have seen, the field
reserves its judgment: [e.g.,Botticelli moves to the
forefront]" (pg. 332). Is measuring a child's ability to improvise on the piano in relation to some stimuli really testing his creative ability? According to Csikszentmihalyi, it is
not.

As previously mentioned in the discussion about the possibility of divergent thinking not being as important as
some would assume in creativity (Weisberg, 1986), one has
to wonder if divergent thinking tests do justice to the
measurement of creative thinking.

Webster points out that an important premise of the measurement of creative musical thinking is that it is not related
to the measurement of musical aptitude (i.e., a musical
creativity test does not measure the same things a music
aptitude test measures). In a study by Charles Schmidt and
Jean Sinor (1986), a relationship was found between the
Primary Measures of Music Audiation (PMMA) (Gordon,
1977 cited in Schmidt & Sinor, 1986) rhythmic subtest and
the MCTM. The authors concluded, "that although these relationships are moderate in strength, they are not easily ex-

plained" (pg. 171). Is there some correlation between the MCTM and the measurement of musical aptitude? Is the MCTM really measuring musical creativity or just certain aspects of musical aptitude? Is musical aptitude necessary for musical creativity?

A final potential problem with the MCTM has to do with another finding from Schmidt and Sinor's study. They obtained a significant difference for sex across three of the four dimensions of the MCTM (i.e., musical flexibility, musical syntax, and musical originality). Quite possibly, they hypothesized, some of the MCTM tasks have a sex bias. For example, it may be argued that tasks that call for students to produce truck or robot sounds, or to create music that depicts a trip into outer space, are biased in favor of males.

Despite (or perhaps, in spite of) the inherent weaknesses and problems of measuring musical creative thought, more research and exploration is needed. It is only by critically examining the existing methods of measurement and by suggesting new and different alternatives that these problems will be solved. Or perhaps, as David Hargreaves (1986) suggests, the "problems of establishing the reliability and validity of musical creativity tests may unfortunately turn out to be overwhelming" (pg. 178). The problems certainly seem to be overwhelming now, but through the efforts of researchers like Peter Webster and of his critics, hopefully some sense can be made in the realm of measurement of musical creative thinking and of the concept of musical creativity in general.

Conclusion

As is evident, there is no, one, universally accepted definition of creativity, yet alone of musical creativity. However, the phenomenon of creativity does exist. One aspect of a definition which seems to be essential is the notion of cultural and social contexts. Without such contexts, the judgment of creativeness would not be possible and, therefore, creativity could not exist. Also needed is a *person* who undergoes the *process* of creating some*thing*. The questions, then, are; (1) "How does one create?"; (2) "Does everyone have creative potential, or is it an inborn trait?"; and (3) "How does one (or, is it possible to) measure creative ability?" A fourth question might be "Why would one want to measure creative ability?"

On the surface, these may appear to be simple questions, but they require much more than simple answers. The answer to each could be a book in itself. Indeed, much of the literature reviewed here has attempted to answer these questions, but none of the authors have done so definitively. Perhaps there are no definitive answers. For example, different people may have different methods or styles for creating that is unique to them. Or, possibly, everyone has the potential to be creative, but some possess more of a "flare" than others. If this is the case, music educators have a responsibility to cultivate as much creative ability in students as possible. Possibly, musical creative ability may not be measurable in statistical terms (Botticelli's case, for example).

The implications of creativity for music education depend upon the answers to these questions. That is why it is of vital importance to investigate, theorize, and build models of creativity. Asking the right questions is the first step to finding the correct answers. In order for music educators to teach effectively, they must first know what to teach *for*.

References

Amabile, T. M. (1982). Social Psychology of Creativity: A Consensual Assessment Technique. *Journal of Personality and Social Psychology 43,*(5), 997-1013.

Csikszentmihalyi, M. (1988). Society, Culture, and Person: A Systems View of Creativity. In R. Sternberg (Ed.), *The Nature of Creativity.* New York: Cambridge University Press.

Dawkins, R. (1976). *The Selfish Gene* New York: Oxford University Press.

Elliott, D. J. (1990). The Concept of Creativity: Implications for Mu sic education. *Proceedings from the Suncoast Music Educa tion Forum on Creativity.* Tampa: University of Southern Florida, 14-39.

Gardner, H. (1989). *To Open Minds.* New York: Basic Books.

Gardner, H. (1988). Creative Lives and Creative works. In R. Sternberg (Ed.), *The Nature of Creativity*. New York: Cambridge University Press.

Gorder, W. D. (1980). Divergent Production Abilities as Constructs of Musical Creativity. *Journal of Research in Music Education* 28,(1), 34-42.

Hargreaves, D. J. (1986). *The Developmental Psychology of Music*. New York: Cambridge University Press.

Hennessey, B. A., & Amabile, T. M. (1988). Conditions of Creativity. In R. Sternberg (Ed.), *The Nature of Creativity*. New York: Cambridge University Press.

Perkins, D. N. (1988). Creativity and the Quest for Mechanism. In R. Sternberg & E. Smith   (Eds.), *The Psychology of Human Thought*. New York: Cambridge University Press.

Perkins, D. N. (1981). *The Mind's Best Work*. Cambridge, Massachusetts: Harvard University Press.

Richardson, C. P. (1983). Creativity Research in Music Education: A Review. *Council for Research in Music Education Bulletin 74*, (Spring), 1-21.

Schmidt, C. P., & Sinor J. (1986). An Investigation of the Relation ships Among Music Audiation, Musical Creativity, and Cognitive style. *Journal of Research in Music Education* 34,(3), 160-172.

Tardif, T., & Sternberg, R. (1988). What do we know about creativity? In R. Sternberg (Ed.), *The Nature of Creativity*. New York: Cambridge University Press.

Vaughan, M. M. (1977). Musical Creativity: Its Cultivation and Measurement. *Council for Research in Music Education Bulletin 50*, (Spring), 72-77.

Wallas, G. (1926). *The Art of Thought*. New York: Harcourt, Brace, and World.

Webster, P. R. (1994). *Measure of Creative Thinking in Music: Administrative Guidelines*. Evanston: Northwestern University.

Webster, P. R. (1992). Research on Creative Thinking in Music: The Assessment Literature. In R. Colwell (Ed.), *Handbook of Research on Music Teaching and Learning*, (pp. 266-280). New York: Macmillan.

Webster, P. R. (1990). Creativity as Creative Thinking. *Music Educators Journal 76*, (May), 22-28.

Webster, P. R. (1987). Conceptual Bases for Creative Thinking in Music. In J. C. Peery, I. W. Peery, & T. W. Draper (Eds.), *Music and Child Development.* New York: Springer- Verlag.

Webster, P. R. (1979). Relationship Between Creative Behaviour in Music and Selected Variables as Measured in High School Students. *Journal of Research in Music Education,* 27,227-242.

Weisberg, R. W. (1986). *Creativity: Genius and Other Myths.* New York: W. H. Freeman and Company.

Chapter 4

A Curriculum for the Creative Imagination

Austin Clarkson

AUSTIN CLARKSON, M.A. (Eastman), Ph.D. (Columbia), is professor of music emeritus, York University, where he helped design the B.Ed. program, Fine Arts in Education. His interdisciplinary fine arts course, *Foundations of Creative Imagination*, led to the formation of the *Milkweed Collective*, a community of artists and writers which gives public shows of artwork and provides workshops on creativity for children and adults. Members of the group collaborated in writing the book *The Intelligence of the Imagination: Personal Stories of the Creative Process* (forthcoming). His writings on contemporary concert music, especially the composer Stefan Wolpe, have appeared in many books and journals. He is general editor of the composer's music and writings.

> . . . *When your voice*
> *decides to quit its day job, which is mostly*
> *door to door, to take its little sack of sounds*
> *and pour them into darkness, with its*
> *unembodied barks and murmurs, its refusal*
> *to name names, its disregard for sentences,*
> *for getting there on time,*
> *or getting there,*
> *or getting.*
> From "Wings of Song" (Don Mckay).

Introduction

Forty years ago it was widely believed that there was an un-bridgeable divide between the culture of science on the one hand and the culture of the arts and humanities on the other. Northrop Frye disagreed. In a series of talks broadcast by the Canadian Broadcasting Corporation and published as

The Educated Imagination, he argued that an educated imagination is not only a necessity for both cultures, it is vital for all citizens of a free society. He said that we have one type of language for everyday conversation, another for technology, and a third for the arts and sciences. The third, the language of the imagination, is more speculative and imaginative, for it enables us to compare what has been done with what we imagine can possibly be done. Scientists and artists come at their tasks from opposite directions. The former base their data on the world as it is in the here and now and attempt to explain them rationally by means of logic and mathematics. But when they devise possible models for interpreting the data, they reach for metaphors that call on the language of the imagination. (Frye didn't provide examples, but the black holes of astronomy and the Hilbert space of quantum physics would qualify as such metaphors.)

The data for artists, on the other hand, come from imagined worlds, which they then bring them into the world of everyday experience, often with the help of complex technologies. The arts and the sciences both operate with a mixture of hunch and common sense. "A highly developed science and a highly developed art are very close together, psychologically and otherwise "(Frye, 1963:4-11).

Frye goes on to explain that the language of the imagination and everyday language differ in how they deal with categories. Everyday language distinguishes between the subject (the individual) and the object (the thing "out there"), between past, present, and future, between body, mind and spirit, between animal, vegetable, and mineral, and so forth. Such distinctions, Frye states, tend to evaporate when we engage in immediate creative activities, as when we plant a garden or a crop and go to work because we have to, and because we want to produce something at the end of the work. Then the categories become, "what we have to do and what we want to do--in other words, necessity and freedom." Moreover, the language of the imagination dissolves the categories of self and other, thus helping us to understand difference. "In the imagination our own beliefs are only possibilities, but we can also see the possibilities in the beliefs of others. Bigots and fanatics seldom have any use for the imagination." (pg. 32)

For Frye, the creative imagination expands the limits of

what we can conceive from heaven to hell and everything in between. It enables us to imagine a better world or a worse world than the one we actually live in and then to make a moral choice for the one we prefer. Educating the imagination stimulates the moral imagination, thus bringing the individual into relationship with community: "The limit of the imagination is a totally human world. Here we recapture, in full consciousness, that original lost sense of identity with our surroundings, where there is nothing outside the mind of man, or something identical with the mind of man." And so Frye anticipated what we now call ecological consciousness. He supposed that if you were "enough of a primitive to develop a genuinely imaginative life of your own," you'd start by identifying the human and the non-human worlds in all sorts of ways. He also noted the importance of ritual and ceremony as sites for creativity: "weddings and deaths and initiation ceremonies have always been points at which the creative imagination came into focus, both now and thousands of years ago." He emphasized that in teaching literature creativity is as important as intellectual analysis, for "no matter if [the student] only writes a little, he's bound to have the experience sooner or later of feeling he's said something that he can't explain except in exactly the same way that he's said it" (13-14). Here Frye articulated the central reason for educating the imagination, namely, that by creating symbolic forms we express primary meanings that lose some of their import when translated into everyday language.

In the intervening decades educators have not taken up Frye's challenge. An extensive survey of research in arts literacy in Canada gives little evidence of interest in the creative imagination.[1] This may reflect the cognitivist attitude that has held sway for several decades and that (Daston, 1998). It may also mark a fundamental mistrust of the authenticity of the products of the imagination: "The typically postmodern image is one which displays its own artificiality, its own pseudo-status, its own representational depthlessness" (Kearney, 1988:3). Kearney affirms the need for commitment to imagination. "We live in a 'Civilization of Images' where human subjects are deemed less and less responsible for the working of their own imaginations. The citizens of contemporary society increasingly find themselves surrounded by simulated images produced, or reproduced by mass-media technologies operating outside their ken or control" (Kearney, 1995:108). He calls for a return to the unique, authentic image.

Just as Frye predicted, scientists are converging with artists and humanists to justify the value of educating the imagination. Neuroscience is now claiming that images constitute the basis of all mental functioning: "Thought is an acceptable word to denote such a flow of images" (Damasio, 1999:303-304; see also, Edelman & Tononi, 2000:202-206). Educators need to reckon with the fact that the brain is hard-wired to operate by means of symbols and metaphors. This confirms what we've known all along, namely, that for millennia humankind has passed down the values, technology, and wisdom of the clan, tribe, and nation from one generation to the next by means of handicrafts and visual designs, stories and songs, dramas and dances, games, rituals, and ceremonies. A few educators have responded to Frye's and Kearney's challenge. In a series of valuable books Egan advocates what he calls mythic or primary understanding. He provides many strategies for stimulating the imagination in the core subjects of elementary, middle, and high schools. Though he does not deal with the arts as such, Egan emphasizes the importance of narratives and stories for stimulating feelings of empathy, wonder, and awe (Egan, 1988, 1993). This goes part way to implementing fully Frye's program for educating the imagination, but we need to consider going further to engage the deep structure of the creative process.

The Foundations Program

Ideas for a course on the creative imagination accumulated little by little during a career of teaching music at various universities. In 1982 I put forward a proposal and was a bit surprised but delighted that it survived collegial scrutiny and was accepted into the university calendar. The course was offered for the first time in 1984 through the department of fine arts in Atkinson College, the faculty of part-time studies at York University. The basic concepts of the curriculum were then incorporated into the Bachelor of Education program in Fine Arts Education, which was instituted in 1995.

In the full-course format *Foundations of Creative Imagina-*

tion meets one evening a week for twenty-six weeks. The classroom is large enough to have one area with a circle of chairs for presentations and discussions and another cleared of furniture for exercises in creativity. Some sessions are held in an art gallery, a dance studio, and even in a woodlot. The four-hour meetings usually begin with discussions of assigned readings and presentations on the topic of the day. After a break come the exercises and time for processing the results. At the end of the evening a few minutes are set aside for recording responses to the exercises in course journals. Although the curriculum is tightly structured, great latitude is given to the participants in responding to exercises and assignments. The course was taught by a team, with specialists assisting in leading units on body movement, visual art, the structure of the psyche, and the symbolism of myths and fairy tales.

The curriculum is formed around the following concepts:

(1) Personality type is an indicator of the individual's approach to creativeness and shows how each type has particular gifts and particular challenges.

(2) Personality type promotes appreciation of difference in others and understanding of interactions within the group.

(3) Creativeness is a drive directed towards actualization of the innate potential of the individual.

(4) Activating the creative imagination engages the tertiary process, which mediates between higher-order conscious awareness (the secondary process) and unconscious functioning (the primary process).

(5) Engaging the tertiary process evokes felt meanings, symbolic images, and emergent thoughts that have a homeostatic, life-fulfilling tendency.

(6) Such images are multimodal, as they blend sense data, feelings, thoughts, and intuitions; a wide range of media are needed for their expression.

(7) Knowledge of archetypal images in the literature and the arts of various cultures leads to discovery of the connections between personal and cultural meanings of symbols and furthers the symbolic attitude.

(8) A continual process of dialoguing with the products of the creative imagination results in the emergence of archetypal images as personal guides to self-actualization.

(9) The symbolic attitude promotes ecological awareness of the interplay between the inner world of personal images and values and the outer world of cultural and environmental images and values.

(10) Sharing the outcomes of the creative process builds confidence in the individual's creativeness, skill in communicating inner thoughts and feelings, and trust in the group.

(11) Undergoing the cycle of the creative process--preparation, incubation, illumination, and completion--leads to effective management of both the conscious and unconscious phases of the cycle.

(12) The cycle of the ritual process--preparation, liminality, vision, and aggregation--is analogous in structure to the creative process; self-created rituals deepen the significance of the creative process and evoke a sense of community.

The students who enrolled in *Foundations of Creative Imagination* were for the most part completing degree programs that they had been working on part-time for several years. They had families and full-time jobs, and their median age ranged from mid-thirties to early forties. They were discriminating judges of university offerings and did not hesitate to let instructors know their thoughts and feelings on the evaluation forms distributed at the end of each course.

By the fifth time the course was offered, the bugs were pretty well worked out, the students were keen, and the program got off to a good start. By the end of the fall term the students had formed a mutually-supportive group, and as the winter term drew to a close the sense of community had increased to the point where they began to talk about staying together after the course was over. At the end of the last evening, after the presentations were all done and the evaluation questionnaires filled out, they set a date to meet again. I have known many ensembles of musicians who stayed together after graduation, but this was the first time in my experience that a class from an academic program had formed an ongoing group.

Seven years later the group continues to convene at members' homes and at other locales at least four times a year to share personal stories and creative work, plan group projects, engage in further creative exercises, and enjoy a potluck supper. A few of the original class have gone separate ways, while others with like interests have joined.

The group now calls itself *The Milkweed Collective* and has put on public shows of art together with workshops on creativity at community art centres. The group has also collaborated in writing a book about the program. Eleven participants in the course wrote accounts of their experience as chapters for the book, while my contribution was a commentary, from which I have adapted this essay (Clarkson, et alia, forthcoming).

The Creative Imagination

The creative role of the imagination came fully into European culture when the humanists of the Renaissance challenged the authority of medieval scholasticism. Human creativeness was valued as never before, and the discovery that the physical universe is infinite coincided with the awareness of the boundless possibilities of the human mind. Shakespeare gave voice to metaphors for the creative imagination that still resound today. In *A Midsummer Night's Dream* he wrote: "as imagination bodies forth / The forms of things unknown, the poet's pen / Turns them to shapes, and gives to airy nothing / A local habitation and a name" (1984:115-116). In the late play *The Tempest* he personified the creative imagination in the character of Ariel, the fiery spirit who assists the magician Prospero to establish an ideal state ruled by love. Prospero's power arises from his belief that, "We are such stuff / As dreams are made on; and our little life / Is rounded with a sleep" (1955:104). Four hundred years ago Shakespeare envisioned a society in touch with the symbolic attitude.

The scientific rationalism of René Descartes divided the mind from the body and dismissed the imagination as irrelevant, but in time Immanuel Kant returned the imagination to its former position as the very foundation of the mind's functioning (Rundell, 1994: 94-96). The idea of creative imagination as a primal drive was elaborated greatly during the succeeding era.

In a novel published in 1796 Goethe wrote: "There lies deep within us this creative force which is able to call into being what is to be and does not let us pause or rest until we have given expression to it outside ourselves or about ourselves, in one way or another" (1977:173). For William Blake, "a man's imagination is his life" (Frye, 1947:19). Samuel Taylor Coleridge, who praised Shakespeare's *The Tempest* as a miraculous drama of the imagination, wrote that the imagination provides a reflection in the human mind of "the eternal act of creation in the infinite I AM."

The concept of the imagination as the source of creativity was linked to the newly-emerging knowledge of the unconscious dimensions of the mind. By the end of the nineteenth century four main functions of the unconscious were identified: (1) the creative function; (2) the conservative function, for the recording of memories and unconscious perceptions; (3) the dissolutive function, by which some conscious phenomena become automatic and habitual, while others persist and interfere with normal processes; and (4) the mythopoeic function, which creates fictions and myths that may remain unconscious, or may appear in dreams and reveries (Ellenberger, 1970:317-18).

In the early twentieth century several educators—among them Arnold Gesell, Maria Montessori, and Heinz Werner—pioneered theories of development that maintained a balance between the reason and the imagination while promoting self-directed maturation (Crain, 1992: chs. 2-5).

Education in the arts was furthered greatly after World War I by the artist-teachers of the Bauhaus at Weimar who established a program that respected the basis in the unconscious of the creative imagination. The Russian painter Vassily Kandinsky sought to revive the spiritual dimension of art, saying that the artist must listen for "the inner voice that tells what form he needs, whether inside or outside nature. Every artist who works with feeling knows how suddenly the right form comes" (Kandinsky, 1955:75). The Swiss painter Paul Klee wrote: "The power of creativity cannot be named. It remains mysterious to the end. But what does not shake us to our foundations is no mystery."

We ourselves, down to the smallest part of us, are charged with this power" (Klee, 1961:17). Their colleague, the Viennese painter Johannes Itten, said that the main task of the art teacher is "to liberate the creative forces and thereby the artistic talents of the students" (Itten, 1975:12). Itten gave his students exercises in relaxation, breathing, body movement, and vocal toning before letting them do spontaneous drawings. These teachers were elaborating methods for co-ordinating the deep structure of the creative process with the reason.

At about the same time in Zurich, C. G. Jung was developing a therapeutic method for bringing unconscious contents into conscious awareness by means of spontaneous drawing, body movement, and automatic writing. His "active imagination" method called for inducing a presentational state in order to release the creative imagination, which he referred to as the "transcendent function" because it transcends the standpoints of consciousness and the unconscious. He found that the active imagination method generates a life process that expresses itself in images out of which arise new conscious attitudes: "For here the conscious and the unconscious flow together into a common product in which both are unified. Such a fantasy can be the highest expression of a person's individuality, and it may even create that individuality by giving perfect expression to its unity" (Jung, 1971: 428).

The Foundations program is based on the idea developed by the artists of the early decades of the century and by Jung that the spontaneously generated symbolic image points the individual to his or her authentic path.

After World War II the theory and practice of holistic education propounded by the philosopher John Dewey was sidelined by theories of development that privileged cognitive over noncognitive processes. Jean Piaget believed that symbolic thinking of children was a passing phase, and that mature thought should be rational and relatively free of symbolic representations (Piaget, 1962:289). Jerome Bruner, a disciple of Piaget, warned against arousing unconscious, creative impulses in children, referring to such approaches as "pedagogical romanticism" (Bruner, 1966:147).

Resisting the tide of cognitivism, some educators in the 1960's and 1970's emphasized the domains of feelings, values, and the imagination in what came to be called "confluent education" (e.g., Jones, 1968). But schools seem now to be focusing on problem-solving, computer-based instruction, and outcomes-based learning. The curriculum is carved up into ever smaller and more discrete modules for the purpose of standardized testing, which is imposed at increasingly younger ages. Critical thinking is now being taught at the earliest opportunity, leaving little room for imaginative, self-directed, creative play. Howard Gardner's theory of multiple intelligences is symptomatic of this trend. Gardner diversified greatly the notion of intelligence, but his system reinforces a cognitive and product-oriented theory of creativity. His system finds little room either for the language of the imagination or for the deep structure of the creative process that evokes empathic and spiritual feelings, self-actualization, and ecological consciousness.[2] Techniques for coordinating voluntary and involuntary mental and physical processes are now widely used in athletics but are still viewed with skepticism in the core curriculum. Some of the students I have worked with, from elementary school to the university, are surprised to find that they even have an imagination and that they can access it for creative purposes. It is a crucial moment when they discover how to let the conscious attitude open up to the symbolic images coming from the inner and outer worlds.

As one participant in the Foundations program put it, "outer events quite beyond conscious control seem to correspond to and give form to unconscious trends that are striving towards expression." The students are keen to learn the language of the imagination so as to understand the fascinating and often awesome images that flow into their expanding field of awareness. The study of archetypal symbolism in myths, fairy tales, and a variety of art forms proceeds in tandem with the experiential exercises. As the students learn the symbolic attitude, they find that their energy and motivation for creative work increases greatly. A photographer discovered that she was spontaneously making photographs that later turned out to be core images for her process. Another student accidentally cut her finger on a broken window, whereupon a poem flowed out that embodied the main topic of her year's project. A third student kept noticing blue jays in her daily life. During an active imagination exercise in which she chose the blue jay as her image, it transformed into an eagle, which became her principal symbol. After a while students begin to realize that the creative imagination is a source of images that can become an integral part of one's everyday conscious awareness. They begin to trust that the meanings of images will become clearer as one continues to practice the creative process. In this way they learn how to let images become their teachers.

Personality Type and Creativeness

Many traits have at one time or another been associated with creativity—divergent thinking, introversion, self-esteem, tolerance for ambiguity, willingness to take risks, behavioural flexibility, emotional variability, ability to absorb imagery, and even the tendency to neurosis and psychosis (James & Asmus, 2001:150-151). Attempts to isolate traits that are predictors of creativity assume that there is some ideal type of creativity associated with a particular type of personality. On the basis of this cognitive theory of creativity students learn about eminent creators in many fields, but are not introduced to their own creativeness. The result is that a few students are given an inflated idea of their creativeness, while the majority are left with the idea that they have no creative potential at all.

The theory of personality type corrects this situation with the idea that each type has particular gifts and particular challenges and that no single trait is in and of itself more creative than any other. As the most widely used indicator of personality, the Myers Briggs Type Indicator (MBTI) is introduced early in the program to identify the particular approach to creativity of each student (Myers, 1993). The theory of type on which the MBTI is based holds that type is a given of the personality and remains relatively stable through time. When eleven members of the fifth cohort did the MBTI again six years later, their scores were virtually unchanged, which helps to confirm that premise.

Familiarity with the range of personality types in the classroom encourages students to value their own type and to take responsibility for their special gifts. Getting to know one's type and how it differs from that of one's classmates results in many amusing and some tense interactions, but it promotes understanding of how some types prefer to work independently and others in groups; how some take in information through the five senses and others through the intuition (the sixth sense); how some evaluate information logically and impersonally through thinking and others empathically through feeling. In this way type becomes a major factor in understanding both the uniqueness of each individual and what is needed to build community. In the course of the program the participants engage the full range of functions and find out which is their dominant function, their auxiliary functions, and their inferior function. One of the most challenging tasks of the program is to get in touch with the inferior function, the function that is least developed and least manageable. Difficult though it is, engaging the inferior function brings participants in touch with the deepest level of the creative process. The range, richness, intensity, and originality of the imagery in the final presentations is evidence of the extent to which participants have engaged all the functions of their personality.

The Symbolic Attitude

The Foundations course is an immersion program in the creative imagination, and the experiential exercises begin right away with the initial meeting. The first exercise is to make a tissue paper collage. The prospect of having to "do art" so soon makes some apprehensive, and their fears increase when the collages are put up on the wall for viewing. Anxiety subsides when it becomes clear that we are viewing the collages receptively rather than judgmentally, as harbingers of new and intriguing images rather than as objects of aesthetic evaluation. The colours, shapes, and designs immediately begin to take form as symbolic images.

One student has a blue form in her collage that she recognises to be a panther, which becomes the main figure for her entire year's process. Another collage has a patch of red that leads some weeks later to the image of Little Red Riding Hood, then to the story of a fox, and finally to the guiding figure of Aphrodite. The pink that dominates a third collage brings its maker the feelings of the mother.

Many of the collages from that first meeting point the way to what was about to unfold during the next eight months. The second meeting is in a campus art gallery. The students walk around looking at the show until they find a work that attracts them. They are then given an exercise that forms an imaginal bond between the participant and the artwork (Clarkson, 1995). Activating the imagination in the presence of an artwork release strong images and feelings. The results are recorded with crayons and paper and then shared in the group. Students become aware of the wide range of responses evoked by such exercises, and that the resulting images are way stations on an emerging process.

There seems to be no apparent rhyme or reason connecting these initial exercises, but they are fascinating and seem to have beneficial effects. Puzzlement gives way to intense interest when the emergent images and feelings begin to reveal distinctive and recurrent patterns. Another indication that the inner and outer worlds are entering into a productive partnership is the release of powerful energies for the work. Several authors comment that during the early weeks they felt strong motivation for the course without really knowing why. As students become accustomed to activating the imagination, they look forward to the exercises and to the discovery of new and surprising images. Sooner or later they realize that a previously hidden world has opened up, and they become more observant of the symbolic aspect of events in their daily lives for clues to their unfolding story.

Succeeding meetings introduce specific symbols. They bring a stone to class and tell the story of the stone as though the stone itself is speaking. As a cultural symbol the stone represents cohesion and harmonious bonding with the self. Its hardness and durability signifies resistance to change, decay, and death. A whole stone connotes unity and strength, while a broken stone signifies dismemberment, disintegration, and infirmity (Cirlot, 1962:299-300). The stone stories weave the meaning of the stone as a cultural symbol together with its personal significance. One stone is pregnant with potential, as if inside it the whole universe is waiting to be discovered. Another stone is incomplete, bearing scars of separation, and in search of wholeness. A third stone came from the ancestral home of Scotland, and though it is small and insignificant, it is useful to others.

Several weeks later the students re-read their stone stories as though they are autobiographies and are amazed that the stones have told them their own stories. In this way the students begin to understand how apparently ordinary things can be transformed by the imagination into metaphors that bring new meaning and knowledge into conscious awareness.

The next evening we proceed to a woodlot on the campus and the students wander about until they find a tree that attracts them. Sitting beside the tree, they enter a meditative state and wait for what the imagination will bring. After an hour they return to the classroom and record the experience with a collage or a drawing and an entry in their journals. One student sees a bear, which becomes her guiding image for the rest of the year. Another student merges blissfully with her tree, which tells her of the inner strength that comes from connectedness with all of life and of the wisdom that is available to those who seek and ask. A fallen tree with new shoots growing from it provides an experience of death and rebirth. As a cultural symbol the forest is the unknown, while the tree signifies the cycle of life, growth, nutritive and degenerative processes, and immortality. With roots in the underworld, the trunk in the here and now, and the crown reaching up to heaven, the tree also signifies the world axis and the totality of the psyche (Cirlot, 1962:107, 328-332).

Subsequent units introduce body movement and music into the mix of media. The music sessions begin with toning to free the voice as a prelude to story-telling and singing personal songs. The students are taken on a fantasy journey based on a sonic meditation taught by the composer Pauline Oliveros. Participants describe the meditation as relaxing, freeing, and enriching, and often wish that it didn't have to end. The words 'beautiful,' 'heavenly,' 'spiritual,' 'serene,' 'entrancing,' 'alluring' sound a constant refrain.

They go to a place where they experience a state of merging and being in flow with nature, and where sounds come to vivid and meaningful life. The scene may be a cottage up north, a place recalled from childhood, an exotic locale, or some place never seen before. The weather is usually sunny and clear, and water is often present as a lake, stream, waterfall, or seashore. There are sounds of moving earth and sand, wind in grass or leaves, insects, animals, and many kinds of birds--the favourite being the loon. Among human figures there are often shepherd boys playing flutes, women playing harps, and choirs of children singing. Familiar music is heard, and original melodies that the musically trained write down in notation. There are instruments both known and fantastic. The students describe the experience in writing and with crayon drawings.

To make a musical performance, a student recites his or her narrative while the rest of the group sings a simple chordal background that is varied by means of *sol-fa* hand signs. In between each solo we sing a short unison song as a refrain in a verse-chorus format. Performing the narratives from the fantasy journey in this way reveals to the group the rich images for music that lie deep in the imagination (Clarkson, 1994a, 1994b). Further musical exercises involve singing personal songs to the accompaniment of hand drums.

Another is to organise a "potlid gamelan ensemble" with metallophones and other metal percussion instruments, along with pots and lids of all sizes brought from home. This exercise demonstrates the power of sound to entrain a group of musical beginners into an effective ensemble.

When singing personal songs, the group provides an improvised vocal and/or instrumental accompaniment using words or sounds extracted from the songs. A "listen-and-tell" session is devoted to listening to recorded music that has brought participants important experiences.

In the middle of the first term the students are asked to select a symbol that came spontaneously during the exercises. They are then to make a series of artworks on that symbol and research its meaning in various art forms and in different cultures. The resulting essay demonstrates the dynamic relationship between the personal associations and cultural meanings of a symbol. Finding the cultural meanings of symbols enlarges their significance beyond the definitions in the usual dictionaries.

The mask project begins early in the second term and continues through the rest of the program. Working in pairs the students make plaster of paris masks. While decorating the mask, it is addressed as the *Other*. Some decorate the mask as the image from the previous term, but the question of its identity is left open and the masks often transform. The students dialogue with the masks, write poems and songs for the masks, construct an environment for the masks, and design rituals for the masks. One evening the students bring costumes and dress up as the masks. The coming-out party for the masks ends with a lively dance. This provides a rich reservoir of material for the final performances. In the process the students learn that it is as painstaking to learn the language of the imagination as any language. By the end of the program most students achieve sufficient competence to continue on their own, but many feel the need for further study. Several wrote in the course evaluations that they wished they could do the course over again, or could pursue the subject at a more advanced level. The formation of the ongoing group in part met the need for further practice in the language of the imagination.

The Creative Process and The Ritual Process

The first half of the program takes one pass through the cycle of the creative process, while the second half takes the cycle deeper. We discuss the creative process according to the well-known model of Graham Wallas (Wallas, 1926:87). Wallas' model is important for the role it gives to the unconscious phase of the cycle. The first and last stages (preparation and verification) comprise the conscious phase, while the second and third stages (incubation and illumination) constitute the unconscious phase. We discuss the difference between the directed, purposeful energy of the conscious phase and the feelings of doubt, stuckness, and depression during the incubation stage. They begin to understand that the broody incubation stage is as natural part of the creative process as the productive stage and that it is essential to wait out the incubation until the illumination breaks through to initiate the final phase of the project. The incubation phase can last a long time and cause considerable distress and even depression. The moment of the breakthrough happens differently for each student, but when it happens they experience a rush of creative energy.

Everything seems to come together as they prepare for the final presentations. They find that they can give up trying to work out problems intellectually and instead put their trust in the confluence of conscious and unconscious forces in the tertiary process.

The theme of ceremony and ritual is touched on informally throughout the program. At times of public holidays-- Thanksgiving, Hallow'en, the Winter Solstice, and so forth-- we discuss their history and archetypal symbolism. Then near the end of the course we study the structure of the ritual process according to the anthropologist Victor Turner (Turner, 1987:4-19). We talk about the use of self-created rituals for important life-events and transitions—birth, childhood to adulthood, marriage, separation or divorce, recovery from illness, mid-life to old age, and death (Hine, 1987:304-326). The task is to design a ritual for the mask that combines aspects of both the sacred and the profane.

Confronting socially acceptable with socially unacceptable values deepens the process. Some students who were raised in religious households have difficulty with the topic of ritual. They think that rituals are phony and unconnected to the lives people actually lead. After the course one such student realized that ritual was one of the components of the course that she valued most highly. She commented that each class meeting embodied a sense of ritual, and that the ceremony of completion which brought the last evening to a close was especially meaningful.

Turner noted that the liminal phase of the ritual process generates a sense of homogeneity and comradeship that dissolves social divisions of rank and class so that all participants feel entitled to membership in the group. He found that ritual forms a community of equal individuals that has about it a quality of sacredness, which he called "existential or spontaneous communitas" (1969:94-96, 132). Attention to the ritual process brings the individual's creative process into a social context and constellates a strong sense of community in the group. The last three meetings of the course are given to the final presentations. It is a time of intense anticipation, adventure, risk-taking, and important discoveries. What until then has been a largely private journey becomes a shared experience. Each presentation takes on the aspect of a rite of passage that affirms the relationship between the individual and the witnessing community. Several presenters involve classmates in their performances, and sometimes invite the whole class to take part. The students become each other's teachers. Whether as witness or performer, almost every participant discovers some new knowledge that marks the beginning of the next stage in their journeys.

Applications in Middle and High School Classrooms

Three participants in the Foundations program have written reports on how it affected their practice as teachers. A teacher of music and art in a middle school wrote that the course increased confidence in her own creativeness, and revealed gifts that she didn't know she had. It also gave her the courage to display her creative potential in front of students and colleagues. "I re-discovered myself as a poet and discovered my brave, leadership self who makes it possible to do my job." It gave her confidence to be a conductor and got rid of the fear of not being good enough to do her job well. The course gave her "the ability to open the creative channels at will without the need for extra stimulation from outside, and the confidence and courage to demand that others make way for as much of the creative process as I can muster in my school setting." She learned to stick her neck out and take creative chances despite the fear of criticism from others.

She is now able to lead her students "to try creative work that seems to them at first to be impossible" (T. Fewster). The head of the art department in a middle school reports that the Foundations program is conducive to a highly creative art-making process for young people and provides a meaningful method for helping them explore the vast potential of their imaginations. He writes that it has become an integral part of his educational practice, and that "it is deeply rewarding to witness the individuality of each student radiate through these explorations" (A. Jahangir).

The former head of a high school visual art department said that the Foundations course gave her "an understanding of what is *Other* and the confidence to transfer personal experiences and understandings" to her students (J. McEwen).

These teachers introduced variously the topics of personality type, active imagination exercises, spontaneous art-making, mask projects, and the study of symbolism and archetypes in the regular curriculum. They comment on the focus, concentration, and ability to stay on task that comes from activating the intelligence of the imagination even with ADD, ADHD, and learning disabled students.

Personality Type. Joanna McEwen outlined the principles of the MBTI and had her students locate their types. After she explained her own type, the students discussed theirs. To explain the problem of the inferior function she had them make drawings with their non-preferred hand. "This exercise had a liberating effect."

Symbolism. "Most of the students are completely bereft of any knowledge of symbolism, which means finding something they can all relate to, like Star Wars, or Greek mythology. The First Nations students have an advantage because they are used to Grandmother Moon and Father Sky. The students can use any medium they please, but I encourage tissue collage, regular collage, watercolours, and oil pastels. I ask them to do a whole series of exercises in which nothing can be literal: (1) Any emotion using only colour; (2) Lines denoting only peace (anger, etc); (3) Images only of the feminine; (4) Images only of the masculine; (5) Images of the Child or the Trickster. I broach the idea that we have these many parts inside us. At first they got so enthralled with the idea of symbolism and archetypes that the artwork tended to get somewhat clichéd and predictable. The concepts of type, different paths inward, and archetypes came up over and over, and I was able to remind them of the self and of their outer masks. In retrospect I think the most outstanding revelation for me was that they were ready to pay heed to moderate inner work. I believe that if this were included somehow in our curriculum, how much more wellness of being and becoming there would be" (McEwen).

Mask Projects. In adapting the mask project Ali Jahangir had a group of grade eight students construct plaster masks. He asked them to consider the masks to take on imaginative extensions of their personalities, either real or fantasy, which they wished to explore. They responded with tremendous interest and chose qualities for their masks that ranged from being magical, to challenging gender stereotypes, to expressing deeply personal issues. He then asked them to find a quiet place and begin listening to their masks and write down what they "heard." Some found this quite a challenge, while others wove wonderful stories.

"Students who did not normally enjoy writing were suddenly completely engaged in the writing process". McEwen had her students make plaster masks and line the inside with sculpture wax. The plaster then was the negative mask and the wax was the positive. The problem she posed was: "To create a sculpture using the two masks in which you present two points of view based on an issue that is very personal to you. One mask will be your outer stance, and the other mask will be what you really think way down inside." The students were then partnered and wrote about what their partner's sculpture said to them.

The partners then shared their reactions with each other. The teacher received a copy of their writing. She reported that it was tough going, but the students loved it. It was undoubtedly the most successful unit that she taught.

Movie Projects. It is preferable if the students select the story, invent the plot, and write the script, instead of using a known plot from a current movie. One possibility is to read the beginning of a story out loud and then ask the students to complete the story on their own by making a storyboard (a sheet of cartridge paper or newsprint folded into eight panels). Each panel has one scene of the story in words and drawings. One or more of the storyboards is selected and the class divided into teams to write the scripts and produce the skits (Clarkson, Durlak, & Pegley, 1993).

Fewster comments on two movie projects that she conducted in her middle school. She found that it worked best to select a story that is not well-known so that the students have to work out their own plots and scripts. "The learning was endless and had deep impact. I was astonished at how an unruly, undisciplined group of kids pulled together to create an experience they will remember for a long time. My principal came into the school shaking her head in amazement after finding my students (some of the more difficult ones among them) searching diligently in the school yard for small stones with which to make an avalanche. Every child was focused and on task independent of the teacher, who was inside setting up the shot with the camera crew. They learned that if you don't write a script, no one knows what to do. They learned about themselves, their language, their culture, the media, and especially how to rely on each other, to commit to a task, and to finish it. Most of all they learned a lot about who they are as human beings, and what their place was in the class. It was a revelation to most of them. Some kids still come back and ask to see their movie."

Among the recommendations that come out of these applications of the Foundations program are the following: (1)
The concept of personality type helps students to understand themselves and their relationships to the other types
in the classroom, including that of the teacher; (2) Working
with type gives the individual confidence in their particular
creative gifts; (3) Activating the creative imagination stimulates the production of images and felt meanings that have
personal value and produces a high level of concentration
and the ability to stay on task in all students; (4) Developing the knowledge of symbolism was instrumental in getting beyond clichéd images to more personal images; (5)
Collaborative projects, such as videotaped "movies," builds
both authentic identity and teamwork and stimulates a
high level of motivation; (6) Teaching the language of the
imagination can be done with any age group.

Conclusion

The personal stories of the participants in the Foundations
program affirm the value of acquiring the language of the
imagination. and of showing and telling one's experiences in
the intimacy of the group. The program puts into practice
Kearney's insistence on the need to cultivate the narrative
imagination: "current pronouncements on the end of narrative notwithstanding--our postmodern society of spectacle
and simulation has more need than ever of narrative imagination. Without it, we would be deprived of the power to
refigure historical memory and to transform self-identify
into an ethical mode of selfhood. Narrative imagination . . .
possess[es] a singular capacty to commit us to a dimension
of otherness beyond ourselves--a commitment that, in the
moment of decision, invites the self to imagine itself as
another and to imagine the other as other" (1995:106). Re-
counting one's stories is for Kearney the basis of poetic freedom and ethical judgement, and, I would add, of creative
community.

Notes

1. Case 11 (173-74) and Case 23 (190-91) reported research on the creative imagination. The latter was the present author.

2. Howard Gardner's study of seven eminent twentieth-century creators reveals the problems of the purely cognitive system of the intelligences. He assigned his intelligences as follows: linguistic and personal intelligences for Sigmund Freud; logical-spatial intelligence for Albert Einstein; spatial, personal, and bodily intelligences for Pablo Picasso; musical and other artistic intelligences for Igor Stravinsky; linguistic and scholastic intelligences for T. S. Eliot; bodily and linguistic intelligences for Martha Graham; and personal and linguistic intelligences for Mahatma Gandhi. This fails to take account of some of the more notable gifts and failings that Gardner himself describes in his sketches of their careers. He mentions Einstein's famous thought-experiment in which he imagined travelling on a light-beam, the experiment that led him to the theory of relativity. But Gardner does not include the imagination as a factor in Einstein's (or anyone else's) creativity. Secondly, Gardner assigns high functioning in personal intelligence, defined as "understanding of one's self and the others around one," to Freud and Gandhi. And he narrates numerous instances of their dictatorial and arrogant treatment of members of their families and immediate circles of associates. To score high in personal intelligence it was sufficient for them to deal with thoughts and feelings on a purely rational level. The ability to sustain richly empathic and nurturing personal relationships does not rank as an intelligence in Gardner's system. Gardner also documents Gandhi's remarkable gifts as a spiritual leader but has no intelligence of spirituality. Gardner recently added an eighth intelligence to his scheme, that of the naturalist who observers and classifies natural phenomena. At the same time, he discussed the possibility of admitting spiritual intelligence into his roster, but concluded that spirituality can be an intelligence only when it is purely speculative and intellectual. Gandhi's gifts as a spiritual leader therefore do not qualify as a spiritual intelligence (Gardner, 1993:35, 336, 360-363; Gardner, 1999:60-64).

References

Bruner, J. (1966). *Toward a Theory of Instruction*. New York: Norton.

Cirlot, J. E. (1962). *A Dictionary of Symbols*. New York: Philosophical Library.

Clarkson, A. (1993). "Imaginal Intelligence: The Basis for Arts Literacy." *The Recorder* (December), 35-37.

----- (1994a). "Exploring the Audial Imagination." *The Recorder* (Winter/Spring), 71-74.

----- (1994b). "Uncursing the Silence: An Exploration of Sonic Imagination." *Musicworks* 57 (Winter), 38-46.

----- (1995). "The Sounds of Dry Paint: Animating the Imagination in a Gallery of Art." *Musicworks* 63 (Fall), 20-27.

----- (2001). "The Intent of the Musical Moment: Cage and the Transpersonal." In Bernstein, D. & Hatch, C., eds., *Writing through John Cage's Music, Poetry, and Art.* Chicago: Chicago University Press, 62-112.

Clarkson, A., & Pegley, K. (1991). *An Assessment of a Technology in Music Programme.* Technical Report 91-2, revised version. Toronto: York University Centre for the Study of Computers in Education.

Clarkson, A., Durlak, J., & Pegley, K. (1993). *Creative Applications for Multi-sensory Interactive Media.* Technical Report 93-1. Toronto: York University Centre for the Study of Computers in Education.

Clarkson, A., et alia (forthcoming). *The Intelligence of the Imagination: Personal Stories of the Creative Process.* The book consists of chapters by eleven participants in the Foundations program plus a commentary.

Crain, W. (1992). *Theories of Development: Concepts and Applica tion,* 3rd. edn. Englewood Cliffs: Prentice-Hall.

Damasio, A. (1999). *The Feeling of what Wappens: Body and Emotion in the Making of Consciousness.* New York: Harcourt.

Daston, L. (1998). Fear andLoathing of the Imagination in Science. *Dædalus, 127,* 73-95.

Edelman, G. M. & Tononi, G. (2000). *A Universe of Consciousness: How Matter becomes Imagination.* New York: Basic Books.

Egan, K. (1988). *Primary Understanding: Education in Early Childhood.* New York: Routledge.

Egan, K. (1993). *Imagination in Teaching and Learning: The Middle School Years.* Chicago: Chicago University Press.

Ellenberger, H. F. (1970). *The Discovery of the Unconscious: The History and Evolution of Dynamic Psychiatry.* New York: Basic Books.

Fewster, Tracy. "Creative Visioning and Self-discovery through the Arts." In Clarkson, A. et alia (forthcoming).

Frye, N. (1947). *Fearful Symmetry: A Study of William Blake.* Princeton: Princeton University Press.

----- (1963). *The Educated Imagination.* Toronto: CBC Publications.

Gardner, H. (1993). *Creating Minds.* New York: Basic Books.

Gardner, H. (1999). *Intelligence Reframed: Multiple Intelligences for the 21st Century.* New York: Basic Books.

Goethe, J. W. v. (1977). *Wilhelm Meister's Years of Apprenticeship,* trans. H. M. Waidson. London: John Calder.

Hine, V. (1987). "Self-Created Ceremonies of Passage." In *Betwixt and Between: Patterns of Masculine and Feminine Initiation,* ed.

Mahdi, L.C., Foster, S. & Little, M. La Salle, IL: Open Court, 304-26.
Itten, J. (1975). *Design and Form.* New York: Van Nostrand.
Jahangir, A. "Celebrating Imaginal Intelligence." In Clarkson, A., et alia (forthcoming).

James, K. & Asmus, C. (2001). "Personality, Cognitive Skills, and Creativity in Different Life Domains." *Creativity Research Journal* 13/2.

CJones, R. M. (1968). *Fantasy and Feeling in Education.* New York: Harper and Row.

Jung, C. G. (1971). *Psychological Types. Collected works,* vol. 6. Princeton: Princeton University Press.

Kearney, R. (1988). *The Wake of Imagination: Toward a Postmodern Culture.* Minneapolis: University of Minnesota Press.

Kearney, R. (1995). *Poetics of Modernity: Toward a Hermeneutic Imagination.* New Jersey: Humanities Press.

Kandinsky, V. (1955). *Concerning the Spiritual in Art (1912).* New York: George Wittenborn.

Klee, P. (1961). *The Thinking Eye,* ed. Spiller, J., trans. Manheim, R. New York: George Wittenborn.

McEwen, J. "Projects for the High School Visual Arts Curriculum." In Clarkson, A., et alia (forthcoming).

McKay, D. (2000). *Another Gravity.* Toronto: McClelland and Stewart.

McIntosh, R. D., Hanley, B. A., Verriour, P., & Van Gyn, G. H. (1995). *Arts literacy in Canada: A report prepared for the Canada Council and the Social Sciences Humanities Research Council.* Victoria, B.C.: Beach Holme Publishers Ltd.

Myers, I. B. (1980). *Gifts Differing.* Palo Alto: Consulting Psychologists Press.

Myers, I. B. (1993). *Introduction to Type,* 5th edn. Palo Alto: Consulting Psychologists Press.

Piaget, J. (1962). *Play, Dreams, and Imitation in Childhood.* New York: Norton.

Rundell, J. (1994). "Creativity and Judgement: Kant on Reason and Imagination." In *Rethinking Imagination: Culture and Creativity,* ed. Robinson, G. & Rundell, J. London: Routledge.

Shakespeare, W. (1984). *A Midsummer Night's Dream*, ed. R. A. Foakes. Cambridge: Cambridge University Press, 1984.

----- (1955). *The Tempest*, ed. F. Kermode. Cambridge: Harvard University Press.

Turner, V. (1969). *The Ritual Process.* Ithaca: Cornell University Press.

----- (1987). "Betwixt and Between: The Liminal Period in Rites of Passage." In *Betwixt and between: Patterns of Masculine and Feminine Initiation*, ed. L. C. Mahdi, S. Foster, & M. Little. La Salle, IL: Open Court, 4-19.

Wallas, G. (1926). *The Art of Thought.* London: Jonathan Cape.

Section 2: Creative Processes

Chapter 5

Creative Process as Meaningful Musical Thinking

Jackie Wiggins

JACKIE WIGGINS is Professor of Music Education at Oakland University, Michigan. Known for her work in children's musical creativity and technology in the music classroom, she has been an active clinician, presenter, and author in local, national, and international settings. She holds two degrees in music education from Queens College of the City University of New York and a doctorate from the University of Illinois. Among her publications are numerous journal articles and four books: *Sound Thinking* (2004, McGraw-Hill), *Teaching for Musical Understanding* (2001, McGraw-Hill), *Composition in the Classroom* (1990, MENC), and *Synthesizers in the Elementary Music Classroom* (1991, MENC).

This new CMEA series addresses the implications of research for practice. In my work as a researcher studying music learning as it takes place in real music classrooms, this is not a directional relationship (research to practice) but rather an interactive relationship. What happens with real students in real classrooms in "real time" is what informs my research, which in turn informs my practice. The relationship is circular and continuous. Since I study individual cases within particular classrooms, my findings are applicable to other classroom situations only to the extent that my readers see their own circumstances in what I describe. What I share in this chapter is based on more than 20 years of practical experience composing and improvising with elementary students in general music classrooms, combined with what I have learned as a researcher, collecting and analyzing data in general music classrooms over the past 10 years.

In this chapter, I consider creative process as meaningful musical thinking and the role of this process in students' music education. First, to be effective, an educational experience must be meaningful to a learner. Students need to perceive learning experiences as meaningful to their lives. They need to feel a sense of ownership of what happens in the classroom. They need to believe that their personal ideas are valued in the educational setting and that their work in that setting connects to their lives outside the setting. Bringing creative process into the music classroom is one way of making music learning personally meaningful to students. Second, all people are capable of many ways of thinking (Gardner, 1983). A complete education has opportunities for students to grow in all their ways of thinking. A successful education is one that enables learners to think in multiple ways, in ways that are meaningful and personal, generating ownership and fostering growth. Musical thinking is one unique way in which people think. Musical creative process enables learners to engage in musical thinking in ways that are personally meaningful.

The ability to engage in musical thinking is central to one's ability to engage in and understand music. Musical thinking is thinking in sound and understanding the organization of sounds in relation to other sounds and to the contexts in which they occur. The extent to which an individual understands the ways sounds are assembled to create music determines the sophistication of his or her ability to engage in music and musical thinking. Gardner (1983) characterizes musical intelligence as sensitivity to the structure of music that enables an individual to make decisions appropriate to the music of his or her experience, which includes sensitivity to musical properties, sensitivity to interrelationships among musical ideas, and expectations about what makes musical sense (pp. 107-8). We might say that musical thinking is musical intelligence in action.

In a music classroom, students engage in musical thinking as they listen to, perform, and create music. All three musical processes require students to pull together the various aspects of their understanding of music and its contexts. All three are creative processes. Performers may produce their own original music or reproduce music originally created by others, but the process of performing is creative in that it involves personal interpretation and meaning making on the part of the individual. Listening is a creative process in that individuals hearing and interpreting a piece of music recreate the music in their minds as they listen, bringing personal interpretation to the experience which makes it meaningful. Creating original music through composing or improvising can be a totally creative process. When composing or improvising, individuals may initiate new, original musical ideas that are developed and set into a context in new and original ways. A creator of music can also utilize thematic material that was previously created by another, but set it into a new context and develop it in new, original ways. Whether performing, listening, or creating, the extent of an individual's prior musical experience, the sophistication of his or her ability to think in sound, and the sophistication of his or her ability to understand the perceived sound in context will determine the sophistication of the musical experience and/or product. Therefore, assessment of students' creative products and processes can reveal a great deal about the level of sophistication of their musical thinking and understanding of music.

The Nature of Students' Musical Thinking

Much of my understanding of the nature of students' musical thinking has been gleaned from study of data collected in music classrooms during actual music teaching/learning experiences. Over the past ten years, I have audiotape- and videotape-recorded students' verbal and musical interactions as they engaged in learning in music classrooms (Wiggins 1990, 1992, 1994, 1995, 1998, 2000). These data have been analyzed for what they reflect about the nature of students' ways of thinking in sound, thinking about music, and learning to understand music.

The most important theme to emerge from analyses of these data is the overwhelmingly holistic nature of children's conception of music. This is reflected in almost everything they do. For example, one audiotape captured a fifth grade general music student's attempt to teach himself how to play the melody of *America* on a xylophone, following an iconic representation of the melody and using his knowledge of the song to guide his playing. While he was learning to play the melody, he was also carrying on a conversation with two peers about which instruments his group would use to compose a variation on the melody. As he played the melody, he would occasionally pause to make a verbal comment to his peers, but then return to the melody in the exact place where he had left off. Finally, he ran away from the xylophone to secure a coveted drum for his group, and then returned to the xylophone to play the final "Let freedom ring" in the same tempo as he had been playing the rest of the melody—as though he had never left. This is only one example from data I have collected that reflects students' drive to complete whole musical statements.

From my practice as a teacher, I was also aware that whenever students tried to figure out how to play a melody by ear on a classroom instrument, they would repeatedly play the melody in its entirety. For example, if I noted that a student was repeatedly playing last phrase of a song incorrectly and brought that to the student's attention, he or she would invariably return to the beginning of the melody as part of the process of fixing the problem in the last phrase. If I tried to show them how to play only the last phrase, they seemed unable to begin at that that point; they needed to start from the beginning in order to understand how to fix the problem. It seemed as though the ability to conceive of only one part of the melody entailed a more sophisticated conceptualization process than did playing the whole melody. If we consider how much music teaching tends to focus on segments of melodies, we can see how important it is for teachers to understand this from the students' perspective.

From extensive analysis of students' processes as they compose and improvise original music as part of class projects, I have found that the holistic nature of their musical thinking is particularly evident in their compositional processes. First, whether composing independently, in a small group, or whole class setting, students' initial decisions often reflect broad organizational elements such as texture, form, and sense of ensemble. Second, as they begin to conceive of thematic material for their work, it is always conceived in "chunks" (Davidson & Welsh, 1988; Sloboda, 1985), often articulated in some way by a student before it is actually played on an instrument (sung or chanted), often conceived in relation to other ideas of the individual or of peers, sometimes sung or spoken rhythmically as the student plays the theme for the first time. Students who are composing original songs without instruments often sing long portions of the song on their very first attempt, although this initial statement is often altered through a long path of permutations before the student(s) settle(s) on what the final product will be. At the very least, their initial idea is invariably articulated as a phrase, complete with lyrics and expressive qualities.

Throughout their work, students make constant references to musical ideas sounding "good" or "no good" based on their individual or group conception of how the final product will sound. As the work begins to take form, new ideas are always judged in terms of their appropriateness to the overall character of the work in progress. When students who are engaged in a group project choose to work independently on a particular idea (developing new thematic material for the work or working out details in an existing part), they often request (or demand) to hear the "whole thing" so they can hear how what they are doing will fit with the ideas of others. A key issue throughout their work seems to be the need to relate individual ideas to a vision of the whole (the group's vision or the individual's vision). It is this vision of the work in progress that gives meaning to the musical ideas.

I include this example from data I have collected to show that even first-time composers can think in sound and hold a holistic concept of the work in progress. The following data were drawn from a fourth grader's first experience composing with a small group. Her initial work was done without her peers, begun as soon as she chose her xylophone. Her first utterance was a short phrase, probably to test the sound and working of the instrument:

Ex. 1

She giggled and then, without a word, began playing her first melodic idea:

Ex. 2

In the last measure or two, a new idea was emerging, but evidently the octave placement did not match what she was hearing in her head and she immediately switched to the lower octave and played the new idea in its entirety:

Ex. 3

Satisfied with the new idea, she returned to the first rhythm, played on different pitches and extended a bit in length:

Ex. 4

At this point, she stopped briefly to remind the group that they needed to make a plan: "All right, what do we want? We gotta figure out something guys!" She then returned to playing her melody in a variety of permutations and, moments later, said, "I like the one I picked out." These instances are the first of 68 repetitions of her melodic ideas that occurred across two days. Note that the idea emerged in its entirety, as a chunk, after one initial "doodle," and that it maintained its syncopated pattern, length, meter, tempo, phrase structure and character across the various permutations, almost always played on three pitches, always involving some repeated tones. I share this example because it is typical of what I have found. It shows that even inexperienced composers are capable of inventing thematic material and need to have opportunities to do so if a composition assignment is to be personally meaningful to them.

Not only is students' conception of musical ideas holistic in nature, but in many ways, their common understanding of the work in which they are engaged is broader than the ideas of each individual. I have written elsewhere about the role and nature of shared understanding in students' creative work (Wiggins, 2000). A group's shared vision of a work in progress is generally larger than the ideas of individuals in the group (Beals, 1998; Mehan, 1984). Group members judge the merit and appropriateness of individual ideas against their personal interpretation of the shared vision of the work in progress. The group's shared vision of what is appropriate reflects cultural influences, including influences of the media and the music of their world.

Students' work in composing or improvising with peers is dependent upon their shared understanding of the work in progress, of the nature of the teacher's assignment, of their joint experience with the music curriculum, and of the music of their cultural experience. Shared understanding is reflected in the ways students talk about the music they are creating—often using few words and engaging more in musical conversation than in verbal conversation. This is fueled by their common understanding of the music of their experience, drawing to some extent on what they have experienced in the music classroom, but drawing much more from their common experiences with music of the media and other non-school sources. Shared understanding is also reflected in the musical elements of their products as they share, extend, vary, and answer one another's musical ideas. Sometimes, in the initial conception of thematic material for a work, students operate on such a high level of shared understanding that one student will finish a phrase that has been initiated by another (often interrupting the first student who is singing or playing the idea).

What Makes a Creative Experience Meaningful to Students?

As students work to solve creative problems, the nature of their creative process depends on the nature of the task. In an educational setting, the teacher usually determines the task. The nature of the task that teachers design is affected by their perceptions of and understanding of the nature of the processes students will use to carry them out. This is the critical piece. In order to design compositional and improvisational problems that will foster and enable creative musical thinking, it is essential that teachers understand the broad, holistic nature of students' conception of musical ideas and the holistic nature of their work processes.

In their attempts to make creative problems accessible to students, teachers sometimes design problems that emanate from and require the ability to think about music in an isolationist rather than holistic manner. Sometimes this takes the form of the teacher providing most of the information and expecting the students to do only one small portion of what needs to be done (e.g., "Using only *sol, mi,* and *la* and the rhythmic fragment, create a melody that is 4 measures long.").

♪♪♩ ♪♪♩

Students tend to approach such a task as a puzzle to be solved rather than as music to be created. I have observed students in a fourth grade classroom engaged in this task—writing the rhythm on their papers and then randomly distributing the three scale syllables over the notes of the rhythms. They then took xylophones and attempted to play what they had written on their papers, their eyes wandering back and forth between paper and instrument. In the process, the rhythm was completely obscured because they could not technically carry out what they were trying to do. Many approached the teacher or me (an observer) asking whether we would play their music for them so they would know how it sounded. This is not composing. It may be some kind of exercise (one whose validity as a music learning experience I would question), but it clearly did not entail the origination of musical ideas. It did not entail musical thinking. In fact, the nature of the assignment stood in the way of the students' ability to engage in musical thinking.

It is also important to realize that students need opportunities to conceive of their original music as it will *sound* and not as it will *look* on paper. Compositional problems cannot be notational problems unless students are able to function at the very highest levels where they are able to conceive of musical ideas from notation (hear music in their heads from the page the way a highly-experienced musician can).

If composing is originating musical ideas, then the compositional tasks must be designed to enable and support this process. Creative problems must be designed in ways that allow opportunity for the flow of musical ideas.

This means, first of all, that teachers should not restrict the pitches or rhythms that students may use to compose or improvise. Students thinking in sound are often unaware of which pitches or rhythms they are using. They are simply singing ideas in their heads. If they are not permitted access to all pitches and rhythms, they may be unable to perform the ideas they have in their heads. Since students' creative process entails the development of thematic material that is then set into a context, sometimes the best creative problems are those that deal with the parameters of the context. If the teacher sets some of the characteristics of the context, students are free to develop what they perceive to be appropriate thematic material to fill that context. This kind of assignment tends to free students to generate musical ideas. A well-designed assignment makes free-flowing musical thought possible.

In setting contextual parameters, teachers might ask students to compose or improvise in a particular form, texture, meter, or mode. They might ask students to develop a work with contrasts in dynamics, tempo, articulation, timbre, or range. Students might be asked to create a piece of music that will generate a particular mood or audience response (scary, peaceful, agitated). In carrying out any of these kinds of creative problems, students would be free to conceive of and develop whole thematic ideas and set them into the specified context. They would invariably find that some ideas were more appropriate to the context than others, and therefore make evaluative decisions to reject some ideas and embrace others. Solving these kinds of creative problems enables them to operate in ways of musical thinking that are most natural to them.

When students are permitted to think freely in sound to generate and develop their own thematic material, they feel a strong sense of ownership of the musical work they are producing—something the students who were writing *sol, mi,* and *la* over rhythm patterns did not. When students have ownership of the music they are creating, the experience becomes meaningful to them—connected to their lives. When students are permitted to initiate and develop original musical ideas in the music classroom, they know that their ideas are valued in that classroom. The music learning experience becomes personally valuable and meaningful to them.

References

Beals, D. E. (1998). Reappropriating Schema: Conceptions of Development from Bartlett and Bakhtin. *Mind, Culture, and Activity: An International Journal, 5*(1), 3-24.

Davidson, L. & Welsh, P. (1988). From Collections to Structure: the Developmental Path of Tonal Thinking. In J. A. Sloboda (Ed.), *Generative Processes in Music: the Psychology of Performance, Improvisation, and Composition* (pp. 260-85). Oxford: Clarendon Press.

Gardner, H. (1983). *Frames of Mind: the Theory of Multiple Intelligences.* NY: Basic Book.

Mehan, H. (1984). Institutional Decision-making (pp. 41-66). In B. Rogoff & J. Lave (Eds.), *Everyday Cognition.* Cambridge: Harvard University Press

Sloboda, J. (1985). *The Musical Mind: The Cognitive Psychology of Music.* Oxford: Clarendon Press.

Wiggins, J. H. (1990). Case Study: Musical Decisions of Two Fifth Graders. Unpublished pilot study, conducted at University of Illinois at Urbana-Champaign.

Wiggins, J. H. (1992). *The Nature of Children's Musical Learning in the Context of a Music Classroom.* Doctoral dissertation, University of Illinois at Urbana-Champaign.

Wiggins, J. H. (1994). Children's Strategies for Solving Compositional Problems with Peers, *Journal of Research in Music Education,* 42(3), 232-52.

Wiggins, J. H. (1995). Building Structural Understanding: Sam's Story, *The Quarterly Journal of Music Teaching and Learning,* 6(3), 57-75.

Wiggins, J. H. (1998). Recurring Themes: Same Compositional Strategies—Different Settings. Paper presented at the Southeastern Music Education Symposium, Athens, GA.

Wiggins, J. H. (2000). The Nature of Shared Musical Understanding and its Role in Empowering Independent Musical Thinking," *Bulletin of the Council for Research in Music Education,* 143, 65-90.

Wiggins, J. (2001). *Teaching for Musical Understanding.* NY: McGraw-Hill.

Chapter 6

Creativity and Motivation

Geoffrey Lowe

GEOFFREY LOWE is the Executive Director of the Western Australian Youth Orchestra Association, a post taken in 2001 following two years of post-graduate research in England in the area of motivation in music education. He also lectures part-time in Music Education at the University of Western Australia, and has written a number of books on music education andis in demand as an adjudicator and clinician. As an educator, Mr. Lowe is the former Head of Music at United World College of South East Asia, and Head of Performing Arts at Wesley College in Perth. He is also an experienced administrator, teacher and conductor with a deep commitment to youth and youth music-making.

Introduction

Music educators have examined extensively the philosophical and educational value of creativity in school-based music programs, but creativity has not been widely considered from a motivational perspective. Worldwide, there is evidence that music education programs in schools often fail to motivate and stimulate students (Ross, 1995; Ross, 1998; Austin & Vispoel, 1998). Without motivation, effective learning simply cannot occur. The general music education literature infers that creativity may help stimulate student interest, but is this the case? Can the use of a creative approach help music teachers stimulate student desire for greater musical involvement? This chapter seeks to explore the relationship between creativity and motivation.

Definition

Motivation functions as drive or desires, and is manifest largely in action and behaviour. Action and behaviour is guided, biased and influenced by attitudes; attitudes therefore are central to the motivation equation. While attitudes are a hypothetical construct which cannot be directly measured and whose existence can only be inferred, there is general consensus that they include a cognitive component, an affective component and an evaluative component (Reber, 1985). Therefore, by implication, attitudes derive from conscious beliefs, emotional and instinctive feelings, and exist on a positive / negative continuum. In simple terms, attitudes can be described as what an individual believes about an object, what an individual feels about an object and the positive or negative strengths of those beliefs and feelings.

Expectancy-value Theory

There has been a considerable amount of research undertaken into the concept of attitudes and motivation in general education, with over 4000 dissertations being published in the US alone between 1990 - 1994 (Asmus, 1994). However, surprisingly little research has been undertaken in the music education domain. The general field of achievement motivation, which seeks to understand the desire to succeed or otherwise, has been a popular research area. One of the most enduring and widely applied theories has been expectancy-value theory (Eccles, 1983). Originally designed to explain motivation in maths for lower secondary school students, it has since been applied across a number of subject domains, including both classroom and instrumental music (Lowe, 2001; O'Neill, 1996; Wigfield, 1994).

While a detailed examination of the theory is beyond the scope of this chapter, the theory seeks to explain the development of attitudes from the broader social milieu to more immediate, task-related setting. Eccles describes attitudes as deriving from both values and competence / expectancies. Values are defined in terms of an individual's cognitive and affective assessment of an object, in this case, what the individual thinks and feels about music, and is largely subjective. Thus, values are derived from a personal assessment of music itself. In the school setting, these are influenced by the tasks that teachers set. Further, Eccles describes values as having four components. (see Figure 1)

Fig 1 Definition of the components of value, Eccles (1983)

VALUE COMPONENT	DEFINITION
Attainment value	The importance of doing well on a given task. This includes characteristics valued by the individual. i.e. the need for a challenge, a forum for achievement, power and social needs.
Interest value	Inherent enjoyment gained from doing the task. This is a very important component.
Utility value	How the task fits into future plans or related goals. It is often influenced by long-range goals such as career plans, educational plans and social plans.
Cost	What an individual has to give up to undertake the task. If the amount of anticipated effort necessary to succeed increases in relation to the amount of effort considered worthwhile, the task value decreases.

Eccles notes that value components are moderated by broad achievement goals, including long-term career goals or behaviours associated with gender characteristics, such as gender stereotypes.

Competence / expectancies relate to an individual's perceived beliefs about their abilities to interact with an object, in this case, music, and their abilities to improve. Examined through attribution theories which describe beliefs regarding the cause of success and failure, this has been a popular general field of research (Asmus, 1994). While values may be summarized as how the individual feels about an object, competence may be summarized as how good the individual thinks they are at interacting with the object, and expectancies as how much better they think they can become. Eccles' model acknowledges that while competence relates to current beliefs, expectancies for the future is an integral part of attitudinal development in young people. They tend to be naturally optimistic about their ability to improve.

For teachers, the implications are clear. The expectancy-value model suggests that attitudes are key determinants of motivation. They are shaped in turn by values relating to perceptions of music itself, and competence and expectancy beliefs relating to the individual's perceptions of their musical abilities. Facilitating positive engagement to enhance both these states is critical. Both research and observational studies have revealed the importance of teachers' task designs in shaping values and competence/expectancy beliefs. Critically important are the type of tasks that teachers set, and the way they are delivered.

The Link with Creativity

An examination of the literature suggests that creativity may be a naturally motivating process. Clare's (1993) summary definition states:

[Creativity is] engaging in a process which produces objects or ideas which are novel or original, aesthetically pleasing and functionally appropriate for the creator. (p. 22)

This definition implies that the creative process is enjoyable for the creator, and suggests that it is a deeply personal process of exploration. Therefore, the 'functionally appropriate' end product must impact favorably upon the values component in Eccles equation. Clare continues:

> ...the actions an individual performs on the object...in order to make some changes in that object...these processes influence development of skills, knowledge, competencies, communication and enforcement of values and norms. (p. 22)

While stating that the creative process does influence competencies, Clare infers that creative engagement must enhance competence beliefs as musical skills and knowledge develop. Why is this the case?

Bowman (1994) suggests that creativity builds positive attitudes by confirming idiographic independence. One of music's strengths is its idiographic meaning, and by engaging in the creative process, students are able to explore and develop a deeper understanding of musical meaning. Competence beliefs are enhanced as the creative process develops a product which fulfills the personal needs of the creator, developing a sense of confidence and achievement. Values are enhanced as knowledge of music through creative exploration is taken to a deeper level of personal understanding and appreciation. Therefore, creativity may well be a process which enhances attitudes by allowing students deeper insights into personal musical meaning.

Music education, particularly class-based music programs, has been criticized in the past for their inability to facilitate student engagement beyond the superficial level of factual acquisition (Sherman, 1991). Students are 'knowledgeable about' music, rather than 'know in' music, and this is often cited as a reason for poor attitudes towards music in traditional school-based programs. The problem of attitudinal decline is particularly strong around the transition to secondary school and the succeeding two years (Wigfield, 1994). While a decline in the values and competence components of attitudes is apparent across most subject domains, researchers have highlighted a disturbingly strong decline in attitudes towards school-based music, particularly when compared against other subject domains (Wigfield, 1994; O'Neill, 1996).

Many attribute a primary cause for attitudinal decline to the use of traditional, passive, non-creative curricula. Limited quantitative evidence presented by Pogonowski (1985) suggests that creativity may stem the downward attitudinal spiral. In an examination of a Process Oriented Music Curriculum (POMC), he found lower rates of attitudinal decline among year 5 - 7 students. However, there was no guarantee that the examined POMC was creative, although a degree of creativity may be assumed by implication. However, Pogonowski's study was of general attitudinal variables, and was not specifically related to creativity. Thus, the improvement in attitudes may have been attributed to other causes. Some observational evidence has been cited in the UK by Mills (1996) who notes that student attitudes are largely determined by the nature of the tasks being undertaken, and the most effective tasks are those which provide a challenge, and permit personal, self-guided creative exploration, as cited by Pogonowski and Bowman.

Students and Creativity

There has been little direct examination of student attitudes towards creativity. Given that attitudes contain an evaluative component, student responses should offer valuable insights into the positive or negative attitudinal potential of creative activities. Lowe (2001) found that students rated activities involving creativity highly. Students described creative exercises, which they defined as composing, improvising and performing, as important and fun.

Creative work is more...more fun so you should do more of it so then you can make people like music more.

However, in exploring why creativity was considered fun, it became clear from student interviews that creativity did not operate in isolation from other motivational perspectives. While there is a paucity of research in this area, other key perspectives included the need for degrees of choice and practical involvement. Choices were important for developing a sense of ownership, leading to a deeper personal sense of achievement, and practical involvement was seen as the means by which this was achieved.

Yes, it is fun, its much better than just being given a piece of music and told just do that because if you get to have a word in it, you can make it more of your own piece.

Creativity is sort of constructing work where you are actually doing something practical.

Creativity operates as a gateway to deeper understanding in music, as long as the student maintains a degree of ownership, and therefore a greater personal stake, in both the process and product.

That you get to do it personally and that you don't get to watch the teacher doing it. It's that you get to do it personally.

That the creative process is more important as a means of achieving greater understanding was also evident.

I think that being creative is actually more important than the actual piece that comes out at the end.... You can still know inside yourself that you put a lot of effort into it and learned a lot.

Despite the high rating given to creativity, students also identified areas for careful consideration, including the need for skill acquisition to allow creative fulfillment. Students identified the need for practical skills, but only to a level necessary to permit deeper creative exploration. This further emphasized the link between creativity and practical involvement in music.

I think it is important to learn a bit before you play, because if you go on to it straight away, you might not have a clue what to do...

...when you come down to composing, you've got more skills and are capable of producing a better piece

Therefore it is important for music teachers to find a balance between complete creative 'freedom', and some form of structured technical skill development. Here is potentially rich ground for exploring the role of technology in enhancing access to the creative process.

The student responses generally supported the theoretical assumption that creative exploration in music education improves attitudes. Students indicated a valuing of creative activities - they are seen as fun and interesting, and most significantly within the context of the expectancy - value model, important in developing a greater understanding of musical meaning. Further, the creative process was identified as positively affecting competence beliefs. However, creativity may only enhance competence beliefs as long as students have sufficient skills to allow effective exploration. Conversely, competence beliefs may decline if students feel inadequately equipped to explore at the level they desire as a sense of creative frustration sets in. However, the full impact of creativity upon all values components and competence / expectancies remains to be fully explored.

The Role of Task Design

Research suggests that task design is the critical element in the motivation equation (Lowe, 2001). While teachers may acknowledge the need to incorporate creativity into the tasks they design for philosophical and educational reasons, there are parametres within task design which need to be negotiated for enhanced attitudes to occur. It is important to acknowledge student desire for a degree of control over and ownership of the creative process and product.

Teachers need to be careful not to unwittingly impose their own ideas, but rather design tasks which offer students the flexibility to explore in their own way. Students need to be guided through the creative process by questioning and self-appraisal at each stage in the process (Ross, 1995). Ross notes the value of encouraging reflective thinking, teacher modelling and verbalization. Thus guided, values, through a deeper understanding of musical meaning, and competence, through greater confidence, may be enhanced.

There is also the need to negotiate the role of skills acquisition in allowing effective creative exploration to take place. Burnard (1995) suggests an effective strategy of separating activities into clearly delineated taught technical prerequisite activities and guided creative activities. As it is clear that one of the most motivating aspects of creative involvement is the opportunity for practical involvement, maintaining the practical base for creative activities is important. Students love doing music - generating, experimenting, refining and extending. The fault of too many traditional music programs is that they are based upon theoretical talk, and not practical action. The most effective method of creative exploration is with an instrument of some sort at hand.

Further, where possible, these experiences need to be authentic (Swanwick & Lawson, 1999). For example, students creatively exploring popular music genres need performance access to popular musical instruments. Reproduction of popular music on metalophones or even pianos does not sound 'real' in their ears, and the activity is devalued accordingly. Again, this suggests an important role for technology in allowing authentic sounding reproduction.

While these parameters indicate potential for understanding the role of creativity in shaping student attitudes, it is framed within the narrow student understanding of what constitutes creativity (Balkin, 1991, Webster, 1991). Creativity should embrace all aspects of music education, including traditionally passive activities such as listening and aural analysis. Too often, creativity is seen as being merely 'composing'. Creativity can embrace all aspects of task design. For example, if the desire to generate deeper musical meaning is fundamental to the teacher's teaching philosophy, then extending the creative process into creative listening is important. This again involves the teacher guiding the student through various listening stages, commencing with what the student hears (surface listening) through to how the music creates an effect (value judgments) to why the composer many have desired that effect (personal meaning). Students arrive at a personal level of understanding, just as they did through the guided compositional process.

While it is beyond the scope of this chapter to further explore the breadth of creativity in task design beyond the superficial level, the basic assumption that creative involvement acts as a conduit for generating a deeper understanding of music meaning should act as a guiding principle for all teachers when designing tasks.

Summary and Conclusion

There is no question that creativity is educationally important. However, qualitative evidence appears to support the theoretical assumption that creativity also enhances student attitudes towards music. Creativity, by developing idiographic meaning, can be naturally motivating and may have a significant role to play in reversing the worldwide motivational problems associated with many class music programs. Expectancy-value theory gives the teacher a framework for understanding the parameters of attitudinal development.

However, it is not enough to assume that creativity alone will be naturally motivating. How creativity is introduced remains critical. Given that interaction with the task is the central factor in determining student attitudes, for creativity to have a positive impact, teachers need to design creative tasks carefully in conjunction with other motivational perspectives, namely choice and practical involvement. Creativity needs to be guided, not taught, be practically based, be authentic and infuse all areas of the curriculum. Only then will it achieve the educational goal of developing a deeper understanding of musical meaning in students, while impacting positively on values and competence beliefs. Only then will it help allay the criticisms that school music programs are demotivating.

References

Amus, E (1994). Motivation in Music Teaching and Learning. *The Quarterly Journal of Music Teaching and Learning,* 5 (4),5 - 29

Austin, J. & Vispoel, W. (1998). How American Adolescents Interpret Success and Failure in Classroom Music: Relationships between Attributional Beliefs, Self-Concept and Achievement. *Psychology of Music,* 26, 26-45

Balkin, J. (1991). What is Creativity, What is it Not? In Hamann, D. (Ed.) *Creativity in the Music Classroom.* Music Educators National Conference, Reston, VA, 35-39

Boswell, J. (1991). Comparisons of Attitudinal Assessments in Middle and Junior High School General Music. *Bulletin of the Council for Research in Music Education,* 108, 49-57

Bowman, W (1994). Sound, Sociality and Music (parts 1 and 2). *The Quarterly Journal of Music Teaching and Learning,*5,(3)50 - 67

Burnard, P (1995). Task Design and Experience in Composition. *Research Studies in Music Education,* 5, 32 - 46

Clare, L (1993) The Social Psychology of Creativity: The Importance of Peer Social Processes for Student Academic and Artistic Creative Activity in the Classroom. *Bulletin of the Council for Research in Music Education,* 119, 21-28

Eccles, J. (1983). Children's Motivation to Study Music, pp 31-38. In *Motivation and Creativity: Documentary Report on the Ann Arbor Symposium on the Application of Psychology to the Teaching and Learning of Music; Session 111.* Reston, VA : Music Educators National Conference

Lowe, G. (2001). *Task Design and Student Attitudes towards Class Music: A Study of Year 7 Music Students in an English National Curriculum Context.* Unpublished masters thesis, The University of Western Australia

Mills, J. (1996). Starting at Secondary School. *British Journal of Music Education,* 13 (1), 5-14

O'Neill, S. (1996). Factors influencing children's motivation and achievement during the first year of instrumental music tuition. Unpublished doctoral thesis, Keele University

O'Neill, S. (1999). The role of motivation in the practice and achievement of young musicians. Paper presented at the 5th International Congress of Music Psychology Conference, Seoul, Korea

Pogonowski, L. (1985). Attitude Assessment of Upper Elementary Students in a Process-Oriented Music Curriculum. *Journal of Research in Music Education*, 33 (4), 247-257

Reber, A. (1985). *The Penguin Dictionary of Psychology* (2nd ed.). London : Penguin

Ross, M. (1995). What's Wrong with School Music. *British Journal of Music Education*, 12, 185-201

Ross, M. (1998). Missing Solemnis; Reforming Music in Schools. *Brit ish Journal of Music Education,* 15 (3), 255-262

Sherman, E. (1991). Creativity and the Condition of Knowing in Music, pp 7-22. In Hamann, D (Ed.). *Creativity in the Music Classroom.* Reston, VA : Music Educators National Conference

Swanwick, K. & Lawson, D. (1999). 'Authentic' Music and its Effect on the Attitudes and Musical Development of Secondary School Students. *Music Education Research* 1, 47-60

Webster, P. (1991). Creativity as Creative Thinking, pp. 25-31. In Hamann, D.(Ed.). *Creativity in the Music Classroom.* Reston, VA: Music Educators National Conference

Wigfield, A. (1994). Expectancy-Value Theory of Achievement Motivation: A Developmental Perspective. *Educational Psychology Review*, 6 (1), 49-77

Wigfield, A., O'Neill, S. & Eccles, J. (1999). *Children's Achievement Values in Different Domains: Developmental and Cultural Differences.* Paper presented at the 1999 biannual meeting of the Society for Research in Child Development, Albuquerque, New Mexico

Chapter 7

Creativity: A Fundamental Need of Adolescent Learners

Sandra Reid

SANDRA REID has taught both instrumental and vocal music in the Ontario school system as well as in the Faculty of Education, Nipissing University. Dr. Reid has presented at national and international music conferences and is author of the book, "How to develop your child's musical gifts and talents" published by McGraw-Hill.

If teachers are going to incorporate more creating in their lessons, we must first consider the benefits. " They themselves like to create". It is active, involving all students, and provides potential transformational experiences. The creative process connects what they are doing in the classroom to real life outside the classroom, and reinforces music concepts. It can be a way of helping you find out strengths and talents".

Beliefs in the ability to be creative and valuing creativity are key attitudes needed to increase the likelihood that creativity will happen. The benefits of including the creative process in our music plans are deeper understandings about music works, teamwork, problem solving, and pleasure by students. "By introducing improvisation and composition, children come to see how composition and performance are connected" (Upitis, 1992, pg. 37).

"It is time for every parent's organization to state unequivocally its belief in children's creative potential and the importance of making it possible for the creativity to emerge" (Pitman, 1998, pg. 48). Personally, I believe it is time for every music teacher to plan their lessons so that the creativity of adolescent learners is given the opportunity to emerge and teachers should provide the audience and venues for demonstrations. In this century children are now encouraged to make up their own music instead of always playing someone else's and we should see and hear this is our schools.

Creativity: A Fundamental Need of Adolescent Learners

In the last half dozen years, many provinces in Canada have introduced new Arts curriculum for all grades. The music curriculum in each of the provinces of British Columbia, Ontario, Nova Scotia, and Saskatchewan, has a creative strand outlined for all grades. In particular, adolescents in grades seven, eight and nine are expected to "demonstrate their abilities, skills, and techniques in creating" (Nova Scotia, 1998, pg.10). When interviewing grades 7, 8, and 9 music teachers and students in various provinces about the artistic and aesthetic needs, the need and importance of creating in music emerged as a theme in the analysis of the research. Hopefully things have changed since the 1980's when children were not encouraged to make up their own music (Walker, 1985). First I will outline some beliefs about creating in music. Barriers and benefits to incorporating creative activities in music will be mentioned. Practical strategies for teaching music creativity to adolescents are suggested.

Beliefs About Creating

I believe that creating is a craft and as such is teachable in music, just as we teach students to write stories or poems in language arts, or draw pictures in visual art. Taylor (1987) finds the notion of craft unappealing and Hamann quotes Sherman, "Creativity can not be taught, but in the proper environment and with the proper guidance and support, it can flourish and grow" (1991, pg.7). My opinion on teaching creativity is supported by Carl Orff. "Sound patterns may be constructed arbitrarily and then organized into forms to create compositions. The principle of 'improvisation unfettered by knowledge' is upheld until very late in the process "(Choksy, Abramson, Gillespie, Woods, York.2001, pg.337).

The comprehensive musicianship method also supports

teaching composition early in their programs. Environmental sounds of "found" sound sources may be organized into form to produce spontaneous improvisations. These may of may not be charted in invented graphic notation to that they may be read later (thus becoming compositions). Traditional reading and writing, while desirable skills, are not necessary for improvisation and composition (Choksy et el. 2001, pg.337).

Barriers and Benefits

Since music curriculum expects creativity and adolescents want creativity, the question that must be answered first is, "What are the barriers to teaching the creative process in music?" Traditionally, teachers may have experienced only performance in their school experiences themselves and so fall into a comfortable pattern of repeating the way they were taught. Some teachers may not have experienced teacher training using creativity in music, do not have confidence, and so are not comfortable risking. Many feel that they do not have the time necessary for performance and theory requirements. "I have not had a lot of experience for composition and writing. As far as reasons why, no, I guess the main one being that we do not have the time. I see the students twice a week every six days for 45 minutes. When you have scales to be taught, ensembles, you cannot do it all". (Teacher 4)

One does not need a lot of new resources or materials to incorporate creativity into music programs for adolescents. Time in the planning process is the main requirement.

If teachers are going to incorporate more creating in their lessons, we must first consider the benefits. "They themselves like to create" (Teacher 17). It is active, involving all students, and provides potential transformational experiences. The creative process connects what they are doing in the classroom to real life outside the classroom, and reinforces music concepts. "It can be a way of helping you find out strengths and talents" (Student 4).

Beliefs in the ability to be creative and valuing creativity are key attitudes needed to increase the likelihood that creativity will happen (Cornett, 1999, pg.24).

Suggestions for Starting Creativity

Often a teacher will be teaching music to adolescents who have come from 'feeder schools' and this creates a variety of readiness in music. A creative activity at the start of the year is a good way to involve all students quickly and successfully. A lot of kids do not arrive with skill in band or strong voice skills.

Some start off with next to nothing. "I start with Orff instruments because they are least difficult even singing the right pitch is difficult. I start with something they know. It could be a nursery rhyme and then play the melody. Finally, I let them loose in small groups and they can use instruments and sing (they get bonus points for singing). They take a rhyme like *Row, Row, Row Your Boat.* They find out how important a steady beat is and how important it is to start and stop together and listen to each other". (Teacher 6)

Another method of introducing creativity at the start of the year is to start with beat and rhythm. "I think rhythm is the starting point for many of them. Then going to pitch is a natural progression" (Teacher 9). Take a familiar song like "O Canada" and have the students put the beat in their feet. Ask them how the beats are grouped. Next put the rhythm of the words in their hands. Practice until students are confident in the difference between beat and rhythm. Students can then be put into groups of four having two students keeping the beat in their feet for eight beats and the other two students creating rhythm body percussion for the eight beats. Each group is to repeat their creation without losing a beat, for a total of 16 beats. After about ten minutes practice, each group will perform their creation. Some feel that moving to music is the first creative response we should consider. This is the Jaques-Dalcroze philosophy, "Movement is the first level of creativity" (Choksy et al. 2001, pg. 336).

Movement for middle school is really important. They pretend they do not want to, but really they do "show what the music does with your bodies. Then we look at pictures and created sound shapes. Grade 6 and 7 did graphic notation. They took their compositions and performed for their parents"(Teacher 16). Creating, by moving to music is also mentioned by students. "Suddenly there is a different energy *moving to music* it is like I enjoy it. We personalized the Joseph song. In the middle there is a part we don't sing so we just bounced around. Spontaneous--it came from us" (Student 29).

Moving to music might also be introduced by having students view a *Stomp* video to answer the question, " How does this group make music?" Students are then put in groups of 5 or 6 to create their own *Stomp* version with all using the same found sounds (books, pens, and shoes) and creating organized movements to their creation.

Suggestions for Continuing Creativity

Once students have an understanding of beat and rhythm, one can teach *Rondo* form by the teacher performing a rhythm pattern of specific length and students responding with their own improvised rhythm of the same length. I would suggest starting with two bars in common time. The whole class claps the 'A' pattern and individual students improvise a 'B', 'C', and 'D' pattern for the ABACADA form. After improvisations on rhythms are secure, use only one or two pitches in the improvisation of a rondo form.

Once students are comfortable improvising a short passage for the rondo form, put students in pairs to create a melodic sequence to portray a conversation.

An understanding of rhythm can also lead to creating by having students take a known song and change the rhythm. Composing variations in this manner can be either written or performed, or both.

Students need to re-create first and create music that is challenging, yet within their abilities. "Composing and improvising involve creating something new but it is not something profoundly new. It is based on what a person knows and their experience" (Teacher 14).

Another successful creative activity is to give students the rhythm of a piece they are going to study and have them write the melody within a given key. While students need some structure to their creativity, it need not be all the rules of harmony. "My best classes are where I give them really strong borders and lot of freedom in the center and let them fly" (Teacher 18). Because consciously thinking of all these things at one time would be very inhibiting to the creative process, students find it easier to solve compositional problems that involve fewer specifications established by the teacher (Wiggins, 2001, pg.86). Composition can also be taught by giving students a short piece or phrase and asking them to create the last few bars, or the ending. "When I first teach composition I say it can be eight bars and then we look at what makes it work. What will make it sound better" (Teacher 4). Students need guidelines within which there is freedom to experiment.

Performance and Creative Decisions

Another strategy to teach creating is how we get students to perform pieces musically. "Creativity is very much a learning skill. Look at things from a different perspective" (Freed, 1992). We need structure our lessons so that we are asking students what to do to make the piece musical.

"My biggest thing is they really want you to tell them what it is supposed to sound like. I want to get them to problem solve on their own. I ask them for ways of enhancing the sound or tempo or whatever. At the end of a piece what is their emotional response? Get them to verbalize and comment on it". (Teacher 7)

Give students responsibility of interpretation. "We were working on a piece the other day, it repeats and the second time it has a counter melody. I ask 'What can we do?' It is getting kids involved in the process of interpreting or shaping the piece" (Teacher 1). "This morning we were doing *Largo* from Dvorak's *9th symphony*. There was a whole note that the kids were just playing and I said, 'Let's do something to make this more interesting'" (Teacher 1). Sometimes we get into a bad habit of always stating and directing the interpretation of a piece, and not allowing students the pleasure of deciding which interpretation will be best. Giving students ownership of the interpretation of a piece is also teaching creativity.

"We have these options articulation, tempo what would we do? By experimenting in rehearsal, they get to create. It is ownership they were part of the interpretation" (Teacher 2).

Students at any grade level can create a soundscape to a poem, story, piece of art, or short video. This can be done with found sounds, voices, or instruments.

"Last year I did a project with student teachers called *The Creative Act* and it was so exciting! My kids were finger-painting a collage and it developed over a period of 8 weeks into a performance piece at the end. The creative act, it was a gradual process of discovering whom you are and how you're going to express that. The kids loved it" (Teacher 5). Another creative process is described by first listening to music, responding, and then creating.

"In studying music I have four quadrants: (i) draw a picture of what this music is about, (ii) what do you hear, i.e. instruments, (iii) what terms are demonstrated that we have discussed in class, i.e. dynamics, (iv) what emotions are you feeling and why? This leads to composing, which is one of the most important of artistic needs. With composing you make rules and sometimes they follow the rules and make a really pathetic composition because they do not have the ear for what flows. That's where their own experimenting and listening skills and practice comes in: does this piece flow and connect? They can recognize so in examining they learn. In the beginning that might not make a lot of sense to them so they have to hear what is beautiful first. Like in writing, you have to go beyond the first draft if they only do rough copy they are only going to get a rough copy story. Keep trying new notes, reflecting until you get something you've done that is beautiful. Even great composers had to learn the rules" (Teacher 1).

Our task is to instill the process and not necessarily to produce a professional product.

Journals

Journal responses to music should be a routine in planning a music course for adolescents. This activity ensures that students "explore, develop, formulate and express thoughts and experiences and feelings" (Nova Scotia, 1999, pg.10) about music. Journals also provide students with opportunities to "communicate their thoughts and feelings about music" (Ontario, 1998). "Looking at the decisions made by professional composers or performers helps them to be better decision makers in their own work" (Wiggins, 2001, pg.86).

"Students (adolescents) need to feel comfortable with themselves. We need to help them . . . so they can express themselves. That is why journaling is so important in music" (Teacher 1).

Listen to a piece of music and ask, "What emotions are you feeling?" Then we discuss "Why?" This leads to composing which is one of the most important artistic needs. Kids need to be able to create their own music and then they connect with music in a deeper way, and they understand the rules better. (Teacher 14)

Fooling Around

Sometimes the creative process occurs outside of the structured lesson and music class. The safe and relaxed environments of lunch hour jam sessions, or being at home seem to stir the creative process. "Sometimes it's 'improvisation' someone playing a piano and others joining in" (Teacher 4). "I started playing with people in grade six, and then it was really fun. Since then we play at talent shows. Then it is more fooling around we've written our own songs then we go skateboarding" (Student 5).

"When I go home, I play my guitar. On three chords I can play my whole day's emotion. Music can be used to speak up without disturbing the peace there's always a message whether there are words or not" (Student 4). This is supported by Hamman (1991), "most, if not all genuinely creative activity takes place outside the areas of institutionalized learning" (pg.10). However, the school music program should provide some basis and encouragement in improvisation and composition.

Conclusion

The benefits of including the creative process in our music plans are deeper understandings about music works, teamwork, problem-solving, and pleasure by students. "By introducing improvisation and composition, children come to see how composition and performance are connected" (Upitis, 1992, pg.37).

"It is time for every parent's organization to state unequivocally its belief in children's creative potential and the importance of making it possible for the creativity to emerge" (Pitman, 1998, pg.248). Personally, I believe it is time for every music teacher to plan their lessons so that the creativity of adolescent learners is given the opportunity to emerge and teachers should provide the audience and venues for demonstrations. In this century children are now encouraged to make up their own music instead of always playing someone else's and we should see and hear this is our schools.

References

British Columbia Education. (2000). HYPERLINK "http://www.bced.gov.bc.ca/irp/music810/8tf.htm" www.bced.gov.bc.ca/irp/music810/8tf.htm

Choksy, L., Abramson, R., Gillespie, A., Woods, D., York, F. (2001). *Teaching Music in the Twenty-first Century.* 2nd edition. New Jersey: Prentice-Hall Inc.

Cornett, Claudia. (1999). *The Arts as Meaning Makers.* New Jersey: Prentice-Hall Inc.

Freed, Dale. (1992). *Living Creatively.* The Toronto Star, November 15, G1,3.

Hamann, Donald. (1991). *Creativity in the Music Classroom.* Reston, VA.: MENC.

Nova Scotia Ministry of Education and Culture. (1999). *Foundation for Arts Education.* Halifax:

Ontario Ministry of Education and Training. (1998). *The Arts.* Toronto: Queen's Printing.

Pitman, Walter. (1999).*Learning the Arts in an Age of Uncertainty.*
Aylmer, ON: Aylmer Express Ltd.

Saskatchewan Education, Training and Employment. (1994). Arts
education. Grade 8. Regina.

Taylor, Marlene. (1987). *Creativity, Imagination and Originality: Three
lenses for viewing creative potential.* Canadian Journal of
Research in Music Education. 29. 21-30.

Upitis, Rena. (1992). *Can I Play You my Song?* Portsmouth, NH:
Heinemann,

Walker, Robert. (1985). *In Search of a Child's Musical Imagination.*
Canadian Music Educator. 26, 4.

Wiggins, Jackie. (2001). *Teaching for Musical Understanding.* New
York: McGraw-Hill.

Chapter 8

Creativity and its Origin in Music Improvisation

Rafael Prieto

RAFAEL PRIETO ALBEROLA holds degrees in Orchestral and Choral Conducting and Composition and a Ph.D. in Music Education. He studied in Spain, Salzburg Mozarteum (Austria), Hungary and the Universities of Tucson (Az), Tampa (Fl) and London.

His scientific works have been published in various Spanish and European journals and congresses of music education. He also published books on conducting and elementary composition.

Dr. Prieto is a conductor of bands, choirs and orchestras, and toured as a pianist with the American group, Up With People.

He is a Professor (Catedratico) of Music at the University of Alicante (Spain) and he is supervisor of music education research and theses.

1. Introduction

Creativity is a very important issue in almost everything in modern times and specially in education but the word creativity has been overused and sometimes misunderstood. It has been said that it is an impossible subject to teach or to learn however some authors with whom I agree, like Balkin (1990), established that this is an "acquired behaviour, learnable (and) teachable".

Orff, Dalcroze, the British National Curriculum, the Manhattan Curriculum Project, the Contemporary Music Project, the Ann Arbor Symposium, the Suncoast Music Education Forum and the American National Standards as well as the Spanish Music Education Law, defend the place for creativity in music education. Authors such as Webster (1990), Moore (1990), Kratus (1994) and Kaschub (1997) also show evidence of the importance of creativity in the Music Education Curriculum. They say that is motivating, stimulating while developing aesthetic sensitivity, human curiosity and the divergent thinking of the students. Shehan Campbell says that creativity is a "high quality" found among the greatest musicians of all traditions. The same author compares musical creativity with the gradual development of verbal language trying to communicate structured thoughts. However, social academics structures still resist accepting this kind of "creative thinking". Ed Costa says that the teacher needs to be a questioner rather than a teller, the teacher is only the one who facilitates the child discovering himself. To teach divergent thinking is hard and difficult to measure and justify.

The origin element for a composition can be very varied, a painting, a landscape, a story, the head of a musical theme, etc. Hickey suggests a "template" giving the student, for instance, the first and the last note of the composition. The same author advises us to use what he calls SCAMPER which is an acronym for substitute, combine, adapt or add, minify (diminution) or magnify (augmentation), put to other uses (other instruments), eliminate, and reverse or rearrange (Hickey 1997). Shehan Campbell cites some standard techniques such as repetition, sequence, extension, call and response, and fragmentation.

There are lots of different types of compositional approaches. Improvisation can be one of them. Haydn, César Franck and Stravinsky became inspired while improvising on the keyboard. There are different theories about inspiration for instance, by some philosophers such as Baumgarten, Kant, Hegel, Hanslick, or artists such as Mendelssohn, Mengs, Goethe, Schiller, Wagner, etc. Inspiration has been involved with mysterium and the divine. From ancient times it was considered that music originated from the gods. For this reason one can find in any culture, melodies or musical fragments of divine origin: Indian Raga, Arabic Maqam, and the Iranian Dastgah and Gushah. Improvisation was not discovered by jazz musicians, it is as old as humanity itself. Since times of the ancient Greeks we know about improvisation contexts. Bach, Mozart, Beethoven, Schubert, Chopin were good improvisers as were, of course, the Jazz legends such as Louis Armstrong, John Coltrane, Charlie Parker, Dizzy Gillespie, Miles Davis, etc.

2. Methodology

The students' creative process is of a holistic nature, that is why it is not advisable to make them work in "watertight compartments". It is better to use the globalization of different musical knowledge, but give them only one direction at a time. According to Wiggins, students need to make their own music without unnecessary teacher control. To compose with pencil and paper or in a spontaneous way such as in improvisation, it is very useful to analyze the works of authors of different aesthetics. Kaschub advises the use of folk songs where the student is expected to change one element at a time: the melody rhythm, the dynamics, etc. After listening and analyzing, the student should then transfer the knowledge to his own compositional vocabulary.

The teacher should participate by asking questions that help the student to follow a compositional path. It is important that objectives should be clearly established. Balkin talks about the "3 p's" of the "creative education": "person, process and product". The personal component: originality, fluency, flexibility, elaboration and expressivity. The process component: problem detection, generation of ideas, modify and evaluate possible solutions, exploration, improvisation, composition and creative performance. The product component: form, timbre, tonality, texture, rhythm, pulse, dynamic, repetition, development and contrast. (Balkin 1990).

3. The composition of a school song with improvisation as a starting point

1. After some previous breath and vocal warm-ups exercises, in a circle the students and the teacher balance on one foot then the other in time with the rhythm, maintaining the pulse. The teacher improvises, by clapping some rhythm patterns and the students imitate this. Later they do the same with melodic patterns. The students' self assessment takes place while they listen to their fellow students and compare the different performances. "Imitative exercises.. involve the student in actively internalizing the musical experience" (Kaschub 1997). Every pattern is recorded.

2. Selection of recorded patterns. Students are not inhibited while they improvise their pattern to be recorded because,

when they listen to it they hardly know who the student is who is playing at any particular moment. Every time a reproduced pattern pleases a student he or she put their hand up. The whole group votes whether or not they want it to be included in the composition.

3. Transcription. The students should do this in their notebooks and the teacher on the board.

4. Writing the lyrics. The teacher or the students suggest a theme. The group writes an essay from which they extract the key words and put them together in a kind of short poem. They are expected to take special care with accentuation and the relation between music and words. Every student shows his work to the class and the verses that seems to be more suitable are chosen.

5. Melody learning. The teacher plays the resultant music on the piano and the students move around the classroom in time with the music. They develop their sense of pulse, rhythm and expressive musical character. In order to repeat the same melody without boring the students, the teacher modulates and does some harmonic or rhythm variations keeping the same melody in order for it to be clearly learned.

6. Singing. The students read the final version of the melody, using the Kodaly technique. Later they sing it with the words and finally with solfa.

7. Basic harmonization of the melody with I, IV and V chords.

8. Chords inversion in order to make it easier for the players and trying to get a better musical sound.

9. Orchestration. The students should write for four parts:

- Recorder and voice.
- Tuned percussion instruments. (Orff).
- Untuned perfusion instruments.
- Guitar or keyboard.

10. They perform the music within the cited groups together with some students that prefer or are better prepared for dancing. The recorders and the singers can also form

two different groups. If it is convenient, another group can improvise some patterns, or ostinatos in order to use them as a reference for future arrangements of the same song.

4. Assessment

Assessing creativity is not an easy task. Johnstone is aware of the assessment problems when he said that "objective criteria for assessment evade definition, and a general impression decides the grade" (Johnstone 1995), However, the Arts Propel theory states that the assessment of creativity is very important. The assessment of creativity is very important to evaluate theoretical knowledge, and furthermore, the objective is the expression and not only to show what students know.

Practically all current work on creativity is based upon methodologies which are either psychometric in nature or those that were developed in response to perceived weaknesses in creativity measurement. Divergent thinking tests are among the most popular techniques for measuring creativity in-educational settings. However studies may be too short in duration, and inadequate statistical procedures may be employed, a traditional reliance on quantity, etc. shows lack of predictive validity. Amabile designed in 1996 the "Consensual Assessment Technique" using several expert judges.

Creative activities, according to Kratus, produce results that can not be predetermined by the teacher. Since there is no correct model, some teachers consider the effort made by the student to be sufficiently positive. This constitutes a problem because it is therefore impossible to evaluate the learning. On the other hand the Nobel laureate, Sir Peter Medawan in 1969 said that, "the idea that creativity is not possible to analyze is a romantic notion that we must overcome." Kratus suggests looking at the compositions both as a product and as a process. Webster in 1987 developed the "Measure of Creative Thinking in Music" advising us to concentrate on the process. I agree with Kratus, that we should avoid evaluating creativity in terms of "good" or "bad" and concentrate on discovering if the student achieved the behaviours that are described in the objectives.

Conclusions

It seems evident that there is agreement in the literature reviewed that creativity is teachable, at least in its technical aspects, and for this reason it is assessable. Creativity integrates many different musical aspects and for this reason it allows the evaluator to observe the musical knowledge and development of skills, it develops the imagination and the students' self concept.

Improvisation is a good way to begin the composition process, and we should concentrate on this process, rather than on the results to assess the students' progress.

Chapter 9

Creating Music in the Classroom

Patricia Martin Shand

PATRICIA MARTIN SHAND is Professor of Music Education at the University of Toronto, Faculty of Music. Dr. Shand directs the John Adaskin Project (Canadian Music for Schools), which is sponsored by the Canadian Music Centre and CMEA.

The Canadian Music Centre (CMC) has been involved in composer in the classroom projects since the 1960's. As part of its Graded Educational Plan (renamed in 1965 the John Adaskin Project), CMC in 1963 sent a group of composers into Toronto area schools to observe and work with student performers, preparatory to writing compositions for school use. In 1965, CMC presented a seminar which featured concert demonstrations by student performers of music by 10 of these composers. At a 1967 John Adaskin Project policy conference (CMC 1967), there was considerable emphasis, not only on promoting the use of Canadian music in schools, but also on encouraging creativity in music education. Early composer in the classroom projects, like those undertaken and described by Murray Schafer', which emphasized student sound exploration and "ear-cleaning" activities, were held up as models. But, with the influx of funds for commissions for the 1967 Canadian Centennial, CMC turned its attention to these projects, leaving further development of the John Adaskin Project till 1973 when CMEA joined CMC as co-sponsors. At that time, the decision was made to focus the Adaskin Project on promoting and commissioning Canadian music for student performers, without CMC's previous focus on student creativity in music education. It was not till the 1983-4 academic year that the CMC Ontario regional office began its Creating Music in the Classroom (CMIC) program. Prior to that, there had certainly been examples of composers visiting schools. Many of the visits were related to commissioning projects, similar to the 1963 school visits during which composers worked with student performers preparatory to writing pieces for school use.[2] Other composer-in-the-classroom projects, such as the Canadian League of Composers' Visitation Program which began in 1979, were designed to introduce students to the music of contemporary Canadian composers, with the primary focus being on listening.

My main purpose in this paper is to describe efforts to involve students in composing, arranging, and improvising activities, guided by an experienced composer and an interested and committed teacher. I have chosen to highlight Creating Music in the Classroom (CMIC) because it is the longest operating program of its type in Canada.

From the outset, the CMC Ontario regional office has acted as a match-maker for the people involved in CMIC, and as a clearing house for funds flowing from the Ontario Arts Council, private donors, and the participating school or school board. CMC describes the main objectives of CMIC as being to provide opportunities for students "to learn the craft of composing by listening and doing" and "to develop an awareness of contemporary and Canadian music" (CMC 2000).[3] Each CMIC project has been designed to fit the needs, interests and abilities of the participants, but in each case a composer has guided students as they undertake a composition project. Some composers have scheduled weekly visits over some months, while in other projects, students have had a shorter, more intensive period of involvement with the composer.

In some cases, students have worked individually, while in others they have worked in groups. Sometimes the student compositions have been performed by professional performers, funded through CMIC. n other cases, students have performed the compositions themselves. There has been considerable emphasis on listening and analyzing, as well as on manipulating musical materials. Some groups have begun with improvisation, others have developed compositions based on preexisting or student-produced melodies, while others have produced music dramas or multi-media compositions. Some have explored descriptive music, while others have experimented with the manipulation

of various musical elements or have explored specific compositional devices such as twelve-tone technique. The
emphasis has been on problem-solving and musical decision-
making as the composer, teacher, and students have
worked together.

From its inception in the 1983-4 academic year to the 1999-
2000 academic year, CMIC involved 47 composers in 134 residencies, working with elementary and secondary school
students in classrooms across Ontario. With the establishment in 1995 of the Composers in Electronic Residence
(CIER) program with support from the York University and
Simon Fraser Faculties of Education, and administrative as-
sistance from the CMC Ontario Regional office, some recent
composer residency sessions have taken place via the internet, "virtual" residencies rather than "in person" visits by
composers to classrooms. CIER, modelled after Writers in
Electronic Residence, allows students, teachers, and composers to reach beyond a specific classroom, since student
compositions and reactions, composer feed-back and musical examples, and teacher comments can all be shared by
other CIER participants. Gary Barwin, composer and CIER
program director, describes CIER as "an online composition
workshop that links together professional

Canadian composers, music students, classroom teachers,
and music education students from Canada and around the
globe. Students submit their compositions in the form of
standard MIDI files. Composers, classroom teachers, and
other students listen to, comment on, and often submit
their own versions of the original pieces. Often groups of
students along with the composers collaborate on pieces. In
addition, discussions occur among students and teachers
within the local classroom as well as between geographically
remote classrooms as they are inspired by the work and discussions they have received. CIER is also a forum of the ex-
change of new curriculum ideas for teachers, and information concerning hardware, software, and technical trou-
bleshooting" (Barwin 1998).

Since 2000, CMC Ontario has focused its attention on Millennium projects which have had significant educational
benefits (Parsons 2000). The Millennium New Music for
Young Musicians Project has involved the commissioning of
compositions for student performers. As part of that project, some composers have visited Ontario classrooms to

work with student performers. The Music Canada Musique 2000 Project has involved the commissioning of compositions for professional performers, with some of the participating composers visiting Ontario schools in person and/or on-line, introducing students to the newly commissioned music. Some students have also been given the opportunity to attend Music Canada Musique 2000 premiere performances. While educational activities related to these Millennium projects took place mainly during the 2000-2001 academic year, some have been carried out during 2001-2. With the completion of these projects in sight, CMC Ontario Regional Director Sheldon Grabke indicated to me in a personal interview (Jan. 7, 2002) that CMC is considering future directions for its educational efforts. Since CMC's primary aim is to promote the work of its Associate Composers, CMC may choose to focus on school visits by composers, designed to introduce students to the music of those composers, rather than returning to the Creating Music in the Classroom project with its emphasis on student composition. I would personally regret the loss of CMIC, particularly at a time when the Ontario Ministry of Education (1998, 1999, 2000) is mandating creative activities as essential components of elementary and secondary school music curricula. Whatever the future of CMIC and CIER, teachers can learn a good deal from the past successes of these programs, as models of approaches to developing students' creative abilities through active music-making.

Here is an example of a well designed and successfully executed CMIC project from the 1998-9 academic year, as described by the participating composer and teacher.[4] Composer Paul Steenhuisen visited a secondary school in the greater Toronto area for a series of 10 classroom sessions with grade 11 and 12 students. The project goals were "to have the students compose a piece, to learn the skills required to compose music and to gain knowledge of contemporary music." The composer worked with large and small groups, and also with individual students. "In between class sessions, many students had 'email' lessons, where midweek compositional problems were resolved in order for work to progress." The composer described the project as featuring "private and group composition lessons, discussions of instrumentation, orchestration, form, analysis, notation, basic and advanced compositional techniques, and listening sessions. Students were encouraged to be creative and explorative, and given the tools to develop and articulate their musical ideas, as well as to express their needs and feelings about the project as it developed." To supplement in-class composition work, students were given opportunities to hear the Esprit Orchestra and the Toronto Symphony Orchestra performing contemporary works, and to meet composers represented on those programs. The teacher was an integral part of the process, working with the composer to establish project goals, consulting with the composer before and after each classroom session, assisting students between sessions, and "providing support and follow-up material and musicianship lessons as necessary." The teacher also assessed students' work: their creative output in terms of "following parameters discussed and originality," and also their more theoretical work as they developed their written scores ("accuracy, neatness, completeness").

The teacher indicated that if he were to undertake another such project in future, he and the composer could "be more demanding of goals - setting and achieving between sessions" and as the teacher he would "set evaluation/ assessment strategies from session to session so students are on task." The students (only one of whom had previously written a musical composition) produced pieces ranging from two to seven minutes in length, for a variety of instrumentations (solo piano, Chinese harp, string quartet, mixed nonet, full wind ensemble). The completed pieces were performed in concert at the school, and a CD was made. The composer reported: "while the majority of the compositions were relatively conservative, it was clear that each composer's thoughts on music had expanded, and that they were making genuine musical expressions of themselves." The teacher indicated that the main benefits of the project to the students were "understanding the process, using the skills and knowledge of theory in a creative way, and hearing a sonic interpretation of the print." The teacher reported that the students enjoyed working with a professional composer, and some "were keen to further pursue similar writing experiences." For the teacher, it was "great experience," with the process being as important as, if not more important than, the final products of the project. Steenhuisen was "very pleased to have been involved with a school so encouraging and supporting of its students' self-expression and awareness of contemporary music."

At the heart of the project described above was the development of students' musicianship through active involvement as composers, performers, and listeners. This type of multifaceted music-making has characterized other exemplary CMIC projects. In a 1986 article, Lee Willingham, then Head of Music at Agincourt Collegiate in Scarborough, reported on a CMIC project which he co-designed with composer Timothy Sullivan.

> This series of classes ranging over a two year period carefully guided students through the process of creating music -- dealing with such diverse concepts as sources of motivation or inspiration, motivic development and orchestral transposition. Students, many for the first time, gained a first hand glimpse of the painstaking and meticulous work of composing. They also realized the thrill of hearing their work performed by professionals. The project culminated in the commissioning of an original Timothy Sullivan work. Here the tables were turned. As Timothy completed a page of music, it was distributed to the student ensembles for rehearsal. They provided immediate feed-back for the composer and in return they saw many of the techniques, creative and motivational devices from their own experiences put to use in the new composition. (Willingham, 1986, p. 25).

Since the project at Agincourt Collegiate, Sullivan has continued to participate in a variety of projects which involve students in active music-making. For example, he undertook recent projects in several northern Ontario communities which "provided the students with a first-hand experience of music/sound exploration with a professional composer. The creative process was immediate: they were able to suggest ideas, explore them sonorally and, as a group, suggest appropriate places within the growing composition for these ideas to be placed. As a group, suggestions were made, explored and ordered, then, again as a group, the developing composition was played through, and feedback given. In this way, all participants were able to contribute as co-creators, co-analysts and co-performers. Within the 60 or 90 minutes, the class moved from a position of being elementary band students to being co-creators and performers of a new composition." When asked to describe students' responses, he noted the following: "Growing enthusiasm. Interest in qualities of sound. Willingness to experiment and to offer imaginative suggestions. A sense of critical skill in assessing contemporary musical content: the idea and its realization rather than a judgment on the sound materials themselves."

Sullivan's focus on the importance of listening to and making judgments about musical sounds is echoed in the comments of many CMIC and CIER participants. For example, composer Gary Kulesha "hoped to inculcate critical listening habits which will serve the students in whichever style they choose to listen to regularly. I believe that learning intelligent listening habits is a vital beginning" (quoted in Moore, 1988, p. 19). Over the years, whether projects focused more on sound exploration (as was often the case with younger students), or put more emphasis on the development of the discipline and craft of composition (as was frequently the case with more advanced secondary school students), the focus on listening critically to musical sounds has remained constant. To use Schafer's term (1986), students have been encouraged to use "the thinking ear." One high school student remarked: "Mr. Nimmons encouraged us to try to compose our own music. He taught us that music isn't what's on paper, it's what you play and how you play it."

Many participants have emphasized the importance of involving students as decision-makers and problem-solvers as they work with sounds. For example, a music consultant commented: "The development of problem-solving skills is a very strong aspect of the program. The students were discovering various concepts and making decisions about them. No matter what skill level the students were working at, the visiting composers encouraged them to use their own judgment and the skills they had learned in the program to choose one element of the score over another" (Moore, 1988, p. 18). Composer Nic Gotham, in describing students' progress, noted that in most cases their "musical ideas and intentions became clearer and more effective, also more elaborate, refined or sophisticated. In Example: I tended to stress the importance of beginnings and endings as a first step to understanding form. This was because much of the student work I heard seemed to begin and end arbitrarily. Does this mean the students themselves were becoming more 'musical'? According to my own ideas on the subject of music, I'd say yes." A music consultant reported that "the opportunity for pupils to interact with professional musicians and to be involved in the decision-making process of composing with them enabled them to readily take ownership of the task at hand. Not only was the musical growth evident in the students, but, in addition, a number of alternatives were discussed for future exploration by them with their own teacher."

The importance of the teacher in the process is reinforced by many of the participants. For example, one teacher emphasized that "the teacher must be completely engaged and committed to the success of the project. The composer enters a strange situation, and so should have clear understanding of the end goal, the role of all participants and guidelines to evaluate both the process and the product. In the end, the teacher remains the critical member for filling in gaps, helping students with skills required, and mediating among all members. In my experience, the composer created teaching opportunities that might not have been possible in a traditional class or setting" (quoted in Stanberg 1997, p. 12). Composer Gary Barwin believes that students participating in CIER benefit from "interacting with a working composer, with an artist as opposed to a teacher. The assumptions/behaviour of the students are different - they have the opportunity to try to be creative and take chances that they wouldn't necessarily with a teacher. They are afforded the opportunity to work with an artist who considers their ideas.

Since CIER uses text and MIDI file attachments primarily, the students interact about music and composition freed from some of the limited social strictures of the classroom. They also discover along with the teacher what the composer has to say. It's an unpredictable unfolding process which is different than most classroom interactions." With the support of composers and teachers, students can be encouraged to take risks as they develop their creative abilities. Barwin, for example, reported that CIER students with whom he worked "became more risk-taking."[5] As his students worked together on a collaborative project, they "were willing to take chances and follow their ears and intuitions." While emphasizing the value to students of working with a creative artist "outside the social/hierarchical paradigm of the school-as-institution" through CIER, Barwin also emphasizes the important role of the teacher who "can mediate what the 'living flow' of the creative artist brings to the classroom." Composer Nic Gotham reported that participating teachers often found "that the CIER work was a great help in confirming and supporting 'from the outside' as it were, some things the teacher had been saying in class but which the students had not quite fully understood or been convinced of." A teacher with whom Barwin recently collaborated "followed up on the implications of what I wrote and composed. He suggested other options to the students, and kept them inspired and focused on a daily basis."

Although Canadians can be proud of exemplary school music programs which nurture student creativity, it must be acknowledged that these are the exception rather than the norm. The types of projects which I have described have been undertaken by individual teachers who have been interested in having composers work with their students, and who may also have been intrigued by the use of technological tools to assist in creative development. The vast majority of students in Ontario, and indeed across Canada, do not have opportunities to develop their creative potential. That being the case, I conclude by suggesting some ways in which more of those now teaching and those preparing to enter the teaching profession might be encouraged to develop music curricula which will foster students' creativity.

A basic strategy, I believe, lies in actively involving pre- and in-service teachers in the sorts of music-making and problem-solving experiences which help nurture student creativity. To the extent that music teachers have had fulfilling experiences improvising, arranging, and composing as well as listening and performing, they will feel confident in making such experiences available to their students. And to the extent that they have had experience observing and working in classrooms where such activities are carried out, they will feel more confident using similar types of teaching approaches themselves.

As a first step, pre- and in-service teachers should be made more aware of exemplary programs which already exist. With increased networking across Canada, less experienced and confident teachers could learn about workable approaches to developing creativity. Links could be established from the top down (e.g., nationally through CMEA and its publications, or within provinces through Music Educators' Associations or Ministries of Education), or links could be established locally through boards of education. University faculty members could document and systematically evaluate current approaches to the nurturing of student creativity, and could arrange for teachers-in-training to observe exemplary programs in their local communities.

A more fundamental approach to increasing the emphasis on creativity in music education involves changing the focus of our teacher-education programs. Advanced performance training and performance methods courses have traditionally been emphasized in Canadian university music education programs, and as a result, today's specialist music teachers generally feel most comfortable using performance-oriented approaches in their classrooms. In the best of our school music programs, we have achieved high performance standards, of which we are justifiably proud. But too often performance has been developed at the expense of other aspects of a well balanced music curriculum. Most music teachers in Canada today feel ill at ease using sound exploration, improvisation, and composition approaches in the classroom because they have not had this sort of experience themselves. At present, the music theory training which our university music education majors receive, tends all too often to involve the learning of arbitrary rules rather than the meaningful exploration of the materials of music.

Because of specialization within university faculties of music in Canada, it is usually only composition majors who have opportunities to develop their musical decision-making abilities as they manipulate sounds to produce compositions. More emphasis should be placed on this sort of approach in music theory courses for music education majors. More consideration should also be given in methods courses to approaches involving sound exploration, improvising, and composing. In addition, pre- and in-service teachers should be given more opportunities to work with composers in meaningful creative undertakings, producing compositions for specific university, community, or school functions.

If teachers are to feel comfortable using technology for musical and pedagogical purposes, they need experience using a variety of technological tools to make music. For the most part, the music teachers currently using computers successfully in their classrooms have invested a great deal of their own time, first in learning to use the technology, then in developing courseware. If more teachers are to be prepared to use technology to assist their students in exploring and manipulating sound, then Canadian music teacher-training institutions should provide music education majors with experience using computers and MIDI technology both for their own compositional work, and as educational tools. MIDI technology has great potential for assisting students in making music, but educators must be prepared to make informed choices about the use of that technology.

Technology is a mixed blessing. If used to enhance music-making, it can be a valuable pedagogical tool. But it can easily take over, leading to emphasis on developing techno-logical skills for their own sake, rather than as a means to acquiring musical skills and understanding. The ease of pro-duction using MIDI technology may encourage students to rely on the technology rather than on their musical judg-ment. Teachers should be aware of this danger and should help students develop the musical and critical-thinking skills essential for evaluating the compositions which they pro-duce. The immediate feed-back and ease of editing using MIDI technology make it possible for students to experi-ment with musical materials, to explore various musical op-tions, and to revise and refine their compositions, and stud-ents should be encouraged to do so.

Thoughtful consideration of the nature of creativity and its importance in music education, and clear educational goals and objectives should guide teachers as they develop music curricula and select the technological tools to assist them in their work. Music educators, computer programmers, and experts in the use of music technology should co-operate to develop software and hardware which will meet music edu-cation's objectives. In addition, teachers should be active in developing curricular materials to guide students in using the available technology.

Pre- and in-service teachers should be given opportunities to observe school music programs in which teachers lead students from simpler to more complex use of technology in achieving musical ends. In addition, teacher-training insti-tutions should develop libraries of suitable courseware, as models. And, finally, pre- and in-service teachers should be guided in developing such courseware. As technology con-tinues to change, the possibilities for students to be in-volved with music-making will also develop, but the teacher is the real key to fostering creativity in music education, and the teacher's ultimate focus must be on the students and the music, not on the technology.

There will never be one single correct way to nurture stud-ents' creativity, so the more fluency we have as a profession in generating a variety of approaches to fostering creativity, the better. We must study current theory and practice related to musical creativity, not only in our own country, but world-wide, and we must be willing to take risks as we explore various avenues to musical experience. It is a fascinating time to be a music educator -- a time when we need to use our creative abilities to meet the challenges which lie ahead.

Notes

1 Schafer's The Composer in the Classroom, published in 1965, described his work in schools. A series of books followed, documenting his on-going creative work with students. See Schafer (1986) for his collected writings on music education from the 1960's and 1970's.

2 See, for example, descriptions of a variety of such projects in Shand, 1979.

3. My research indicates that CMC has never provided CMIC participants with a theoretical definition of "creating music," nor have participating composers and teachers sought to develop such a definition. Their focus has been on actively involving students in the exploration and manipulation of sound, through improvising, composing, arranging, performing and listening.

4 Unless otherwise noted, quotes are taken from material provided by CMC or sent directly to me by project participants. I acknowledge with gratitude the generous support of CMC and of project participants in my research.

5 One of David Elliott's valuable suggestions for teachers seeking to develop their students' creative potential is "to provide many opportunities for students to exercise their developing musical expertise in a receptive environment that will foster the self-esteem needed to risk producing and the evaluation (both by self and others) of such producing" (Elliott 1989, p. 36). In a slightly revised version of his list of suggestions, Elliott (1995, p. 234) writes that "the development of musical creativity requires a receptive environment that encourages risk taking and the constructive evaluation of students' efforts to achieve creative results."

References

Barwin, Gary. "Composers in Electronic Residence." *Canadian Music Educator*. Vol. 40, No. 1 (Fall 1998), pp. 23-25.

Canadian Music Centre, Ontario Region. *Creating Music in the Classroom: Final Report - 1983-1999-2000.* Toronto: CMC, 2000.

Canadian Music Centre. John Adaskin Project Policy Conference. Toronto: CMC, 1967.

Elliott, David J. "The Concept of Creativity: Implications for Music Education." *Proceedings of the Suncoast Music Education Forum on Creativity.* Tampa, Florida: Department of Music, University of South Florida, 1989. Pages 14-39.

Elliott, David J. *Music Matters.* New York: Oxford University Press, 1995.

Moore, Lisa. "Composer in the Classroom." *Federation of Women Teachers' Associations of Ontario* Newsletter. Vol. 6, No. 3 (January 1988), pp. 17-20.

Moore, Lisa. "Music Makes the Mind Grow Stronger." Forum: T*he Magazine for Secondary School Educators.* Vol. 12, No. 4 (Dec. 1986/Jan. 1987).

Ontario Ministry of Education and Training. T*he Ontario Curriculum Grades 1-8: The Arts.* Toronto: Queen's Printer for Ontario, 1998.

Ontario Ministry of Education and Training. *The Ontario Curriculum Grades 9 and 10: The Arts.* Toronto: Queen's Printer for Ontario, 1999.

Ontario Ministry of Education and Training. *The Ontario Curriculum Grades 11 and 12*: The Arts. Toronto: Queen's Printer for Ontario, 2000.

Parsons, David. "New Music for Young Musicians." *The Canadian Music Educator,* Newsletter 107 (Spring 2000).

Schafer, R. Murray. *The Thinking Ear:* Complete Writings on Music Education. Toronto: Arcana Editions, 1986.

Shand, Patricia. "The Composer in the Classroom." Musicanada, June 1979, pp. 18-19.

Shand, Patricia. "The John Adaskin Project at Thirty." *Notations,* Vol. 3, No. 1 (January 1991).

Stanberg, Andrea. *Composition in the Classroom: A Comparison of the Canadian Music Centre's 'Creating Music in the Classroom' project and the Toronto Symphony Orchestra's 'Adopt-A-Player' Project.* Unpublished Mus. M. paper, University of Toronto, 1997.

Willingham, Lee. "Experiencing a Composer in the Classroom." *Canadian Music Educator.* Vol. 27, No. 3 (March 1986), p. 25.

Chapter 10

Evaluating Creative Processes and Products: Targeting Musical Outcomes

Betty Hanley

Dr. Betty Hanley teaches music education in the Faculty of Education at the University of Victoria. She co-organized the 1989 symposium *Re-Thinking Music Education in Bristish Columbia*, chaired the second National Symposium on Arts Education (NSAE), Victoria 1998; and has published articles in a number of journals. She has authored, co-authored and edited a several publications, including *Musical Understanding: Perspectives in Theory and Practice* (2001). Dr. Hanley is a member at large on the Canadian Music Educators' Association Board, and a member of the steering committee for the National Symposium on Arts Education,Canada.

Introduction

There are many explanations of creativity, ranging from personality descriptions to illuminations of the process. Gardner (1993), for example, provided a definition based on originality and cultural need/appreciation for the product. This explanation is useful when talking about Stravinsky and Freud but less appropriate when applied to education. It has, indeed, historically been difficult to apply main-line creativity research to children. For instance, is children's work original? If not, is it still creative?

A more helpful definition is proposed by composer, David Best (2000), who explains creativity as the "ability to think something up and then to craft it" (p. 6). Here, the focus is on both imagination and craft. For Best, creativity (imagination and craft) is one of three components of mindedness or intellect involved in artistic endeavours. The other two are valuing (sorting, sifting, making choices) and spirit (passion and intensity). Looking at creativity from

Best's perspective allows educators to plan learning opportunities in which students can demonstrate creativity. Children need the tools (craft) and the encouragement (place/time/appropriate praise) that will help them communicate what exists in their rich imaginations.[1]

What are the implications of Best's ideas for the elementary classroom? These are simply stated, if not so easily implemented: We need to nurture our students' imaginations *and* provide them with the tools (the craft) to compose music. The imagination can be sparked through the provision of intriguing and engaging musical problems and a classroom context that encourages risk taking, learning, and pursuit of the best "solutions" possible. The tools include (1) sequential [2] skill development (in singing and playing and music notation), (2) conceptual understanding, and (3) perceptual acuity to let students think *in* music. Clearly, isolated, "fun" composition activities presented by inexpert teachers will not allow children to develop the essential tools for musical composition; there is a need for *progression* in the planning of composition lessons. Furthermore, composition, listening, and performance experiences need to progress hand in hand so that students can develop the mindedness that is at the heart of music education.

While honing their craft, students must also be learning to make appropriate musical decisions. These decisions occur throughout the act of composing, but thinking *about* music allows students to focus on what did or didn't work and why and thus helps them set their own direction. Thinking *about* music, combined with experiences *in* creating music, provides a backdrop for the evaluation of creative process and product.

Can creativity be evaluated? The truth is that we do it all the time. In Gardner's sense, we evaluate creativity in individuals and groups based on their cultural contributions. As alluded to earlier, this sense is not very helpful when we are dealing with children. First, a clarification. By assessment, I mean the collection of data; by evaluation, I refer to the making of judgments about the data. It is the latter that is particularly problematic. For educators, a better question than "Can creativity be evaluated?" would be "Can creative process and products be evaluated?" In my view, they must be—as long as, by evaluation, we mean *the process by which students learn* and *as long as we know what we are doing*. Giving a music composition an A or a B+ with no explanation or feedback to students is simply not good enough; in such cases, music educators could rightfully be accused of subjectivism and even of obstructing a child's education. Having and communicating no acceptable criteria for evaluating student work is equally self-defeating. The kind of evaluation used is, therefore, critical. Making judgments about our work is an integral part of learning.

Application

In the following section, I will provide concrete examples of learning strategies for creative work and two samples of the evaluation of creative processes and products drawn from classroom practice. While much of this material may be familiar to readers, the focus on musical outcomes is less evident in the literature. Thus, the following examples will focus on thinking *in* music (composition activities that necessarily involve performing and listening) and thinking *about* music (the use of questions to promote reflective and critical thinking and the building of habits of mind that generate self-evaluation and instill a desire to improve their craft). Thinking about music should increasingly occur during the process of composing as well as afterwards.

The two examples below assume that students will have sung and listened to music that illustrates solutions to the problem or will do so during or after the composition task. They are also designed to illustrate two levels of student learning—novice and more advanced.

Example 1 looks at a possible experience for novice Grade 3 or 4 composers. As a class, building on prior knowledge of how contrast is generated in music, the children created a composition with two sections. They negotiated in advance how the sections would contrast (e.g., in late for school and bedtime). The sound sources were body percussion and voices. Decisions made included which sounds to use in each section, whether everyone should play all the time, how to get from the A to the B section and how successfully other musical elements were used. The teacher modeled the kinds of questions that could be asked. The piece evolved as children suggested ideas to test out and accept or set aside.

Sometimes they built on each other's suggestions. The piece was performed. The class ended with a discussion of various aspects of the composition, once again led by the teacher. Did they think they got it right? Why? Why not? In the class composition that served as a model for subsequent work, the teacher's role was to coordinate students as they tested ideas, encourage children to suggest alternatives or extensions, and ask "what if" questions.

The questions asked of students in the "debriefing" of their compositions, largely depend on the composition task and the product, and the amount of detail needed in the process depends on the experience of the children. The questions provided below give a general idea of possibilities. In Example 1, the observation process has been kept simple for easier observation of the children in an initial experience. Since this is the first small-group composition experience, the teacher is establishing a baseline for planning future work.

Example 1

Length: 40 minutes [10 for composing and 30 for performance and feedback]

Materials: None

Objectives
1. to create a short composition in AB form
2. to reflect on how successfully the music problem was solved

Outcomes
1. to demonstrate an understanding of AB form
2. [there could be a cooperative learning outcome]

Thinking *in* music

Context: The class ore-identifies two pairs of contrasting feelings (from which each pair of students will select one).
The composition problem: Compose a short piece that has two sections (AB) to show contrasting feelings.
The process: Work in pairs. Choose one of the pairs of feelings. Use body percussion and voices for the composition.

Decide how the A section will sound. Practice it. Decide how the B section will sound. Practice it. Perform the 2 sections together. Can you improve your piece? Does it convey the feelings you chose? Perform your composition for the class.

Thinking *about* music

Feedback from the class
Which story did you hear? How do you know?

Questions that might be asked of the composers immediately after the performance.
Is the music over too soon?
Do you hear enough of ...?
Did that part sound right? How can you tell?
How did you know when to finish the A section? The B section?

Evaluation
Evaluation will be based (1) on the quality of the understanding demonstrated by the student composers in their composition and (2) their responses to the question(s), taking into consideration the possibility that some children might do better at either task.

Observation by teacher [depends on what the class has been learning; including corroborating evidence would be helpful]

Composition
Used an AB form
Contrast accomplished through: [list musical devices]
Music craft demonstrated through:

Process [you may have to limit these observations to a few pairs each time]
Concentrated on the task

Discussion
Expressed thoughts about the composition
Made comments about musical features

A desired outcome of the process is that the questions asked during class discussions will serve as a model for the kind of questions students can ask themselves as they compose. Although the role of language in music is disputed, there is a need to validate students' expression of their personal valuing of music (Mellor, 1999) as we help them learn. It is a good idea to invite students to talk about their compositions before the class or teacher make any remarks or ask questions.

Composing requires that students make sounds/noise. How

much "noise" can be tolerated? Creative solutions based on the school facility and availability of adults to supervise the students are required. Example 1 reduces the "noise" element through the selection of sound sources.

Composition tasks need to be progressively challenging; there is no recipe book. The progression needs to be based on the tools available to students and their level of musical understanding. At the same time, a composition task allows for considerable flexibility in the sophistication of students' responses, thus addressing individual student ability.

Example 2 presents a composition task for a Grade 6 or 7 class with some meaningful experiences composing and with the ability to synthesize what they have learned.

Example 2

Length:

Class 1—establish criteria [see sample rubrics inTable 1], plan, compose, rehearse, and revise the composition

Class 2—perform and give feedback

Class 3—[optional] revise composition in response to feedback

Materials: Classroom instruments (including voices), band instruments (if available and the volume potential can be accommodated)

Objectives
1. to compose a short composition that represents an image
2. to reflect on how successfully the music problem was solved

Outcomes
1. to observe the stylistic features of an image and convey these through a coherent music composition

Thinking in music

Context: Students have previously looked at images and discussed the elements and principles of design in art works. Two images are displayed: Kandinsky's "Red-Yellow-Blue" (1925) and Improvisation 26 (1912).

The composition problem: Choose one of the images and compose a piece that sounds like the image.

The process: Class establishes criteria for the composition and performance. Work in groups of four. Identify the important features of the image you have selected. Decide how you will represent these features in sound. What instruments will you use? Plan the composition. Get the instruments. Rehearse, revise, rehearse, perform.

Thinking about music

Feedback from the class
Which image do you think the group chose? How do you know?

Questions that might be asked of the composers immediately after the performance.
Which features of the painting struck you as most significant?
How successful do you think you were in representing the image?
Is the music over too soon?
Do you hear enough of ...?
Did that part sound right? How can you tell?
Why did you select...(instrument)?

Feedback from the class
The discussion would either reinforce or challenge the composers' view of their work.

Evaluation

Student Self-Evaluation
Oral—students provide a self-evaluation in the debriefing)
Journal entry—students reflect on what was successful, how they improved, what they could work on next
Self evaluation form (using rubrics [3] for rehearsal, performance, and composition)

Observation by teacher [depends on what the class has been learning and criteria established; rubrics could be used]

Composition
Response to the art work (features identified
Musical features and devices (tempo, melody, phrasing, form...)
Quality of performance

Process [you may have to limit these observations to a few pairs each time]
Commitment to the task
Ability to work with others toward a goal
Willingness to try out musical ideas

Engagement in the project

Discussion
Thoughtfulness of responses
Reference to musical features of the composition
Openness to feedback
Identification of successes and areas for improvement

The kind of evaluation suggested in this chapter requires respect, empathy, and honesty to promote a desire to learn. The evaluation for example 1 was informal and formative; for example 2, the evaluation is more formal and could be formative or summative.

Table 1. Possible Rubrics for Example 2 [developed by the teacher or with the class]

Composition

1	No attempt is made to reflect the elements of the image in the composition.
2	One or two features of the image are represented in the composition. The music focuses on one or two music elements and the parts don't fit together well.
3	Three or four features of the image are represented in the composition. The various sections of the work are musically attractive, but the sections do not flow together well.
4	Many aspects of the image are reflected in the music composition. The composition used many musical elements in a coherent and effective manner.

Discsussion

What is the teacher's role while students are composing? According to Byrne et al. (2001), neither using directive teaching strategies nor leaving the students to manage on their own is appropriate. Unfortunately, the teachers in their study "did not have the confidence to prompt students to think more widely about the significance of their work" (p. 72). Scaffolding, "holding the task constant while simplifying the learners' role through the graduated intervention of the teacher," is an effective alternative to directive and laissez-faire teaching (p. 71) through the use of "questions and prompts, suggestions of where to look for inspiration, and advice" (p. 71).

Should the compositions be individual, group, or class work? Do the students know how to work in cooperative groups? Working in pairs is more manageable for first attempts and may be the better choice for some assignments. Group work offers the benefits of sharing (Wiggins, 1994, 1999/2000). Music teachers, however, should not assume that children will work well together in groups without some direction; the group process needs to be addressed in planning. And finally, regardless of the value of group work, the purpose of evaluation is (1) to provide feedback for individual students so they will recognize their accomplishments and look ahead to new challenges, (2) to help teachers plan for progress, and (3) to inform parents and administrators of the learning that has taken place. Although it is possible to evaluate student progress in groups, individual composition assignments and evaluation should be part of the music program.

The examples in this chapter could not address many opportunities available to teachers and student composers: the possibility of (1) taping the performance so the composers can listen in a different way; (2) using notation, either invented or traditional; or (3) using technology. All these possibilities contribute to the richness of experiences available to students and have the potential to enhance their learning. In addition, the two examples were intended to exemplify the best learning conditions and should be suitably modified depending on the children and the learning context. Regardless of the context, the focus should be on musical outcomes.

Conclusion

Many people believe that the ability to compose music is a talent reserved for relatively few individuals, that composing is simply beyond ordinary people. Yet, there seems to be no such restriction when it comes to writing an English essay! The purpose of composition in music classes is not primarily to develop a Beethoven or a Paul McCartney.⁺ The purpose is to provide students with another path to music involvement. The teacher must be *willing* and *able* to judge student work. In the process described in this chapter, students are very involved in the judgment process. The criteria are not secret. Part of the process is to share the basis for judgment as a means of enhancing learning.

A key element of using composition in the music class is the need to provide experiences that will foster student learning over time. How many music teachers are composers or have composed? If they are not composers themselves, they may be uncertain about how to help children. Teachers need skills in planning progressive composition lessons and in managing individual and group composition, and in evaluating students' work.

The problem is that we have mystified the act of composition and the nature of creativity to such a degree that we are afraid to address the topic. Yet music teachers regularly evaluate the re-creative act of performing.

Experiences such as the ones described in examples 1 and 2 allow students room to use both their imagination and craft, to value what they do, and show their spirit. If we claim to be educators, then we must evaluate the progress of our students—in composition as well as in other musical engagements.

Notes

1. Whereas Best acknowledges the creative nature of performance, I will restrict my discussion to what creativity usually refers to in schools—composing (and improvising).

2. By sequential, I do not mean a pre-programmed sequence of events. I refer, rather, to the need for student development over extended periods of time and a progression of learning activities that fosters growth.

3. *Learning, Teaching & Assessment in Fine Arts*, produced in 1996 by the Calgary Board of Education and the Calgary Catholic School District, provides some helpful suggestions for rubrics in the area of rehearsal and performance. The document is available from the Calgary Board of Education,

Research and System Development, 3610-9 Street S.E., Calgary, AB T2G 3C5.

4.   See Wiggins (1995) for a description of the learning of one child in a group composition setting.Such a discovery would be a bonus.

References

Best, H. M. (2000). Arts, words, intellect, emotion Part 2: Toward artistic mindedness. *Arts Education Policy Review, 102* (1), 1–10.

Byrne, C., Halliday, J., Sheridan, M., Soden, R., & Hunter, S. (2001). Thinking music matters: Key skills and composition. *Music Education Research, 3* (1), 63–75.

Gardner, H. (1993). *Creating minds.* New York: Basic Books.

Mellor, L. (1999). Language and music teaching: The use of Personal Construct Theory to investigate teachers' responses to young people's music composition. *Music Education Research, 1 92),* 147–158.

Wiggins, J. H. (1994). Children's strategies for solving compositional problems with peers. *Journal of Research in Music Education, 42* (3), 232–252.

Wiggins, J. H. (1995). Building structural understanding: Sam's story. *The Quarterly Journal of Music Teaching and Learning, 6* (3), 57–75.

Wiggins, J. H. (1999/2000). The nature of shared musical understanding and its role in empowering independent musical thinking. *Bulletin of the Council for Research in Music Education, 143,* 65–90.

Chapter 11

Fostering Creativity in Dance Students

David Spurgeon

DAVID SPURGEON currently coordinates the University of NSW
Dance Degree Program. He has taught improvisation, composition
and various dance styles to primary,secondary and tertiary students
for the last 25 years.

He is the author of "Dance Moves" and "Dance 'till you drop".

This chapter is the result of many years teaching dance and
movement improvisation to students of all ages. After a
brief introduction and a consideration of some of the characteristics of creative people I will detail seven guidelines
(techniques? strategies? procedures?) for encouraging
creative students. I am assuming that a creative teacher is
one who actively promotes these behaviours and uses them
to assist and enhance students' learning. My topic is dance
improvisation but I believe that the principals outlined below hold true for music and other arts.

Movement improvisation is an essential part of the choreo-
graphic process and yet it is all too frequently ignored in
dance education so that a major problem for dance educators is shifting student choreographers away from repro-
ducing what they already know towards the creation of the
new, the unseen, the innovative. In the University of New
South Wales dance education program that I coordinate, a
movement improvisation class is a compulsory part of the
first year's studies. The new students, mostly straight from
school will contain only a small number who have improvised and been encouraged to experiment. Most have spent
obedient years being told what to do as they perfect and refine their instrument - the body.

I thus find myself with a delicious pedagogical irony- how do you teach freedom, the unknown, divergency? It may seem impossible to those for whom teaching is didactic and prescriptive; however a broader view of teaching certainly encompasses the teacher as guide, facilitator and enabler. My quest for ways in which to structure movement workshops that would best promote students' creative improvisational responses has lead me to consider methods as much as content. What I do in the classroom (in my case, the dance studio) is tempered by reading and research, dialogues with practitioners and active participation as a student in other teacher's movement improvisation workshops but is informed mostly by past practice i.e. by teaching movement improvisation and critically reflecting on both students' behaviours and my own teaching.

Improvisation in dance refers to spontaneous, unplanned movement. The immediacy and lack of premeditation usually provokes a creative response. To a certain extent, to teach dance improvisation is to teach creativity.

For the purposes of this chapter, I am assuming that creative people possess most, if not all of the following characteristics:
• An openness to new experiences i.e. readiness for change
• An internal locus of evaluation
• An ability to play with both elements and concepts
• Evidence of skill acquisition and self-discipline
• A willingness to take risks - to toy with the unknown
• A high level of flexibility and adaptation

I recommend consideration of the following seven guidelines for encouraging creativity.

1. Invoke 'the pretend'

The eminent biologist J.Z. Young in his book *Programs of the Brain* [1978] details the two realities for human beings: the external world we inhabit and the world inside our minds. He explains that by synthesizing what is seen and experienced into symbols, the brain makes sense of these realities; it 'fits' the external world to "the programs of our expectations" [Young, 1978, 233]. Young continues by drawing a parallel between symbolism in the brain and symbolism in art. He sees works of art as evidence that the symbol producing power of the human mind is functioning normally. Child development theorist John Gabriel carries this analogy further. He contends that there is a 'symbol-creating mode of thinking' inherent in play and that this lies at the centre of both artistic thought and scientific discovery. For Gabriel, there is a direct correspondence between 'the pretend' of children, the symbols of art works and the hypotheses of the sciences. "In play you are relaxed and flexibility poised for change- this is a very good state to be in for learning" [Gabriel, 1976].

Play in all its manifestations is fundamental to movement improvisation. The 'lets pretend' of children is invoked in an improvisation workshop where there is a willing suspension of the normal rules of social behaviour. Since the artistic instrument _is_ the human body you pretend that you can't speak: a movement problem is solved with a movement solution. You don't smile, nod or wink to others as you constantly pass by, you pretend that they are not your friends and colleagues; they are movement material to be experienced. The 'role play' of movement improvisation means you don't apologize when you brush or bump someone as you would in everyday life since playing with others in movement involves frequent accidental bodily contact.

I invoke the testing, trying, fiddling with objects that is part of play by giving my students a comprehensive set of exercises designed to illustrate just how many ways there are for two people to relate in movement [lead, follow, copy, contrast, balance, support, instruct...etc]. They are then well placed to enjoy what I call a 'kinelogue'- a dialogue of movement. In this improvisational form [allied, I believe, to 'question and answer' in musical improvisation] two or more dancers can play with each other in an infinite movement conversation during which new shapes, new movements and new patterns usually emerge.

I invite - implore - my students to play with each other in the improvisation class; to allow their imaginations to run riot; to push the boundaries, challenge the status quo, take risks; to be open to new experiences; to constantly ask "I wonder what would happen if..."

2. Encourage 'Chutzpah' and Humour,

Defined by the dictionary as 'impudence' or 'gall', 'chutzpah' is a Hebrew word that I use to mean 'cheeky' in a positive sense, i.e. the ability to see something new and different and to try and see what happens. I like to think of chutzpah as a 'metaphysical tickling'. A student with this attribute will sense an improvisation that has become 'stuck' or slightly self indulgent and go in and completely change the boundaries so that something new can evolve.

This 'positive cheekiness' is also evident in the best of Australian Humour. Humour is very culture bound and can be quite specific so a brief explanation is necessary. If we are to believe the reaction from most of the world's press, the Sydney Olympics was generally regarded as a success. Unbeknownst to many overseas spectators the Olympics was preceded by a TV comedy series called 'The Games' and accompanied by another daily round up of significant events called 'The Dream'. Both shows - one scripted and prerecorded the other improvised and live - evidenced two of the main characteristics of Australian humour. Firstly, a biting satire and general disrespect for authority and secondly the use of a spiralling flight of fancy; building layers of complexity upon a simple ludicrous premise so that the end result is a triumph of absurdity. This has its immediate roots in Monty Python and the English Goon Show and historical antecedents in medieval carnival where the lord pretended to be a servant, the layperson was a bishop for the day and known society was - for a short while - a world turned upside down.

A few students arrive with this ability to be cheeky, to dabble with the absurd and they are to be encouraged. However, in the absence of these students I have been experimenting with some set structures to encourage chutzpah. One, is to appoint a student as 'dance police' for the session, charged with looking out for and stopping/ altering/ preventing the mundane, the everyday, the self-indulgent.

Another is to invite students to cheat in improvisation. By 'cheat' I mean to substitute a movement response to a problem when you don't know or can't do what is required. The very act of brazenly 'faking it' in public is very much akin to chutzpah. Another strategy is to invite students to go outside the dance studio for a coffee break during which time they are to 'steal' a movement from a member of the general public i.e. look out for, and able to reproduce, a particular movement which can then form the basis of improvisation. A further strategy I used is to ask a pair or trio who have composed a short (30-40 seconds) movement phrase to show it to the assembled class and then repeat the showing, only inserting ten seconds of improvisation upon hearing a handclap. The point of such structures is to encourage the unusual, the slightly bizarre and to show that you, as a teacher, are open to positive cheekiness.

3. 'Leave Home'

I am, of course, talking metaphorically. ' Leave home' is an exhortation to go outside your discipline/area of expertise and to ask "what do others do? How do they solve this problem?" In Australian schools and universities dance is taught as an art form so examples of pertinent questions are "How do musicians improvise? What drama improvisations can I use, alter for dance? How do drawing students view the body? If painters teach line and colour can I use their ideas and methods in dance?" In my improvisation classes, students have experimented with music visualization - literally 'moving to the music'. This is even more exciting with a live pianist and better still if the pianist does dance visualization - transcribing as literally as possible the dancer's improvisation into sound. Using the dance elements of gesture, shape, pathway and dynamics a painting, sculpture, environment or any visual input can be transcribed into dance. I have held an evening of dance and food called 'Saute' where the choreography sprang from images of food, kitchens and cooking and where the six different courses were inspired by movement and dance. Guests alternated between eating and watching dance. I am currently experimenting in a collaboration with a music lecturer- Robyn Stavely. Robyn watches me teach movement improvisation to first year dance students. She then teaches 'music for dancers' to these same students the following year. I either watch or join in these classes. This process has led me to insights into the process of teaching itself as well as an increasing number of links between dance and music. Robyn makes suggestions on the many ways music can be used in dance and I prompt her to physicalise musical concepts.

I am not only advocating cross-art stimuli but suggesting that creative insights can be gained into one's own practice by considering the practice of others. What happens when you give a sculptor the opportunity to compose a dance? What can they do with 'moving clay'? If 'Theatre Sports' can assist with spoken improvisation and be fun to watch can 'Dance Sports' do the same? If a drama student can direct a play [i.e. interpret a written text] and a music student can play a concerto [again, interpret a written text] what happens when a dancer interprets the text of an already choreographed dance?

4. Provide Protection

I believe that one of the greatest barriers to creativity is fear: fear of making mistakes, looking foolish, being embarrassed or compromised. This fear can be more acute in physical subjects such as P.E, drama, and dance because mistakes are out in the open - in the public arena for all to see. There are several procedures that a teacher who hopes for a creative response from students can put into place. All are intended to provide protection for students. I advise that, as a teacher, you:

> • Never compel students to show [i.e. perform for others] class work
> • Ask for volunteers to demonstrate an activity rather requiring specific students to do so
> • Use empowering statements such as 'I probably didn't explain that very well' rather than 'You did that incorrectly'
> • Avoid inappropriate imagery by explaining movement tasks in clear unambiguous terms
> • When appropriate, join in the movement improvisation yourself
> • Explain that there is no right or wrong; only movement to be discovered

An atmosphere that provides protection is aided by emphasizing the need for total focus and concentration on the task at hand during the improvisation classes. Obviously, it is also assisted when students perceive their teacher to be committed, sincere, knowledgeable and approachable.

5. 'Just Do It'

A recurring problem for dance improvisers is the way in which the conscious mind - the logical rational part of the brain - interferes with a movement response by mentally working out what to do. Some of the best and most creative movement responses occur when the intuitive part of the brain is allowed free rein. Oliver Sacks, the author and neurologist, talks of the body's internal sense of its own physical self being derived from the vestibular system and from proprioception [1985-68]. These two, together with sight, give instant feedback on what the body is doing. Clearly the body has its own kinesthetic sense, or, bodily kinesthetic intelligence. I view 'Just Do It' as allowing intuition and kinesthesia to take over. The problem is; how do you STOP the conscious, rational mind from planning and plotting?

I use three allied strategies which I term 'overload', 'otherload' and 'immediacy'. 'Overload' refers to giving the conscious mind so much to think about that the movement response has to be kinesthetic / intuitive. The American dancer Lisa Kraus introduced me to one such technique. A dancer is required to recall, aloud, a particular vivid experience and to move at the same time. Another overload I used is 'impediments'. Dancer A focuses on showing dancer B a composed phrase of movement lasting for approximately one minute. At the second showing B impedes, interrupts, interferes as much as possible - an ideal situation to encourage chutzpah! Dancer A has to continue whist allowing for and, if necessary, incorporation B's impediments.

Similarly, 'otherload' refers to setting up an exercise where planned composed movement is interspersed with periods of improvisation. Music with a regular beat can be very helpful for this. For example I play a piece of music in 5/4 and invite pairs to walk along the diagonal using the pattern: walk for 5, stop for 5. This gradually can be made more complex with examples such as 'walk for 5, make any shape for 5', 'Walk for 5, make any bodily contact shape with your partner for 5'. Most students are so busy keeping the beat and counting that they cannot plan for the shape to be made.

'Immediacy' refers to any situation where the response must immediately follow the stimulus. The Sydney improviser Andrew Morrish uses 'change' as an example. Dancer A focuses on moving a particular body part in a specific direction. At any time, dancer B can call out 'change' whereupon A must change both the body part and the direction immediately. I use the whispered word as another device. The task is to improvise from one corner of the room to another interpreting two or three words. These words are whispered into the ear by the person standing behind whereupon the movement improvisation must immediately commence.

There are, of course, many other strategies. The aim of all of these is that of preventing the rational mind from logically dictating what will happen.

6. 'In Tuition'

The philosopher David Best says "intuition in art is the result of tuition" (1978:1). An oft-quoted aphorism in dance is that 'good choreography is the result of 5% inspiration and 95% perspiration'. My point here is twofold. Firstly, that to be creative you have to have something to be creative WITH. The intelligent acquisition of dance vocabulary must precede its creative use. Secondly, by denying students the opportunity to be creative and intuitive we dance educators are in danger of encouraging perfect technicians who have nothing to say. I cannot speak for drama and music but a constant topic for dance education is the relationship between, and relative amounts of, discipline and freedom.

At varying times in the 20th century dance educators have mirrored their dance performer colleagues by rejecting the old and embracing what is different and new. Discipline and freedom have seesawed their way through the decades. This age old dichotomy is further intensified by an essential difference between the performing arts of dance, drama and music and other arts of image production and object construction. In the performing arts the act of DOING is usually separate from the act of CREATING/MAKING. Most painters who go into a studio to do painting are also making a painting. A sculptor constantly practices making and composing a sculpture. I don't know the situation with music or drama but certainly in dance hundreds of dance schools - public and private - spend thousands of hours requiring their students to practice and refine their physical dance technique, their 'instrument', their bodies.

Many of these dancers emerge having never made a dance or thought about dance. They remain locked inside their bodies: prisoners of technique. In rebellion against this, other schools of thought encourage the younger student to play with movement, endlessly fortified by the belief that whatever the child does is somehow sacred.

A dance education conference may well feature staged performances of both ends of this spectrum. On one stage is the technically precise dance devoid of any originality or creativity. On another stage, happy children jump, roll and frisk about demonstrating a wonderful ability to play but a lack of any aesthetic quality.

What I am strongly advocating is a proper balance between the acquisition of the technique of an arts discipline and the encouragement to be intuitive and creative. This balance is usually age dependant for the growing child but certainly by adulthood the dancer should be given equal encouragement to do and make. Creativity in dance springs not only from the practice of what I have written so far, but from the acquisition of skills, knowledge and competencies in dance. To paraphrase David Best 'intuition is in tuition'.

7. 'Structured Flexibility'

I realise that this is essentially an oxymoron but the creative teacher needs to develop these two skills; provision of a structure for a lesson so that skills are learned and planned outcomes are realised together with a willingness to 'seize the moment' and go with an idea that is either offered by a student or the result of sudden inspiration. There are several procedures that can encourage this teaching trait. Firstly, practice creativity yourself. Be a student wherever possible. If you teach dance improvisation go to other dance improvisation classes or, invite in guest teachers and join in. Being creative yourself, being 'in the moment' refines both your planning skills and your divergent ideas. As a teacher yourself you can both do the exercises and analyse / speculate on the efficacy and intention of the problem at hand.

Secondly, practice 'reading people' so that you know as a

teacher, when to stop or redirect an activity or when to let the improvisation continue until it has run its course. There will be times when your planned lesson will be delightfully subverted by an improvisation that totally engages the group and seeming acquires a life of its own. These moments are to be savoured!

A third way was taught to me by a very gifted Australian dance teacher Margaret Chapple. It needs a teacher with a lot of experience (and a certain amount of courage!). Simply put - go in empty. Don't plan the lesson. Start the students on a fairly simple task such as walking around the room and then watch carefully what they do and trust yourself to 'feed off' what you see. This is creative teaching at its most immediate and it provides a wonderful way in which students' creativity can be fed back to the group. Margaret used a particular teaching technique derived in part from Viola Spolin's 'side-coaching' (1963:392). This involves giving a group of improvisers fresh tasks or instructions whilst they are focused on a particular problem so that the teacher instruction does not interrupt the improvisation but assists, alters or redirects it. Combined with 'walking in empty' it allows the perceptive, creative teacher to notice an interesting student idea and then to use this idea as fresh input for the group. Quite lengthy and fascinating improvisations can develop.

Another procedure came from the improvisation teacher Julyen Hamilton who advocates that you, the teacher, invent your tasks and exercises to suit the occasion, the group and its needs. The large number of useful resource books for teachers and frequent in-service courses would seem to attest to the belief that it is possible to purchase the ultimate set of exercises and procedures to teach whereas it can be just as exciting to invent your own.

In the true spirit of creative teaching and creativity I trust that some readers will find this chapter interesting and useful and that others will be 'cheeky' in their adaptation of the contents to fit their teaching. You are invited to use, alter, discard the contents and allow thoughts on dance improvisation teaching to inform and alter your own practice.

References

Best, D. [1978]. Unpublished lecture at Australian Association for Dance Education Seminar. 17th September 1978. Sydney.

Gabriel, J. [1976] Unpublished lecture at Macquarie University, Sydney, 8th April, 1976

Sacks, O. [1985] *The Man Who Mistook His Wife For A Hat.* London, Picador.

Spolin, V. [2963]. *Improvisations for the Theatre.* Illinois. Northwestern.

Young, J.Z [1978] *Programs of the Brain.* Oxford O.U.P

Section 3   Creative Pedagogy

Chapter 12

Finding the Music ' Within':
An Instructional Model for Composing
With Children

Francine Morin

FRANCINE MORIN, Ph. D., is Associate Professor of Music and Movement Education at the Faculty of Education, University of Manitoba. Currently, she is Acting Head, Department of Curriculum, Teaching and Learning and President of the Manitoba Choral Association. Recently, she received the 2001 Morna June Morrow Award for Excellence in Music Education in Manitoba, the University of Manitoba Outreach Award for significant and sustained contributions to the provincial and national music education community, and the 2002 Special Recognition Award from the Mantioba Music Educators Assocation. Dr. Morin is active in teaching, conducting research, presenting at conferences, adjudicating arts festivals, and serving the professional community in a variety of ways.

Perhaps the most powerful justification for the inclusion of the arts in education is the development of children's creative abilities (Edwards, 1997; Goldberg, 2001). Most educators contend that "childhood is a time when creativity flourishes" (Jalongo & Stamp, 1997, p. 61). Children are thought to be engaged in creative behavior when they use symbol systems or languages to express ideas, images, feelings, or experiences (Engel, 1989). Here the music classroom serves an important function. It can provide the playground for encouraging the development of imaginative, metaphoric, and creative thinking in sound. The music composing process embraces innovation, technique, and the projection of new or alternative approaches to solving artistic problems. Creative products are records of children's intellectual development and are viewed as evidence of their emerging abilities to make aesthetic decisions and organize ideas in musical forms.

Creative learning now dominates the educational landscape with stronger emphases placed on the development of creative thinking and problem solving in curricula across disciplines. This trend is echoed in the field of music education where mainstream journals, such as the *Music Educators Journal,* have published numerous articles on the topic over the last decade or so. The advent of the National Standards for Music (Music Educators National Conference, 1994), which has influenced music curriculum reform in Canada, provides further evidence that the profession acknowledges the importance of addressing the creative process in today's school music programs. Despite the legislation for including improvisation and composition as curriculum goals for all music students K-12, research shows that there is some dissonance between theory and practice. Henry (1996) cites several studies which found that creative learning experiences are seriously lacking in the majority of music classrooms. Similarly, the National Assessment of Educational Progress in the Arts revealed that eighth graders in the United States have achieved only limited abilities in creating music (Lehman, 1999).

As a music teacher educator, I have the opportunity to visit many early and middle years music classrooms. Sadly, my observations of music teaching substantiate the notion that creative activities are rarely employed in classrooms. Conversations with teachers reveal that this situation may be attributable to: a) incomplete knowledge of the creative process; b) lack of personal experience with composition; c) limited instructional time for composition; d) lack of tools and strategies for assessing creative work; and e) a tendency to view creative work as a personal enterprise, often accompanied by a hesitant attitude towards using a fixed approach for composing music with children. On the other hand, music specialists are often disappointed with children's creative works that have evolved immediately, free from contemplation and structure. They realize that valid composition is dependent to a great extent on the teachers' ability to provide solid grounding for flights of creativity, as well as instruction that genuinely enables and supports children's efforts to make their own music.

If creativity is to be given more attention in music classrooms, teachers must increase their understandings of the process and be offered more open-ended instructional models for guiding the process. From more than two decades of direct experience working with children and teachers, active research, and an ongoing review of related literature, I have increased my understanding of teaching music composition. In this chapter, a three-component instructional model for composing music with children will be presented. The presentation will include separate discussions of each component which will focus on:

  a) developing and expanding the compositional base;
  b) selecting aesthetic content for children's musical works; and
  c) outlining a sequential composing process. A sample learning plan for children's creative idea development in the music classroom will be shared to provide a context for illustrating the model.

Expanding the Compositional Base

Knowledge and skills are the vehicles that enable creative ideas to flow, and are clearly fundamental to promoting creativity in music. The work of Edwin Gordon (1993), for instance, reminds us that the extent to which children can be creative depends upon a learned storehouse of melodic and rhythmic patterns. The larger the reservoir of musical images and tools that children possess, the better equipped they will be for creative work. Davidson (1990) goes further in saying that a broad knowledge base also increases the child's ability to evaluate and revise their creative work in more profound and meaningful ways.

The music composing process then, begins with, and is supported by, the ongoing development of a compositional base (See Figure 1). This encompasses children's total music repertoire; a working knowledge of music elements, fundamental music skills, musical styles, as well as knowledge of the communicative aspects of music.

Naturally, as children progress through a music program, the compositional base from which they can work expands. Valid, artistic products are dependent to a great extent on developing this music skill and knowledge foundation. Fortunately, the professional environment is very supportive of teachers who want to design the kinds of foundational learning experiences that follow (For example, see Anderson & Lawrence, 2001; Hackett & Lindeman, 1995; Richardson & Atterbury, 2001; Rozmajzl & Boyer-White, 2000).

Figure 1 - An Instructional Model for Composing Music With Children

I.   *Expanding the Compositional Base*

- rhythmic ideas (beat, meter, rhythmic patterns)
- melodic ideas (pitch, intervals, scales)
- harmonic ideas (polyphonic, homophonic accompaniments)
- fundamental music skills (listening, singing, playing, moving, performing)
- historical/cultural music styles (features, music-making skills)
- communicative ideas (expressive devices, form, compositional devices)

↕

II.   *Selecting Aesthetic Content*

- children's interests and ideas
- curriculum themes (music or general classroom)
- auditory sources (natural, musical, environmental sounds)
- literary sources (poems, word pictures, stories, folk tales, legends)
- visual sources (pictures, film, photographs, paintings, sculptures, artifacts)
- children's personal stories and lived experiences
- children's shared experiences (social issues, local events, current newsworthy topics)

↕

III. *Composing Music*

- exploring and improvising
- selecting, refining and extending motifs
- organizing and structuring form
- editing and polishing
- notating and rehearsing
- publishing, performing and recording

A core working knowledge of music elements requires a rudimentary, but intellectual grasp of rhythm, melody, and harmony. This branch of study will give young composers a basic music vocabulary and provide the scaffold for thinking and knowing about how music works. Rhythm refers to the temporal or mathematical aspect of music and comprises essential ideas about beat, meter, and rhythmic patterns. Melody is the horizontal aspect of music, a linear succession of tones integrated with rhythm that forms a complete musical idea. It is the tune of a musical piece that requires the child to apply concepts related to pitch, intervals, and scales. Harmony, in contrast, is the vertical dimension of music. It results from the blending of two or more sounds that when added to a melody produces a polyphonic or homophonic backdrop.

A second critical strand in the compositional base - fundamental music skills - focuses on listening as well as the manipulative or physical skills of singing, playing, moving, and performing music. Fundamental music skills can be thought of as the technique or "how to" of music. They can be taught in isolation, but are best advanced "actively" with children in relation to cognitive learning about music. The mastery of music-making skills essentially provides the modes through which children come to express themselves creatively and imaginatively.

Like all art forms, music has a culturally and historically rich stylistic dimension that deserves some attention when developing children's compositional base of knowledge (Shehan Cambell & Scott-Kassner, 1995). A musical style is created by using the musical elements in characteristic and unique ways. This third critical strand can be taught by linking a concept-based and performance-based approach to instruction. A concept-based approach focuses on the identification and analysis of the features and purposes of musical works that are representative of different historical periods and cultures. A parallel performance-based experience gives children the opportunity to extend their music repertoire by participating in some of the distinct rhythms, melodies, and music-making practices of people from other times and places.

A fourth critical strand of the compositional base concerns the various communicative aspects of music, such as expressive devices, form, and the aesthetic principles of composition. This strand helps children explore ways of clearly com-

municating their musical intentions by giving those intentions appropriate nuances and structures. A study of expressive devices includes techniques and concepts related to
tempo, dynamics, and tone color. The ordering of musical
ideas into forms involves learning about both sequential
(e.g., binary, rondo, theme and variations) and contrapuntal
designs (e.g., ostinato, canon, fugue). As each form is introduced, the more generic aesthetic principles of composition
- such as repetition, variation, contrast, climax, proportion,
balance, transition, logical development, and unity - can be
applied more specifically to creative idea development in
music.

Selecting Aesthetic Content

Elliot Eisner (1981), a well-respected educational thinker and
strong advocate for the arts, asserts that "the realm of
meaning has many mansions" (p.52). Music, then, can be
thought of as a particular communicative channel available
for shaping and representing ideas through sound. The aesthetic content of any art work refers to these underlying
ideas which are of special significance and meaning to the
creator. More simply, it is what the music is about - what is
being communicated through the sounds that are selected
and performed.

In order for children to become engaged in the process of
creative work in music, they must have something to express. Although many music teachers begin with pre-deter-
mined music problems for children to solve creatively, research tells us that it is important for children to be a part
of the decision-making process when it comes to selecting
the content for a music composition. For instance, DeLorenzo (1989) found that the degree of children's personal in-
vestment and levels of absorption and engagement directly
affected the success of their compositions. It seems sensible
to begin by inviting children to share ideas that hold special
interest for them, as well as experiences that they think
might be expressed most meaningfully through musical
sounds. Teachers can guide children in selecting content
from a range of stimuli presented within current curriculum
themes emerging from the music or general classroom.
Ideally, such themes will connect to children's first-hand
learning experiences and curiosities, have relevance and immediacy, and yet be broad enough to offer young composers diverse possibilities for musical composition. Colleagues

in arts education caution that a narrow stimulus can block the creative process every bit as much as it can stimulate it (Lovell, 1999, Wiggins, 1999).

Direct auditory, literary, and visual sources about the theme are obvious points of departure for children's creative work in music. For example, children who are excited about studying "The Rainforest" can respond musically to auditory stimuli such as: natural recordings of rainforest sounds; recordings of traditional music from rainforest regions of the world; recordings of sounds that children have gathered themselves from a locally simulated rainforest environment. Simple musical works of short duration can also result from celebrating in sound the messages of short poems or word pictures related to a curriculum theme such as "Oceans." Longer and more elaborate storytelling through an interplay of elements drawn from both music and drama can serve to communicate longer poems, folk tales, and stories, and legends about oceans. Other ideas for musical compositions might be stirred by children studying a different theme, like "The Night Sky," by using visual stimuli such as objects, picture books, paintings, film, photographs, sculptures, or other artifacts.

There is an array of other potential stimuli for getting children started with musical composition. For example, they can be invited to tell stories about their personal connections to curriculum themes like "Extreme Weather Disasters," "Inventors," or "Music Preferences." Opportunities to use music as a way to share what they learned from lived experiences like field trips connected to classroom or music studies, such as "Communities," "Rivers, " or "The Orchestra," often work well. Other stimuli can be drawn from curriculum themes based on local events or social issues like "Recycle, Reduce and Reuse."

Composing Music

Hickey and Webster (2001) describe the creative process as "the thinking that takes place as a person is planning to produce a creative product" (p.20). Culled from the work of Wallas (1926), a theoretical pioneer on creativity, music educators have come to view the creative process as a series of steps or stages through which a person proceeds when addressing a musical problem, working though it, and coming up with a satisfying solution (Balkin, 1990; Cornett &

Smithrim, 2001; Webster, 1990). Wallas proposed four stages in the creative process (preparation, incubation, illumination, verification), to which Balkin added a fifth (refactor - rethink, reconsider, replace, refine, redo, reaffirm, reprocess, rewrite, reconceptualize). Studies in music education reveal that children move through similar stages when they compose (Henry, 1996). The outcome of the creative process is the creative product, a vocal piece, instrumental work, or other tangible musical representation of a person's thoughts or feelings.

Once children have something to express, they have a genuine and meaningful reason for producing a musical composition. Their ideas will provide the motivation for an initial period of exploration and improvisation, in essence, free music play. The critical link between music play and creative thinking is well-established in the music education research (Littleton, 1991; Scott-Kassner, 1993; Smithrim, 1997; Tarnowsky, 1999). In the rich sonorous environment of the music classroom, exploration allows children to put ideas into sounds, flesh out the potential of sounds, test connections between them, and build a range of raw musical images and referents for possible use. This kind of experimentation is immediate and transient, an in-the-moment response to a stimulus. It is often the most important response because children become highly engaged and absorbed in the musical aspects of an idea, rather than the non-musical associations. Studies suggest that children involved in this kind of creative "search and research" feel at ease considering many musical alternatives before bringing closure to their work (Kratus, 1991; Levi, 1991a).

According to Campbell Stabley (2001), exploration becomes improvisation "as the student becomes more conscious of his or her efforts and actions" (p. 29). Improvisation, as defined by Brophy (2001), is "the spontaneous creation of music without the intent to revise" (p. 34). Kratus (1996) proposes that children move through seven distinct stages as they develop their improvisational skills: a) exploration; b) process-oriented; c) product-oriented; d) fluid; e) structural; f) stylistic; and g) personal.

To facilitate children's efforts to explore and improvise, it is important to provide open-ended musical problems that are both linked to children's expressed interests and ideas, and set within an exploratory framework. These challenges must accommodate children's current compositional base of knowledge, skills, and experiences, as well as employ sound sources and materials appropriate for the aesthetic content of their works-in-progress. Although improvisation is a very useful step in the composition process, children find it difficult to remember their ideas. They should be encouraged to maintain a composer's log and use conventional or invented notation to record the musical ideas they want to preserve. In combination with the logs, audio-taping with small micro-cassettes, as well as videotaping can help to capture critical "in-process" ideas and facilitate reflection all along the way. It is the intent to create new music by reflecting upon and revising these ideas that truly moves children into the act of composing music (Brophy, 2001).

Some music material resulting from the exploration and improvisation step will then be selected and refined into motifs for each section or layer of the composition. A motif is "a short musical idea, melodic, harmonic or rhythmic, or all three. It may be of any size but is generally regarded as the shortest subdivision of a theme or phrase that maintains its identity" (Sadie, 1988, p. 503). Since they are the critical ingredients for a musical composition, the choice of motifs needs to be guided by relevance, interest and potential for further development. Young composers will need opportunities to take each interesting musical idea and explore it further, draw it out, let it evolve, follow it through to see where it leads. This involves continuous cycles of selection, exploration, and refinement, with each cycle taking the child down new musical roads. Some disorder is desirable because it enhances discovery and keeps the process open and organic. It is important, however, for children to understand the importance of making decisions and selecting a few ideas to extend further. In her music teaching, Wilson (2001) finds that "limiting ideas is usually the hardest thing for beginning composers to learn to do" (p. 29).

Research evidence suggests that one critical factor which affects the success of children's composing is their capacity to sense the musical possibilities (DeLorenzo, 1989). Music webs and charts can be useful strategies for helping children extend and develop motifs. They begin by placing their sound motif in the center of the web using invented or conventional symbols and continue by generating a web of words that takes into account various known musical elements, expressive devices, and compositional principles. Figure 2 shows how a web serves to evoke a range of ideas that can be considered and investigated further in sound

Figure 2. Extending Motifs Through Webbing

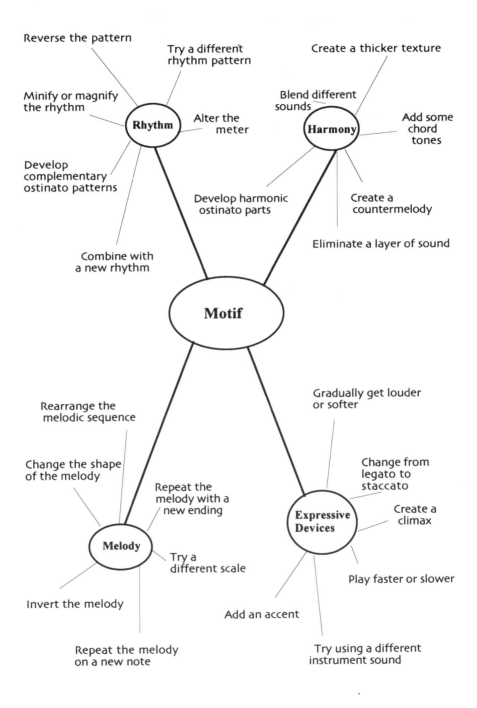

play. Similarly, Hickey (1997) uses a strategy called SCAMP-ER, which is "an acronym for substitute, combine, adapt or add, minify (diminution) or magnify (augmentation), put to other uses (other instruments), eliminate, and reverse or rearrange" (p. 19). Directive prompts or side coaching can also be a support for children who are working to extend and develop motifs: What idea are you trying to communicate? What mood or quality do you want to produce for the listener? How can the musical elements be used to create that mood? What is your central musical idea? What do you like about it? Is it the rhythm? Dynamics? Timbre? How do you want to proceed with your idea? Why did you pick this sequence of sounds?

These extended motifs will result in longer sections of musical material which can then be organized into an overall form. Sometimes the overall design of the composition is predetermined by the aesthetic content. For instance, children might be composing music for events, legends, or poetic verses which clearly and logically define the sequence. It is also possible that children will have begun with a specific form in mind, like a rondo, canon, or theme and variations. In these situations, it is most likely that children can organize their music material quite independently. Other children will benefit from their teacher's guidance when establishing how their composition might unfold: What section is most interesting? What part do you think the listener will want to hear again and again.? What section provides the most contrast or variety? Do you have too many different ideas? What parts complement each other best? How can the sections be sequenced so the composition is balanced and unified? Whatever the case, children should be given many opportunities to play and hear their compositions-in-process while they are rearranging and combining musical sections into more final forms.

Research results show that the creative process for music and language are quite similar (Garrett & Wilkinson, 1992; Levi, 1991b). As in the language writing process, children's draft compositions need to be edited and polished in preparation for bringing them into the public arena. Students can be guided to enlarge, reduce, add, delete, or change musical material for the purpose of conveying their intentions more clearly. Using what they are learning about the principles of composition, they can be encouraged to make decisions about all aspects of their creative work, and this may require moving through all of the steps in the composing process again and again. For example, they might reconsider the contribution of each part to the whole, retain what is most exciting, heighten central ideas, give some thought to a title for their work, or establish a clear introduction, coda, or interlude.

At this point in the process, children can benefit immensely from inviting, receiving, and giving constructive feedback. For those exploring technology-assisted composition, the feedback loop can be augmented by using the Internet to connect children with composers and/or music teacher candidates who are willing to respond to draft music files with suggestions and critiques (Reese, 2001). For those who prefer face-to-face interactions, teachers and peers can help by redirecting, nudging, or offering solutions. Despite the strategy used, it is crucial to understand that young composers often need to be assisted in overcoming frustrations, staying with their projects, as well as realizing moments of euphoria. Interaction with others can give them the chance to learn that their ideas can change for the better, or that new perspectives can keep the composing process fresh and energetic. Most importantly, collaboration prevents children from bringing closure to their creative work too quickly.

Once their music compositions have become more or less fixed, children will need time to notate and rehearse their creative works. They should first be encouraged to make final scores of their compositions by transcribing the draft copies recorded roughly in their composer's logs onto manuscript or blank paper. Research evidence shows that, when given opportunity, support, and tools, children are very capable of using strategies such as icons, letters, numbers, spaces, colors, works, complete sentences, as well as traditional music symbols to represent their musical ideas (Burns, 1997; Davidson & Scripp, 1988; Garrett & Wilkenson, 1992; Upitis, 1987; 1990; 1992). Naturally, the extent to which children can be expected to use conventional notation is dependent upon their music literacy skills and developmental level.

Displaying the final musical scores on a bulletin board or "publishing" them in a class album of music compositions are good initial avenues to celebrating the children's creative productivity. The most authentic celebration, however, for any music creator, is when the composition "jumps" off the page and onto the stage in a concert-like setting. Using these final scores as references, children should then be given time to practice so that performing their compositions can be as reflexive, skillful, and musically satisfying as possible. They will likely need to work on the technical aspects of the performance such as creating appropriate dynamic changes, developing clean transitions, smoothing phrases, reviewing complex rhythms, fingerings, or mallet patterns, and so on.

The culminating step in the composing process is to perform and record the final products. Music teachers can establish an authentic sense of ownership by giving composers the responsibility for setting up their own final concert committee and making all the necessary preparations for a public performance. These preparations would include developing a program, targeting an audience, exploring different avenues of publicity, gathering and organizing instruments and other materials, managing the performance area, setting up a sound system if necessary, choosing an emcee, scheduling rehearsals, and arranging for audio-taping or videotaping the final concert.

The performance is the point at which the compositions are truly "published" or shared with others in their finished, sonorous forms. The exhilaration of the live presentation is usually a true highlight for children as the creative process comes to completion. Teachers should strive for a focused final performance by the children that is executed with a spirit of pride and excitement. After the performance, members of the audience can be invited to participate in a sharing circle, offering personal, positive reactions to the compositions. Later, children should listen to the audio-tape or view the video recording of the performance and be guided in a meaningful discussion of the entire process. In their composer's logs, children can reflect on and write about all that they have learned, including thoughts on what they might want to do differently next time. It is of paramount importance that children's beginning efforts to compose and share with others result in enhanced musical self-esteem, self-confidence, and perceptions of themselves as inventors of music.

The Role of the Teacher

The music classroom functions optimally when teachers and their students are involved collaboratively in creative in-quiry, forming a community of music composers. It is important that teachers understand the creative process and model the excitement of creative exploration for their students. Through professional development and reading books like those by Davis (1998) or Torrance (1984), they should inform themselves of the characteristics of creative children, and promote and support these characteristics in the classroom. Teachers facilitating children's creative work must be good musicians, pedagogues, and amateur composers. It is critical that they are able to identify the musical objectives of young composers, make sound musical judgments, share control and decision-making, and offer appropriate directions and useful instruction. In short, they must learn to invite, initiate, respond, encourage, and converse, but not direct the experience in didactic ways.

The extent of teacher involvement in the music composing process depends on the quality of the ideas coming from the children and on the potential of those ideas to extend students' musical thinking and learning. In most cases, music educators should take on the role of observer-collaborator. In this role, the teacher prepares a safe learning environment where risk-taking flourishes, and works to confront the factors that hamper creativity (Cecil & Lauritzen, 1994; Cornett & Smithrim, 2001; Wiggins, 1999). The teacher must be "as unimposing as possible and resist the impulse to inflict expertise on the student, serving rather as a guide, a creator of musical problems, a resource person, a stimulator for creative thinking, and an astute musician capable of responding to complex musical ideas, all while remaining sensitive to the creative insight of students" (Pogonowski, 2001, p. 27). This role gives the teacher ample opportunity to assess the music-learning context, and it gives young composers access to their teacher's music knowledge and skills. Figure 3 offers several guiding principles for enabling children's creativity in music education.

Figure 3. Guiding Principles for Enabling Children's Creative Work in Music

- Establish an accepting environment that is safe for experimenting, risk-taking and making mistakes.

- Set compositional parameters that are neither too open or restrictive.

- Emphasize that there are many equally valid answers to solving creative musical problems.

• Acknowledge and value the contributions that each child's imagination gives to the composition-in-progress.

• Provide adequate "open space" for children to think reflectively, develop intentionality, and work through music composing processes.

• Encourage children's independence and ownership in composing music.

• Be sensitive to children's sense of choice and individuality.

• Recognize that composing music with children is not always orderly, quiet, or neat.

• Nurture composing with related listening and performance-based experiences.

• Be an enthusiastic, creative model for children.

• Ensure that children's creative efforts are supported and result in satisfying, pleasurable learning experiences.

• Conduct sharing sessions of creative work which are followed by positive, encouraging, constructive responses.

• Explore ways to record and preserve music compositions that do not limit creativity.

• Emphasize process over product, particularly in assessing and evaluating children's music.

• *Trust* that children can invent music, at least in large part, without you.

Sample Learning Sequence: Composing Ojibway-Style Music

It is important at this point to illustrate how the proposed model would unfold in a real music teaching situation. In the music classroom, teachers must design composition experiences for particular instructional purposes by drawing on potential learning from the context of children's ideas and interests. It is from these ideas that educators can stimulate, challenge and facilitate music learning and creativity. Presented below is a fully developed learning plan for fourth grade music students. The plan addresses the three components of the model: expanding the compositional base, selecting aesthetic content, and composing music.

1.   *Expanding the Compositional Base*

• Fourth grade students will have the opportunity to: improvise and compose in aeolian mode (natural minor); explore alternate metric and rhythmic patterns for a given
text; create polyrhythmic texture; combine and organize
sounds; apply understandings of Ojibway-style music; and
read and write music in D minor using invented and conventional notation.

2.   *Selecting the Content*

• Fourth grade students in Manitoba have been involved in
an interdisciplinary classroom study of the Ojibway, a distinct Aboriginal community of people who live primarily in
the grasslands and eastern woodlands regions of Canada.
The music branch of the study has been taking place in the
music classroom, involving ample related listening and music-making experiences. As a way of sharing what they are
learning, students respond enthusiastically to an invitation
to compose their own Ojibway-style music.

3.   *Composing Experiences*

3.1   Cycle 1, Music Class 1

• Ojibway melodies are more often minor than major in
character, so introduce children to the notes of the D minor
natural scale using a notational chart or overhead. Have
them play each note of the scale, ascending and descending,
on recorders or other fixed tuned classroom instruments
(e.g., xylophones, step bells, keyboards). Recorders are preferable because they most closely simulate the sounds of the
flute-like instruments used within Ojibway musical traditions.

• Engage children in a period of echo playback and ques-
tion-and-answer play using short melodic fragments based
on D minor.

• Develop a simple two-measure melodic theme that can be
taught to the class as the A section of a rondo
(ABACADA...). In small groups, have the theme performed
together by the group, and the contrasting sections improvised by soloists.

3.2   Cycle 1, Music Class 2

• Select the English text of a simple Ojibway song such as *The Morning Star* (DeCesare, 1988). This particular song was part of a special spring ceremony held at dawn when the Ojibway prayed to the morning star for a good growing season. In small groups, have children explore the metrical and rhythmic possibilities for the following text: "When it is dawn, the sky is alight; And when it is day, the land becomes bright" (p. 13). Workable ideas should be notated in their composer's logs as shown in Figure 4.

• As a prelude to composing melodies on their own, review the following parameters with the class: a) Use the notes of D minor (D4-E4-F4-G4-A4-B flat4-C5-D5), starting and ending on D4 or D5; b) Draw on the rhythmic material established by your group for the text; c) Ojibway melodies often move from higher to lower, but your melody may at times move up, down, or stay on the same pitch; and d) Use more skips and steps, than jumps and leaps in your melody.

• Using recorders, invite students to explore the melodic possibilities for the rhythmic text. The meaning of the text, rhythmic material, and principles of repetition and contrast will be helpful signposts. The best melodic material evolving from the improvisational play should be recorded like the excerpt in Figure 4. Children can be directed to write the letter names of selected pitches underneath the rhythms already drafted for the text in their composer's logs.

Figure 4, Sample fourth grade rhythm for the text given.

• Provide each student with some manuscript paper and ensure that the D minor natural scale is notated at the top of the page with letter names labeled for student reference. Figure 5 shows how they can begin drafting their compositions more formally by writing in the words beneath the staff and the corresponding rhythms and pitches above.

Figure 5. Sample fourth grade melody recorded using letter names

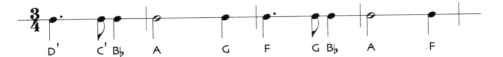

3.3   Cycle 1, Music Class 3

• Have partners share their melodic drafts and offer feed-back to one another. Student composers should make revisions to the melody or rhythm until they are pleased with their work.

• Create a chart with the class that lists the types of non-pitched percussion instruments most widely used in Ojibway music-making (e.g., large ceremonial drums, smaller handframe drums, rawhide-covered sticks, gourd rattles, jingle bracelets, sticks, stones). Also, try to tease out ideas like the Ojibway's preference for natural sounds and the simple, sparing ways in which sounds are traditionally used.

• Have partners experiment with various sound sources available in the classroom that might serve as the accompaniment for their melodies. Give them time to experiment playing their melodies against different accompaniment parts for each other, as well as opportunities to get their ideas down on paper or audio-recorded (see Figure 6).

Figure 6. Reference scale and sample fourth grade melodic draft

When it is dawn the sky is a-light, and when it is day the land be-comes brig

• As children's interest in creating thicker textures becomes apparent, move children into smaller groups for more cooperative, polyrhythmic work. Members of these small groups can also serve as "sounding boards" for each other.

3.4   Cycle 2, Music Class 1

• Create a web with the class to generate ideas for extending their compositions (e.g, create an introduction and
coda, add an interlude, compose a B section for speech or
nonpitched percussion sounds, write original text for additional verses).

• Give children more open work space and support for creative idea development, both alone and in small groups. Encourage children to seek help from the teacher, ask questions, and interact with each other as they continue the
more final editing and polishing of their compositions.

• Challenge children to make decisions regarding the tempo
and dynamics to be used in their pieces, as well as the ways
that these might be indicated on their scores.

3.5   Cycle 2, Music Class 2

• Gradually, a final form will emerge and require formal notation, like the fourth-grade composition in Figure 7. Give
children new manuscript paper and ample time to tran-
scribe their drafts using standard and/or invented notation.
Alternatively, if the technology is available in the school,
children can create computer-generated scores of their
compositions. Display the finished scores on a prominent
bulletin board in the hallway outside the music classroom.

Figure 7. Sample fourth grade ostinato accompaniment for non-
pitched percussion instruments

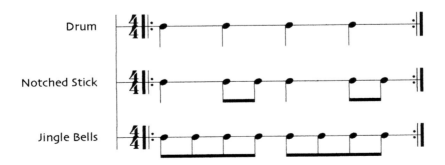

3.6   Cycle 2, Music Class 3

• Small ensembles need to be established, along with a re-hearsal schedule for each composition. Ensure that children have plenty of time to practice, during class time, recess, or before or after school.

3.7   Cycle 3, Music Class 1

• Discuss ideas for a final concert using questions such as: What musical instruments do we need as a large group? How will the performance of the compositions be se-quenced? Is it possible for some compositions to be linked together? How will ensembles enter and exit the perform-ing area? What special jobs need to be done? Who will volunteer to do these jobs?

• Once responsibilities have been assigned, continue making plans to perform "Ojibway-Style Compositions" for another grade four classroom and to have the performance video-taped. For homework, each student should design an invi-tation that can be delivered to members of the other class the next day.

3.8   Cycle 3, Music Class 2

• The compositions are performed as scheduled. Imme-diately after the performance, set up a sharing circle so that members of the audience can offer positive comments to the student composers.

3.9   Cycle 3, Music Class 3

• View the videotape as a group and make judgments about the compositions and performance. Is the Ojibway-style clear in all compositions? In what ways were instruments used effectively? In what ways were the melodies appro-priate for the text? How did the accompaniments serve to support the melodies? Were the performances focused? Technically sound? Musical? Did all members of the en-semble work well together?

• Ask students to reflect on the entire compositional experi-ence through journal writing. Use open-ended statements

Figure 8. Sample fourth grade final score of an Ojibway-style music composition

William's Morning Star Music

Form: Intro ABA Coda

Introduction: Play the handframe drum part for two measures, add the rattle for two measures, then add the jingle bells for two measures. Play the following softly and gently on the wind chimes:

A Section: Play on a soprano recorder at a moderately slow tempo.

When it is dawn the sky is a - light and when it is day the land be - comes bright.

B. Section: Speak clearly and brightly

Star light, star bright. The morn - ing star is quite a sight.

Bring the day, leave the night. Pray up-on this star so right.

Ostinato Accompaniment Parts:

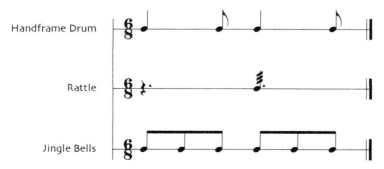

Handframe Drum

Rattle

Jingle Bells

Coda: Reverse the introduction, layer off each instrument, and then end with the wind chimes.

such as: "Through this composition I have learned...," "I can perform the following musical ideas better than before...," "I feel very proud of this composition because...," "Next time I want to get better at...," The best part of the concert was...."

3.8   Assessment and Evaluation

• And finally, teachers should review the children's composer's logs, scores, and performance video for the purpose of assessing each child's creative process and product. Rating scales, like the one developed in Figure 9, emphasize the importance of process by giving it more weighting than the product. The work of Webster and Hickey (1995) is helpful to teachers interested in children's compositions and their evaluation.

Figure 9. Ojibway-style music composition rating scale.

Student Composer:

Total Score: of 85

1.   **Composer's Log and Creative Process of 50**

      • The extent to which musical ideas have been explored openly and thoroughly.
                    5   4   3   2   1

      • The extent to which musical ideas have been extended and developed.
                    5   4   3   2   1

      • The extent to which reflection and revision of musical ideas are evident.
                    5   4   3   2   1

      • The extent to which contributions have been made to others when working in small and large groups.
                    5   4   3   2   1

      • The extent to which personal challenges have been accepted and risks taken.
                    5   4   3   2   1

- The extent to which high levels of commitment and engagement have been demonstrated.

  5   4   3   2   1

- The extent to which high levels of interest and growth in creative work are evident.

  5   4   3   2   1

- The extent to which effective creative work has been undertaken independently and collaboratively.

  5   4   3   2   1

- The extent to which musical intentions are clear.

  5   4   3   2   1

- The extent to which musical decisions are made and rationalized.

  5   4   3   2   1

2. **Composition and Performance of 35**

- The degree to which the composition is rhythmically and metrically cohesive.

  5   4   3   2   1

- The degree to which the composition is melodically cohesive.

  5   4   3   2   1

- The degree to which texture is used as a compositional device.

  5   4   3   2   1

- The degree to which the stylistic features of Ojibway music are present.

  5   4   3   2   1

- The degree to which the composition develops logically with a sense of overall form.

  5   4   3   2   1

- The extent to which the "score" effectively records musical ideas through the use of traditional notation, icons, letters, numbers, and so on.

  5   4   3   2   1

- The extent to which the performance is an accurate and musically expressive enactment of the composer's creative intentions.

  5   4   3   2   1

A Final Word

Creative idea development is an important component of the music curriculum that deserves more attention in the music classroom. To be creative is to think and act openly, to learn and question, to engage every aspect of the child's being to bring into existence something that was not there before. Nurturing active, independent music creators is dependent to a great extent on the development of a strong compositional base, the selection of aesthetic content that engages children, and a clear instructional process that supports and celebrates children's music compositions. As children progress through a comprehensive music program, they will develop the ability to use music as a communicative medium in increasingly crystallized and powerful ways. Consequently, music can become a viable communicative choice for children, moving from playing a marginal to more central role in the literacy development of children in our schools.

References

Anderson, W. M., & Lawrence, J. E. (2001). *Integrating Music into the Elementary Classroom* (5th ed.). Belmont, CA. Wadsworth/Thomson Learning.

Balkin, A. (1990). What is Creativity? What is it Not? *Music Educators Journal, 76*(9), 29-32.

Brophy, T. S. (2001). Developing improvisation in general music classes. *Music Educators Journal, 88*(1), 34-41, 53.

Burns, K. (1997). Invented notation and the compositional processes of children. *Update: Applications of Research in Music Education, 16*(1), 12-16.

Campbell Stabley, N. (2001). Creative Activities for String Students. *Music Educators Journal, 88*(2), 29-33, 57.

Cecil, N., & Lauritzen, P. C. (1994). *Literacy and the Arts for the Integrated Classroom.* White Plains, NY: Longman.

Cornett, C. E., & Smithrim, K. (2001). *The Arts as Meaning Makers.* Toronto, ON: Pearson Education Canada/Prentice Hall.

Davidson, L. (1990). Tools and Environments for Musical Creativity. *Music Educators Journal, 76*(9), 47-51.

Davidson, L., & Scripp, L. (1988). Young Children's Musical
    Representations: Windows on Music Cognition. In J. Sloboda
    (Ed.), *Generative processes in music* (pp. 195-230). New York,
    NY: Oxford University Press.

Davis, G. A. (1998). *Creativity is Forever* (4th ed.). Dubuque, IA:
    Kendall/Hunt Publishing.

DeCesare, R. (1988). *Myth, Music and Dance of the American Indian.*
    Van Nuys, CA: Alfred Publishing.

DeLorenzo, L. (1989). A field study of sixth-grade students' creative
    music problem-solving processes. *Journal of Research in
    Music Education, 14(2)*, 188-200.

Edwards, L. C. (1997). *The Creative Arts: A process approach for
    teachers and children* (2nd ed.). Upper Saddle River, NJ:
    Prentice Hall.

Eisner, E. (1981). *The Role of Discipline-based Art Education in
    America's Schools.* Santa Monica, CA: Getty Trust
    Publications.

Engel, S. (1989). *Children's Bursts of Creativity.* (ERIC Document
    Reproduction Services No. ED 332 796.)

Garrett, S., & Wilkenson, L. (1992). An overture for the year 2000:
    Teaching primary music using a "whole music' approach.
    Manitoba Music Educator, 32(3), 14-17.

Goldberg, M. (2001). *Arts and LeaMning: An Integrated Approach to
    Teaching and Learning in multicultural and Multilingual
    Settings.* New York, NY: Longman.

Gordon, E. E. (1993). *Learning Sequences in Music: Skill, Content,
    and Patterns.* Chicago, IL: GIA Publications.

Henry, W. (1996). Creative Processes in Children's Musical
    Compositions: A review of the literature. *Update:
    Applications of Research in Music Education, 15(1)*, 10-15.

Hickey, M. (1997). Teaching Ensembles toCompose and Improvise.
    Music Educators Journal, 83(6), 17-21.

Jalongo, M. R., & Stamp, L. N. (1997). *The Arts in Children's Lives.*
    Boston, MA: Allyn and Bacon.

Kratus, J. (1991). Characterization of the Compositional Strategies
    used by Children to Compose a Melody. *Canadian Journal of
    Research in Music Education, 33,*95-103.

Kratus, J. (1996). A Developmental Approach to Teaching Musical
    Improvisation. *International Journal of Music Education, 26,*
    27-38.

Lehman, P. (1999). National Assessment of the Arts Education: A First Look. *Music Educators Journal, 85*(4), 34-37.

Levi, R. (1991a). Investigating the Creative Process: The role of regular music composition experiences for the elementary child. *Journal of Creative Behavior, 25*(2), 123-36.

Levi, R. (1991b). A field investigation of the composing processes used by second-grade childen creating original language and music pieces. Unpublished doctoral dissertation, Case Western Reserve University, Cleveland, Ohio.

Littleton, J. D. (1991). Influence of play settings on preschool children's music and play behaviors. Unpublished doctoral dissertation, University of Texas, Austin, Texas.

Lovell, S. (1999). Maximizing the Creative Process in Creative Dance. *Avante, 5*(2), 101-110.

Music Educators National Conference (1994). *National Standards for Arts Education.* Reston, VA: Music Educators National Conference.

Pogonowski, L. (2001). A Personal Retrospective on the MMCP. *Music Educators Journal, 88*(1), 24-27, 52.

Reese, S. (2001). Tools for Thinking in Sound. *Music Educators Journal, 88*(1), 42-46, 53.

Richardson, C. P., & Atterbury, B. W. (2001). *Music every day: Transforming the elementary classroom.* Boston, MA: McGraw Hill.

Rozmajzl, M., & Boyer-White, B. (2000). *Music Fundamentals, Methods, and Materials for the Elementary Classroom Teacher* (3rd ed.). New York, NY: Longman.

Sadie, S. (Ed.). (1988). *The Norton/Grove Concise Encyclopedia of Music.* New York, NY: W. W. Norton & Company.

Scott-Kassner, C. (1993). Musical characteristics. In M. Palmer & W. Sims (Eds.). *Music in pre-kindergarten* (pp. 7-13). Reston, VA: Music Educators National Conference.

Shehan Campbell, P., & Scott-Kassner, P. (1995). *Music in Childhood: From Preschool through the Eementary Grades.* New York, NY: Schirmer Books.

Smithrim, K. L. (1997). Free Musical Play in Early Childhood. *Canadian Journal of Research in Music Education, 3*(4), 17-24.

Tarnowski, S. (1999). Music Play and Young children. *Music Educators Journal, 8*(61), 26-29.

Torrance, E. (1984). Teaching Gifted and Creative Learners. In M. Wittrock (Ed.). *Handbook of Research on Teaching* (pp. 46-51). Chicago, IL: Rand McNally.

Upitis, R. (1987). A Child's Development of Music Notation Through Composition: A Case Study. *Arts and Learning Research, 5(1),* 102-119.

Upitis, R. (1990). *This Too, is Music.* Portsmouth, NH: Heinemann Educational Books, Inc.

Upitis, R. (1992). *Can I Play You my Song?* Portsmouth, NH: Heinemann Educational Books, Inc.

Wallas, G. (1926). *The Art of Thought.* New York, NY: Harcourt, Brace and Company.

Webster, P. (1990). Creativity as Creative Thinking. *Music Educators Journal, 76(9),* 22-28.

Webster, P., & Hickey, M. (1995). Rating scales and their use in assessing children's music compositions. *The Quarterly Journal of Music Teaching and Learning, VI(4),* 28-44.

Wiggins, J. (1999). Teacher Control and Creativity. *Music Educators Journal, 85(5),* 30-35.

Wilson, D. (2001). Guidelines for CoachingStudentComposers. *Music Educators Journal 88(1),* 28-33.

Chapter 13

Creativity in Action

Timothy Sullivan

BIO
TIMOTHY SULLIVAN has been an active composer and educator for over fifteen years. His works for concert, opera, ballet and film have been commissioned and performed widely. His innovative seminars in *Creativity and Music Education* have been given to teachers through the Ontario Institute of Studies in Education and The Ontario Arts Education Institute, and to students through Orchestras Canada, The Canadian Opera Company, The National Ballet of Canada, and others. Timothy Sullivan holds a Doctorate from the University of Toronto, He has taught Theory and Composition at the Royal Conservatory of Music in Toronto and the University of Victoria.

1. Introduction

The purpose of education is to learn to think. By *think*, I mean the ability to solve problems and make decisions, to absorb information and then synthesize this information into useful knowledge which can be summoned up to provide guidance in the solution of further problems, and formulation of future decisions.

Problem-solving and decision-making require the co-operation of the two hemispheres of thought: the logical, and the creative. Education fails when if does not cultivate both of these spheres, yet while there is widespread support for the benefits of teaching students to think rationally, there is little understanding of how to teach students to think creatively. While the education system has developed with an almost exclusive application of logic and reasoning to all subjects, creativity seems to carry with it the dual airs of mystical significance and practical dismissal. I believe creative thinking is as necessary as logical thinking: one sees the parts in the whole, the other sees the whole in the parts.

Creative thinking is imaginative thinking. Rational thought sorts and stores only the necessary information according to systems; creative thought sorts and stores the necessary, but also the causal, intuitive and inexplicable. This information provides the fluid for the many lateral connections and flashes of insight that we associate with creativity. Both rational and creative thinking are fundamental skills which can be developed. Creativity is the skill through which change comes into the world. Its power is awesome and its effects, ubiquitous, but it is a skill with which all people are endowed, and which all people may refine.

Creativity in Action is an approach to teaching creative thinking in the classroom through the most primal of teaching modalities: play. Play is our innate mode of learning. From this magical behaviour spring the pleasures of learning, through exploration, experiment, discovery and analysis. We do not have to be taught to play. It has evolved into our genetic programming for survival. Forms of play, such as trial and error, provide humans with an flexible approach to overcoming the challenges of survival in almost any environment.

The links between play and learning have been well-established.' When I speak of "play", I do not refer to games alone, but to an entire paradigm shift in educative transmission from an *instruction-practice-comprehension-assessment* model to an *information-experience-comprehension-assessment* model. The end result of accountable comprehension has similarly been reached, but via a much different route.

In this model, students are provided with preliminary instruction, are then asked to use these skills in a series of challenges. These challenges require the students to utilize both their rational and creative skills, to gather their collective knowledge to solve problems and to define areas of research where further information is necessary.

Unlike conventional instruction, this approach resembles an investigation or scientific research. It stimulates curiosity and personal initiative. It connects with the natural human play instinct, engaging students in a learning modality with which they are familiar through their experience with sports, computer games, board games and so on.

This model is not intended to replace conventional instruction, but it is also not intended to be relegated to the ancillary role of "entertainment", either. Learning through play need not be conducted only on "rainy days and Fridays", but may be integrated into lesson plans in the conveyance of substantive elements of the core curriculum.

2. Play and the Learning Environment

The use of "play" within teaching practice entails shifts in class management. Play encourages students to be independent, to experiment and take risks; this requires an environment of safety and support. The potential for judgment and shaming exists within the concepts of "winning" and "losing", the "negative" aspects of competition. Safety is established by formulating agreements, arrived at by consensus, setting the "rules" for classroom decorum and behaviour. The appropriate attitudes of mutual respect therefore need to be reinforced daily in order to countervail the fear of ridicule and failure which many students carry from their previous experiences.

From the philosophical position of "treat others as you wish to be treated", students will often be able to articulate such rules, and by so doing, the class "buys in" to a code of behaviour which they themselves have set and which is, therefore, easier to police. This shift from a practice of discipline and conformity to authority, to one of a self-governing respect for each individual and a code of practice for group responsibility, engenders an environment of trust and safety which is vital if creativity is to flourish.

There is also a shift in role for the teacher in this model: from central authority enforcing a strict curriculum-driven timetable, to that of a mentor and manager, who presents objectives and assists teams in acquiring the knowledge and skills to reach them together.

Rather than regard the student as an "empty vessel", the teacher introduces the subject area for the next curriculum unit and makes an inventory of the classes's collective knowledge. The teacher then engages the class in locating their curiosity about the subject: "what do we want to know about this subject? What areas are incomplete in our inventory?"

The principles upon which this approach rests are:

• Establishment of a class understanding of adherence to self-directed responsibility

• With each new unit, the gathering from the class the sum of their collective knowledge of the subject, in order, first, to recognise the extent of this knowledge, and secondly, to assist you (the teacher) to assess the class and tailor your instructional approach;

• The gathering from the class their collective curiosity on the subject, framing questions which may serve to become research objectives. These are the questions which the class will 'investigate'.

As the teacher honours the knowledge, talent and experience which the students bring into the classroom, and enlists this knowledge as a starting point for further study, the students sense that they are co-researchers with the teacher. Each student engages with the course work, because their abilities have been recognised and respected; their curiosity has been aroused, and their play instinct has been directed to the questions they have raised. Their desire to experiment can then be engaged, because risk-taking in the classroom environment has proven to be safe.

This supportive environment satisfies Maslow's *Hierarchy of Needs* for successful learning: 1. for psychological well-being; 2. for safety; 3. for belongingness and love; 4. for esteem; 5. self-actualization. (Abeles, Hoffer and Klotman pg. 226). When these needs are met, students are free to develop their talents to their full capacities. Since we are concerned with the risk-taking inherent in self-expression.

The argument for a more democratic model for the exercise of authority in the classroom is not new. A series of studies by Lewin, Lippitt, White and others from the 1940's and 1950's, that students in more democratic classrooms were more motivated, produced more original work and were more group-minded,unlike their counterparts in more authoritarian classrooms who, while being somewhat more productive, were also more hostile, conformist, and dependent upon the teacher (Liggett and White pg. 220).

3. Games and Imagination

A game is structured play. Each game is an analogy for life. To play well, one learns the rules, practices the skills and develops the strategies. Each game challenges the players to focus their attention, creative energy and knowledge in an attempt to obtain a particular objective. In its broadest perspective, a game is a life-lesson in a simulated real-life experience. The skill set may be very specific (such as spelling, matching cards, clapping a rhythm or catching a ball), but its practical applications to life are never far off (such as locating a store or a city street (spelling); or physical acuity and co-ordination (music performance or sports).

While a game is structured, it is also uniquely open to chance and spontaneity. Unlike teaching activities, wherein students are provided with a prescribed series of steps which lead, if carefully followed, to a "successful" outcome, the game provides a framework for a wide assortment of variables within which the participant "plays", making a series of complex observations and analytic decisions. This process hones the participant's skills and often leads to the acquisition of new abilities. Neither the course of events unfolding during the game, or its eventual outcome are prescribed. Game Theory has plainly demonstrated the depth of the complexity of these variables, as analogies to problems in statistical analysis, economics and politics.[2]

While being a testing ground for life skills, games are also portals to the imagination. The games of "make-believe" are as common in children as hide-and-seek; what possible 'life skills' can pretending teach? Simply put, pretending teaches the life skills of the mind. The ability to imagine what is not actually there is the foundation of abstract thought. As such, the ability to pretend only appears at a certain point in a child's psychological development, where the Id and Ego are clearly differentiated, making it possible to distinguish "I" from "the Other", thereby separating make-believe from reality.

Pretending opens the mind to the world of imagination, visualisation and invention. This is the realm of speculative thought, the "what if" of science and the theatre [3], the "once upon a time" of fables, myth, and fiction, the inner visions of "close your eyes and imagine", which unites children with humanity's great artists, scientists, mystics and philoso-

phers. The imagination is one of humanity's greatest resources, enabling logic and reason as well as music and poetry. Yet the imagination is but the blank tablet upon
which ideas and innovations are written, while the ideas
themselves are received through creativity.

4. Game Types and Models

Incorporating play as part of the learning process takes the
form of a *game* when the play is given an objective. Many
different types of games may be developed to suit differing
needs. I have articulated a few types below, differentiating
each type by the material which it is attempting to teach.
Games may be used with large and small groups, as well as
pairs and individuals.

Skill-Building Games require little background information.
these concentrate on essential music performance skills such
as sensing the pulse, clapping in time, counting, note
matching, singing in tune, and so on. Such games include
clapping games, chanting games, circle games of counting,
divided scale or melody and games requiring rhythmic
movement. Also included are listening games such as "name
that tune" (or rhythm, tempo, key, instrument), find the
wrong note, and so on.

Instructive Games introduce new information as elements
of the game, whether as material to be used in the game, or
within the rules of the game. For example, note values may
be introduce as characters in the game, "Note Baseball". In
the first round, all hits must equal a half note. The batter
steps up to the plate. The pitcher draws a card with a note
value less than a half; it is the batter's job to name the note
value which must be added to this note for the two to equal
a half-note. If the batter is correct, it is a "hit"; if not, it is
"strike one". It is also possible to add elements of excitement to the game, such as: the more quickly the batter answers the question, the harder the "swing", the further the
ball travels. For fielders to "catch" the answer, they must
quickly volunteer to sing or clap it correctly.

Integrative Games help students to make new connections
with information they already have. Such games may be
played by class members, may be combined with movement
or visual art or may be done individually. Examples of Inte-

grative games might be: musical hangman, or crossword puzzles, fill-in-the-blanks games, error correction and editing games, such as incomplete bars or notes missing from chords or famous melodies. Included also are matching games such as notation-to-note-name, or note-to-rest and pattern recognition and completion games. Integrative games also include problem-solving games such as riddles and other puzzles, where all the necessary information is provided, but it is left to the student to organise and connect it to 'solve' the challenge.

For example: a curriculum objective for Grade 8 music " describe some aspects of the historical context of music that they sing, play or listen to (e.g. identify some major political events or philosophical movements, architectural or painting styles)" One can approach this objective in the traditional manner with a lecture or film about a composer, work and time period and test the student's memory, or as an example, one can develop a game, whose objective is to make information chains. Students are given a short narrative which contains all the information required for the game: names, dates, locations, explanations, etc. pertaining to the composer, composition or period being discussed. They are then given a column for each context identified in the curriculum objective: political event philosophy, architecture, painting style. Student teams now assemble information chains, linking all the appropriate pieces together. Challenge may be increased by having the introductory paragraph refer to more than one composition, which therefore requires more than one information chain.

Investigative Games present challenges to students to gather information on a subject. They are sent out on a quest, or given clues and are asked to become 'detectives'. They may be asked to find data, to make a newspaper report, to dramatize an important event, or to investigate other questions which the class has identified. Clues may be left around the school, in the library, on a website, in pieces of music, in textbook chapters. While the investigative game format entertainingly engages the students, it develops their research and analytic skills, which will be required in later life.

A Grade 9 curriculum requires students to: "demonstrate an understanding of the following simple musical forms: binary, ternary, popular song, and two other simple performance forms related to a specific cultural context (e.g. Native drum song, Scottish pipe song)." An investigative game which responds to this curriculum objective might be, for example, one in which the class is divided into teams, each provided with a set of clues to investigate. Each group must follow their clues, gathering information leading to a composer, piece and its cultural context. The group must then determine the work's and any other significant features which come to light in the course of the investigation. Some of these clues may be in the composition itself, so it will be necessary for each group to learn and perform their piece. At the conclusion of the process, each group presents its findings to the class. The objective of the game is to identify the correct piece, and its form, in the most persuasive class presentation. To "win", the class votes on which group was the most accurate and the most convincing.

Performance Games present students with age appropriate challenges to develop their essential performance skills: sight reading and singing, intonation, rhythmic co-ordination, instrumental or vocal facility, and so on. Games may include clapping various metres and metre changes, sight reading or singing famous melodies, singing back a melody and adding solfège syllables. Performance games are distinguished from skill-building games in their use of music notation and the tendency of these games to require participants to present their answers, as though in a performance.

A music curriculum for Grade 4 states: "read and perform simple rhythmic patterns in 4/4 time". A performance game to teach and reinforce this objective would be, for example, a *Magic Knock* relay game, with a number of "magic doors" arranged around the room. The class is divided into groups. One person from each group goes up to one door, is presented with a card containing a short rhythm in 4/4 time, and must perform the rhythm correctly as the magic knock, in order to receive a note value to bring back to the group. The next person from the group cannot go to the next door until the first member has returned. The second person repeats this process, and so on, until all the doors have been knocked upon. The first group to accumulate and arrange sufficient note values to reproduce the rhythm the teacher has written on the blackboard, wins. As a conclusion, the entire class claps the final rhythm in unison.

Improvisation Games place students in the position of creating music 'on the spot'. The objective of Improvisational and Creation games is not so much winning as playing. These outcome of these games is the experience of the creation of music. The process of creating this music, like games, is governed by sets of rules. In theatre improvisational games the character and/or situation is established beforehand, leaving the actors free to create and respond to the changing circumstances they present each other. Similarly, in music improvisation games, certain musical elements are established in advance, while others are left to the musicians to create freely as they respond to each other.

Improvisation games are useful for providing students firsthand experiences with their musical creativity. In a music curriculum for Grade 6, is the objective: "create and accompaniment for a story, poem or drama presentation". This would be a daunting task for a student to create using standard notation: the task of imagining the real-time experience of the story, poem or play, without actors present and trying to work out the co-ordination of music and text expects much from the most talented grade 6 student.

A much simpler solution is to improvise the accompaniment. A group of students, each with a different sound-making device (a musical instrument or found-sound source), respond to a reading of the text. Discussion of the sound elements in the text, any dramatic events within the story, elements of location, passage of time, etc. may all be discussed. The process may lead to the creation of graphic scores of these sonoral 'soundscapes' or they may be left to develop from performance to performance. The students may be told that there is no "correct" accompaniment, just those that are more or less "convincing". It may be instructive to analyse how each piece produces these differing results.

Many aural skills are heightened in an improvisation. Through the challenge of reacting immediately to the element of surprise, the ongoing variables each choice brings, from listening carefully and co-ordinating with others, to-adjusting dynamics, intonation and density in response to the group creation, and so on, all these are skills which, while being developed in improvisational games, will reap huge benefits when returning to the group rehearsal and performance of notated music.

By contrast, a curriculum for Grade 8 contains this learning objective: "Improvise a solo melodic line (accompanied or unaccompanied)." This appears general enough. Improvise vocally or instrumentally? Does the improvisation follow any harmonic or melodic structure? Varying a rhythmic pattern, a melodic motive, a melodic line over an harmonic progression or substituting a new text for the usual words of a familiar melody are examples of improvisation games which provide students with first-hand experience with creating music spontaneously. Such games can easily fulfill learning objectives such as that quoted above. Improvisation games may also be passed around from student to student in a whole-class activity, or may also be conducted in teams, each facing the same challenges yet producing differing results, with plenty of fodder for discussion.

Composition Games provide the student with the task of actually creating music for a specific purpose. The music produced as the result of the 'compositional' process tends to be relatively precise in terms of pitch, duration and form.

This is why themes, harmonizations, counterpoint and complex forms are composed rather than improvised. While composing makes more intellectual demands upon the students,there is no reason for younger and/or less knowledgeable students to be discouraged from attempting it.

Composition is simply the formulation of *what occurs when* in advance. Composition may be practiced in large groups, small groups, pairs or alone. As with the other games, composition games have objectives and rules. The composition game contains restrictions: create using given keys, rhythmic motives, chord structures or progressions, formal scheme, for certain instruments, with given musical gestures, or for sections of a specified duration (in bars or seconds), metres, tempi, and so on. In a composition game, some decisions are made, and some problems are presented to the composers to solve. The challenges presented in a composition game require the planning and reflection that improvisational games specifically avoid.

Composition games therefore stimulate the student's interest in music theory, since so much of it is required in order to compose. The tasks involved lead naturally to an need for organisation and co-ordination, probably requiring some sort of score. Some may want melody and/or harmony, and voices and/or instruments to perform, and this all needs to be notated and/or rehearsed. The compositional task causes the student to call forth everything that he or she knows about music in order to complete the it.

Composition games may take the form of a short creative assignment such as writing a jingle for a given product or creating a theme song or overture for a given play or story. The composition game may be to set a piece of text in one or more musical styles. A music curriculum for Grade 2 under *Creative Work* reads: "create short songs and instrumental pieces using a variety of sound sources". Almost anything might be a starting point for composition games which address this learning objective. Taking the world inside an aquarium for inspiration, groups of students might be asked to create a fish song, for example, making up their own words and using three notes (a simple pattern such as d-r-m or r-f-s might be sung to them as a starting point).

Other examples of starting points might be a short story or a nursery rhyme might be turned into a piece of music by dividing it into sections and assigning a different group to create a musical version of each section, which the class then performs in sequence.

Additional learning objectives from the same grade may be touched upon by these games as well, such as "sing expressively, showing an understanding of the text", and/or "accompany songs in an expressive way, using appropriate rhythm instruments, body percussion, or 'found' instruments" and finally, "produce a specific effect (e.g. create a soundscape as background for a story or poem), using various sound sources (e.g. the voice, the body, instruments)".

5. Creating Curriculum Games

A game, like a work of art, allows for manifold possibilities within a restricted field. A successful game is, in itself, a pleasure to play and is its own motivation. This is why game structure is useful as a teaching tool: students are predisposed to being motivated to play, and therefore learn.

The game itself may be quite simple; as implied before most successful games have a very simple objective. Hockey, for example it is to: "put the puck in the net". The process for accomplishing this, however, demands many complex and highly developed skill sets, which some refine to a professional degree. The skill sets required to perform a piece of music are also complex, but the process of acquiring and refining them is quite different than that of a team sport. Musical games simulate the team sport experience by combining skill-building exercises with entertaining activity.

If a game can teach, it must provide a vehicle for the acquisition and refinement of skills and/or knowledge. Game structure may be applied to any curriculum objective, by defining the skills and knowledge which are required for competence, and then tailoring the scope of the game to the desired skill/knowledge field. The following steps may provide some guidance:

> 1. State the curriculum objective
> 2. Itemize the skills which are required to demonstrate competence with this objective
> 3. Detail any background knowledge which is necessary to reach this objective
> 4. Select a game type
> 5. Select an objective for the game
> 6. Define the procedures (rules and materials) of the game
> 7. Assessment

Let us now apply these steps to the creation of a curriculum game:

> 1. *State the curriculum objective.* At random, I select the follow objective from the Ontario Music Curriculum for Grade 7: "demonstrate the ability to produce the same pitch as others, vocally or instrumentally".

> 2. *Itemize the skills* which are required to demonstrate competence with this objective: In order to match pitch, students must be able to hear the pitch, locate or identify it in some way, and then reproduce this pitch, either vocally or on an instrument. If done vocally, some experience locating pitches through vocal warmups and singing would be helpful; if done instrumentally, prior training on the instrument is nec-

essary, in order to locate and produce selected pitches.

3. *Detail the background knowledge which is required by this objective.* Since most people have some experience singing before entering school, much less background knowledge is required for pitch matching vocally than on an instrument, yet many students have difficulty with vocal pitch location. From my experience, very few people are actually "tone deaf". They hear the note, but are unable to locate the pitch with their larynx. I have solved this problem by allowing them to pick a note which they *can* sing. I then match their note on the piano and have them experience pitch matching. I then move up or down by tone and ask for further matching. Gradually, a larger range of notes they are able to hear and match is established. Matching pitches instrumentally does not require any special training if done on a keyboard instrument but, as mentioned above, requires previous training if done on a string, wind or brass instrument.

4. *Select a game type* (skill-building; instructive; integrative; investigative; improvisation; performance or composition). Pitch matching is a basic musical skill which can be done quickly and without much prior training or explanation. I therefore select the "skill-building" game type.

5. *Select an objective for the game.* What demonstration of skill/knowledge would constitute a "successful" learning experience (There is no one "correct" answer to this question). A correct pitch match is considered "successful".

6. *Define the procedures (rules and materials) of the game.* What game would use these skills to obtain this objective? How does one "play" the game? What constitutes a "win" ? What materials might be required to play this game? This is the portion of the game creation process where your inventive skills are required. The game should use the students' background knowledge while developing the skill set required by the learning objective. Frequently, the adaptation of an existing game can provide a model

upon which to build your game.

For our example, I will use the theatre game *zip, zap, boing* as my model. The object of the game is to match pitches and pass pitches around the circle as quickly and smoothly as possible. Participants stand in a circle. The leader sings a pitch and passes the pitch to another person in the circle by making eye contact, followed by a "tossing" motion. This person receives the pitch by matching the leader's pitch. The second person then selects a nearby pitch (different from the first pitch) and "tosses" it to another person, who matches it and passes on a third pitch, and so on. A pause or mismatched pitch is considered a "dropped ball". In *zip zap*, this person is eliminated from the circle, but this may not be helpful in a teaching situation. Instead, this person may be asked to start the process again.

7. *Assessment.* In this final phase, the teacher can assess the success of the game in teaching or enhancing the knowledge required by the curriculum objective(s). Student engagement and enthusiasm should also be considered as an objective and as a necessary part of Piaget's self-motivation cycle:

Self-Motivating Cycle (as in Abeles pp 216)

1. Play (interacting with the environment)
2. Accommodation (adjusting information to the environment)
3. Imitation (practicing this adjustment}
4. Assimilation (applying new information to standard situations)

In the above example, students had, perhaps for the first time, to sing individually in front of their peers. The fun of "tossing" the matched pitches soon overcame their initial fears. For those students who had difficulty with pitch matching, encouragement was provided. This game quickly boosted the energy and excitement level in the class , it also provides the teacher with a quick and painless assessment of each of the student's pitch and co-ordination abilities, which informs the teacher about those who require extra help, and those who displayed talent.

Footnotes

1. Research and practice concerning the links between play and learning have focused primarily on pre-school aged children. More recent interest has been taken in the manner in which the modality of play opens the entire being to deep participation: the senses, the imagination, the mind and memory. See, for example:

Apter, Michael J., and John H. Kerr.."Chapter 12: The Nature, Function and Value of Play," in *Adult Play* (1991) ed. John H. Kerr and Michael J. Apter Amsterdam: Swets and Zeitlinger.

Bruner, Jerome S., Allison Jolly, and Kathy Sylva.(1976) *Play - Its Role in Development and Evolution.* New York: Basic Books, Inc..

Fromberg, D. P. (2002). *Play and meaning in early childhood education.* Boston: Allyn & Bacon.

Martin, Paul and T.M. Caro. *On the Functions of Play and Its Role in Behavioral Development.* in "Advances in the Study of Behavior" (1985) edited by J.S. Rosenblatt, C. Beer, M.C. Busnel, and P.J.B. Slater

Roschelle, Jeremy. *Learning in Interactive Environments: Prior Knowledge and New Experience.* in "Public Institutions for Personal Learning" (1995), edited by John H. Falk and Lynn D. Dierking, Washington, DC: American Association of Museums.

2. Ironically, interest in play and games has been concentrate at the extreme ends of the learning spectrum: pre-school and post-graduate. Game Theory consists of mathematical constructs of probability based, in part, on stochastics. For example, see:

Owen Guillermo (1995) *Game Theory* Burlington MA Academic Press.

Colman, Andrew M. (1995) Game Theory and its Applications Amsterdam: Butterworth-Heinemann.

Dixit, Skeath K., Skeath, Susan (1999) *Games of Strategy* New York: Norton.

3. See the fascinating discussion of the imagination and the theatrical "what if..." in Stanislavski, C. (1936) *An Actor Prepares* (tr. E.P. Hapgood) New York: Routledge 1989

References

Abeles, Hoofer and Klotman (1995) *Foundations of Music Education* (2nd ed.) New York: Wadsworth

Barrett, McCoy and Veblen (1997) *Sound Ways of Knowing: music in the interdisciplinary classroom* New York: Schirmer Books

Boyle and Radocy (1987) *Measurement and Evaluation of Musical Ex periences* New York: Schirmer Books

Davis, Morton A. (1997) *Game Theory: A Nontechnical Introduction* New York: Dover

Csikszentmihalyi, Mihalyi (1990). *Flow: The Psychology of Optimal Experience.* New York: Harper Collins.

Csikszentmihalyi, M. (1997). *Creativity: Flow and the psychology of discovery and invention.* New York Harper Collins.

Koestler, A. (1964). *The Act of Creation* Middlesex, Arkana (Penguin)

Gardner, H. (1993). *Creating minds.* New York: Basic Books.

Gardner, H. (1993). Frames of mind. The theory of multiple intelligences (10th anniversary ed.). New York: Basic Books.

Jourdain, Robert (1997) *Music, the Brain and Ecstasy: How music captures our imagination* New York: Wm. Morrow and Co.

Paynter, John and Aston, Peter (1970) *Sound and Silence: Classroom Projects in Creative Music,* Cambridge, Cambridge University Press

Chapter 14

A Spider's Web of Intrigue

Charles Byrne

CHARLES BYRNE is a lecturer in the Faculty of Education, University of Strathclyde. As Director of Music in Teacher Education he is responsible for music in education input to a number of teaching courses including the Post Graduate Certificate in Education (Secondary) course. In 1997 Charles established, with Mark Sheridan, the SCARLATTI Project, an action research project investigating the teaching and learning of composing and improvising in Scottish secondary schools. Recent research interests include the development of powerful learning environments, thinking in music and aspects of flow theory in music education. Publications include articles for the *British Journal of Music Education*, the *International Journal of Music Education* and *Music Education Research*

In looking for models of good teaching in composing and improvising and for background reading that could be of use to practicing teachers, we found much of interest in the *teaching thinking* literature, particularly DeCorte's idea of a "powerful learning environment". The purpose of the *Spider's Web Composing Lessons* is not to facilitate the study of children's compositional processes and products, rather, the purpose is to provide opportunities for novice composers to develop skills and strategies in handling musical materials within an organised framework.

Introduction

In 1997, my colleague Mark Sheridan and I established the SCARLATTI Project which aimed to investigate and document the teaching approaches and methodologies used by Scottish secondary school music teachers in the area of Inventing (Composing, Improvising and Arranging) and to share good practice, findings and thoughts with interested colleagues. It was envisaged that a number of teachers would be able to access and share information via e-mail. World wide web based discussion groups and music teachers who subscribed to the project were invited to contribute to the SCARLATTI HyperNews discussion group established at the Clyde Virtual University. HyperNews has the facility to link quickly and easily with other sites. Soon we began to create a bank of information and materials that we hoped teachers would find of some use. It is within this context that we began developing the *Spider's Web* Composing Lessons.

Models for Teaching Composition

In looking for models of good teaching in Composition and Improvisation and for background reading that could be of use to practising teachers, we found much of interest in the "teaching thinking" literature, particularly [first name with the first citation] DeCorte's idea of a "powerful learning environment" (1990). Having been Principal Teachers of Music in busy, urban secondary schools, we recognised this phenomenon as being almost exactly the same as the typical "lunchtime" in our own music departments. A budding rock band is busy learning and perfecting a song; pairs of youngsters are helping each other learn their parts in preparation for the Wind Band rehearsal; two or three guitarists are composing a song together; and a student piano player is leading a small group through songs from the film *Titanic*. In this scenario, capable peers may be working with novice songwriters or performers. The "modelling" of expected levels of performance is given and support, or 'scaffolding' (Wood, Bruner & Ross, 1976) for further learning is provided. Encouragement and advice is offered, and accepted and this 'coaching' gradually gives way to 'fading' when the learner has gained sufficient experience to be able to regulate her own learning (DeCorte, 1990; McGuinness & Nisbet, 1991).

We looked at Guilford's work (1967) identifying the stages in the creative process outlined by[first name] Dewey (1910), [first name?] Wallas (1926; 1945) and [first name] Rossman (1931) and we were intrigued by the emphasis placed on reviewing and evaluating within each of these models. The link between creative thinking and problem solving which, according to Guilford (1967) are essentially the same major operation, led us to conceive of a series of composing lessons consisting of short musical steps. At any point, students would be able to ask questions, solve musical problems and make decisions as to the development of the musical material as a result of their own evaluation and reflection.

Process, Product and Passing Exams

The purpose of the *Spider's Web Composing Lessons* is not to facilitate the study of children's compositional processes and products. Rather the purpose is to provide opportunities for novice composers to develop skills and strategies in handling musical materials within an organised framework.

New approaches to teaching and learning composing often cause teachers to think immediately of problems, usually assessment. Many music teachers in Scotland adopt a fairly short term approach to Inventing; the examination led syllabus dictates that a folio of compositions, improvisations or arrangements must be completed by a certain date so, the product immediately becomes the focus of attention, rather than the process. It may be that some music teachers are uncomfortable "with the prospect of designing activities for pupils which add to their general educational and musical development rather than accomplish the desired objective of preparing a folio of inventions which will secure them a good pass at Standard Grade music" (Byrne & Sheridan, 1998a, p. 299). Barrett (1998) observes that while Kratus (1994) and Bunting (1988) place an emphasis on the compositional process, it is interesting to note that "Bunting (1988) acknowledges that analysis of students' compositional products is an important part of any assessment procedure" (Barrett, 1998, p.14). It seems that it is not only in Scotland that if it moves, we must assess it.

Webster (1988) proposes a theory of creative-thinking in music based on a synthesis of convergent and divergent thinking. Many possible solutions to a musical problem are generated and this focusing on the process, since thinking implies a present tense activity, "becomes a kind of 'structured play' (Webster, 1988, p. 77). Students may have recourse to knowledge or musical concepts already learned and may apply convergent thinking skills in assimilating new and existing knowledge. Such an approach encourages teachers to allow the student "space and freedom to think and experiment, while the requirements of the product for examination takes a back seat. The process, however is under scrutiny and the core skills components of critical thinking and planning and organising, employed in the process can be rewarded" (Byrne & Sheridan, 1999). With the introduction in Scotland of the new Higher Still courses and pathways there has been a slight shift toward assessing the process with the requirement for students to complete a composing log giving details of the compositional processes and techniques used (Higher Still Development Unit, 1997). In these web based composing lessons, the emphasis is firmly placed on the process of composing.

Composers in the classroom

As composers and secondary music teachers, Mark Sheridan and I had over twenty-five years experience of creating materials for our students and we believed that learning to compose could be both stimulating and fun provided that activities were framed appropriately. Our teaching of composing and improvising in the classroom had been based on giving students real musical problems which they were capable of solving rather than mere paper and pencil exercises in the use of notation and chord boxes which, while they may have produced "correct answer" type results, were, it is argued, of little musical significance or value. In a recent study (Sheridan & Byrne, submitted for publication). We describe these "correct answer" type activities as "Closed Critical Thinking Activities" in which the student is given very little opportunity to experiment with or explore different sounds and combinations. Although there may be more than one correct answer within such activities, free and original thought is often excluded due to the contrived nature of the musical problem.

Here is an example of a popular composing activity. (Popular by our teachers' reckoning, we have not yet asked the students!). The class has finished playing *In the Mood* on keyboards and a natural composing activity which develops from this is to create a new melody that fits the chord scheme for "In the Mood" and makes use of the same jazzy, syncopated rhythms (Figure 1).

Figure 1

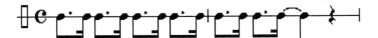

Students are required to use these same rhythms and to select notes from the chord of C major that will fit, creating
their own tune. Chords are often shown in the form of
chord boxes which spell out either the letter names, the
pitches in standard notation or both. Figure 2 is an example
of one format.

Figure 2

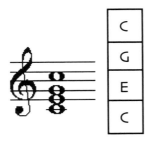

Students are given few rules and are simply advised to use
the notes of the chord to make a new tune. Enlightened
teachers may ensure that students use a musical instrument
during this "composing" process while others will expect
students to use pencil and manuscript paper and to check
their results later, either by themselves, with a more capable peer or with the teacher at the piano. Here is the sort
of result that can be expected (Figure 3):

Figure 3

The contrived nature of activities such as this may be described as "occupying knowledge-restricted problem environments" (Scardamalia & Bereiter, 1985, p. 66). The student is only allowed to use material contained within the
problem to provide a solution. Thinking must therefore be

convergent, since the process involves the solver in selecting one set of permutations which closely match the predicted outcome. The moving around of letter names on the page can, at best, be a logical-mathematical challenge and, at worst, a meaningless and futile exercise. As Elliott puts it "One learns to compose by being inducted into culture-based and practice-centered ways of musical thinking" (Elliott, 1995, p 162) and not, surely, by moving letters and symbols around on a piece of paper without any point of reference in the sound world being established. Composers often use the piano to check material that has already been worked out in their head. Similarly, there is little point in requiring a musical composition to be notated if, as Odam observes, "a child (and possibly the teacher) has interpreted the task of inventing a piece of music on a pitched-percussion instrument as the random playing of pitches and their recording" (Odam, 1995, p 43).

Inventing as part of Standard Grade Music

Evidence suggests (Byrne & Sheridan, 1998a) that the Inventing element of Standard Grade Music (SEB, 1988) is, perhaps unsurprisingly, the area where students achieve poorer grades than the other elements of solo and group performing, and listening. In 1991, 36% of candidates achieved grades 1 or 2 in the Inventing element of Standard Grade Music compared to 53% achieving the same grades for Solo Performance. By 1996, the figure for Solo Performance had risen to 63% while that for Inventing had risen to only 43% (Byrne & Sheridan, 1998a). Teachers often admit to lack of confidence in teaching and assessing inventing work and perhaps this is reflected in the fact that 90 secondary schools are now involved in the SCARLATTI Project which represents nearly 50% of all schools invited to participate. Teachers are always looking for new material and we were happy to use the SCARLATTI Project web based lessons as a vehicle for introducing teachers to some of the ideas discussed in this paper. Data from the University's world wide web server indicate that many individuals are downloading the materials but few are responding to the invitation to submit feedback and evaluation of the lessons.

Spider's Web Composing Lessons

The first lesson in the series makes use of text and graphics only and asks students to make decisions on rhythms and melodic ideas using very few pitches (http://www.strath.ac.uk/Departments/AppliedArts/Spider/compback.html).

Critical responses are encouraged through the use of questions such as "Which rhythm did you like best and why?". Students are reminded that "this is a disposable, process based activity. Remember all the steps if you can, but feel free to forget all of the notes and rhythms which you have just worked with" (Byrne & Sheridan, 1998b).

The second lesson, *Pattern Duet*, builds upon some of the ideas in the first lesson and makes use of sound files (http://www.strath.ac.uk/Departments/AppliedArts/PD/pdback.html).

These were recorded using a Roland Digital Piano and MC-50 Sequencer. Each short segment was then recorded onto a Mini Disc Recorder and converted into AIFF format which can be recognised by web browsers. The music notation graphics for all lessons were produced using Mosaic Composer software from Mark of the Unicorn. Small pieces of notation were clipped using the Flash-It utility and then converted to GIF files in Claris HomePage 3.0 web site design software.

Pattern Duet introduces the notion of combining different melodic ideas; the sound files allow the student to hear the melodic shape of each pattern although not in combination. Teachers and students will have to devise methods of doing this in the classroom, whether by using recording devices or by setting up the activity for small groups of instrumentalists. Individual students could work at a computer workstation, responding to the material on an electronic keyboard with a built-in sequencer. Hyperlinks are included in this lesson in order to provide definitions of new or unfamiliar concepts. For example, transposition is illustrated in the section built around the chord of G major and a definition is also given. Finally, understanding of the concept can be checked by asking the student to make the transposition that will make each pattern fit with the chord of E minor.

The third lesson in the series, *Happy Birthday Mr Smith* illustrates how an effective piece of music can be created using a limited range of notes and some interesting, yet simple chords (http://www.strath.ac.uk/Departments/AppliedArts/ HBMSmith/hbmsback.html). This is an example of an "exploded" composition (individual parts expanded from a piano reduction), allowing the student to feel and hear how a piece has been developed from a tiny musical idea. Textural considerations and instrumentation are explored as users are able to hear parts separately and in combination with each other in the generation of material.

Although these composing lessons represent pitches and rhythms in conventional notation the sound files have been included as additional points of reference. It is important that teachers do not simply treat these lessons as yet another paper-based exercise that can be 'marked' later on. There is, quite deliberately, no emphasis placed on students being either able to, or required to, write down their compositions in any conventional way. Of course, students may want to begin to do this and activities such as these may well provide the motivation for some to learn how to use notation. Salaman (1997) asks " what musical purpose staff notation serves in the lives of average pupils" (p. 148) and if the answer has to do with wanting to record an interesting musical result, then the purpose of learning notation has moved beyond that of acquiring inert knowledge (Scardamalia & Bereiter, 1985).

Feedback and evaluation

So far, there has been little feedback from teachers or students regarding the ease of use of these lessons , the suitability of tasks or the practical implications of their use in the classroom. Electronic evaluation forms are included on the web site although few have been completed and returned. Those that have replied to the request for comments and feedback suggest that the activities are appropriate for secondary years 1 and 2 students and the third lesson, *Happy Birthday Mr Smith* being useful for years 3 and 4 as preparation for, guess what, completion of the inventing folio. As models for the use of text and graphics, they have proved useful for student teachers.

The lessons are no substitute for good teaching and good

teachers will know how much help to give individuals, and when to provide support and advice. Each set of tasks and examples could be done either by individual students or small groups working together. The results of working through *Pattern Duet*, for example, could be a series of MIDI files or a new set of material that could form the basis of another project.

Further development

Other composing lessons are planned, including one which introduces a new thinking tool for composers which draws upon different views of the stages of the creative process (Dewey, 1910; Wallas, 1926, 1945; Rossman, 1931; Weisberg, 1986), as well as the work of Tony Buzan (1974) and Edward de Bono (1976, 1982). The ORIENT thinking tool is intended as an aid for helping students through the composing process. It will not actually compose any of the music but it should help the novice composer organise his or her thoughts and ideas, allowing them the opportunity to check on their progress during the composition process.

Once again, the emphasis is on the process and is offered to music teachers in an effort to move them away from the product-oriented approach in the hope that they will see the importance of providing useful skills in composing and thinking which will form the basis of a continuing interest in creative work in music that students can apply in later life.

References

Barrett, M. (1998). Researching Children's Compositional Process and Products: Connections to Music Education Practice? In, *Children Composing*, B. Sundin, G. E. McPherson & G. Folkestad (Eds.) Malmo: Lund University.

Bunting, R. (1988). Composing music: Case studies in the teaching and learning process. *British Journal of Music Education*, 5(3), 269-310.

Buzan, T. (1974). *Use Your Head*. London: BBC Books.

Byrne, C. & Sheridan, M. (1998a). Music: a source of deep imaginative satisfaction? *British Journal of Music Education*, 15(3), 295-301.

Byrne, C. & Sheridan, M. (1998b). *Spider's Web Composing Lessons*. http://www.strath.ac.uk/Departments/ AppliedArts/lessonmenu/complessons.html
Byrne, C. & Sheridan, M. (1999). Think Music. In, *Effective Music Teaching*. CD-ROM, Edinburgh: Higher Still Development Unit.

de Bono (1976). *Teaching Thinking*. London: Temple Smith.

de Bono, E. (1982). *de Bono's Thinking Course*. London: British Broadcasting Corporation.

DeCorte, E. (1990). Towards powerful learning environments for the acquisition of problem solving skills. *European Journal of Psychology of Education*, 5, 5-19.

Dewey, J. (1910). *How We Think*. Boston: Heath.

Elliott, D. J. (1985). *Music Matters. A New Philosophy of Music Education*. New York: Oxford University Press.

Guilford, J. P. (1967). *The Nature of Human Intelligence*. New York: McGraw-Hill.Higher Still Development Unit (1997). Subject Guide: Music. Edinburgh: Higher Still Development Unit.

Kratus, J. (1994). The ways children compose. In H. Lees (Ed.) Musical connections: Tradition and change, (*Proceedings of the 21st World Conference of the International Society for Music Education*, held in Tampa, Florida) Auckland, NZ: Uniprint, The University of Auckland, 128-141.

McGuinness, C. & Nisbet, J. (1991) 'Teaching Thinking in *Europe*', *British Journal of Educational Psychology*, 61, 174-186. Odam, G. (1995). The Sounding Symbol. Cheltenham: Stanley Thornes (Publishers) Ltd.

Rossman, J. (1931). *The Psychology of the Inventor.* Washington, D.C.: Inventors Publishing Co.

Salaman, W. (1997). Keyboards in Schools. *British Journal of Music Education,* 14(2), 143-149.

Scardamalia, M, & Bereiter, C. (1985). Cognitive Coping Strategies and the Problem of "Inert Knowledge". In, S. F. Chipman, J. W. Segal& R. Glaser (Eds.),*Thinking and Learning Skills, Volume 2: Research and Open Questions,* New Jersey: Laurence Earlbaum Associates.

Scottish Examination Board. (1988). *Scottish Certificate of Education: Standard Grade; Arrangements in Music.* Dalkeith: Scottish Examination Board.

Sheridan, M. & Byrne, C. (submitted for publication). *The SCARLATTI Papers.*

Wallas, G. (1926; 1945). *The Art of Thought.* London: Watts.

Webster, P. R. (1988). Creative Thinking in Music: Approaches to Research. In, J.T.Gates (Ed) *Music Education in the United States: Contemporary Issues.* Tuscaloosa: The University of Alabama Press.

Weisberg, R. (1986). *Creativity: Genius and Other Myths.* New York: W. H. Freeman and Company.

Wood, D. J., Bruner, J. S. & Ross, G. (1976) 'The Role of Tutoring in Problem Solving', In *Journal of Child Psychology and Psychiatry,* 17,89-100.

Chapter 15

Unleashing the 'Ganas' in the Large Ensemble: Developing a Mindful Pedagogy

Gerald King

GERALD KING (B. Mus., M. Mus., Ed.D.) is an Associate Professor of Music and Music Education at the University of Victoria in Victoria, British Columbia. His responsibilities include conducting the Wind Symphony, teaching undergraduate and graduate conducting, and pedagogy courses in secondary music education.

As we enter the 21st Century the prevailing zeitgeist is that "creativity" may replace the focus on information. The notion of a "creative age" is timely, albeit long overdue in my view for those of us in education. Inexperienced and pre-service teachers spend much of their time acquiring information and knowledge often resulting in less time being devoted to exploring ways to "engage" the students we work with so that they can make meaning of the material presented. Each individual's search for meaning involves a creative process—the creative "niche" within each person may be likened to the "ganas" or "spirit" within each human being. Our role as educators is to "unleash the ganas," thus enabling in individuals the desire to learn.

Views of Creativity and Being Creative

Defining creativity has and continues to be a very difficult task. Langer (1989) believes that: many, if not all, of the qualities that make up a mindful attitude are characteristic of creative people. Those who can free themselves of old mindsets...who can open themselves to new information and surprise, play with perspective and context, and focus on process rather than outcome are likely to be creative, whether they are scientists, artists, or cooks. (p. 115) She further states, "a respect for intuition and for the information that may come to use in unexplainable ways is an important part of any creative activity" (p. 119).

Harold Best (2000) speaks of "musical/artistic mindedness" as having "three sides or modes: creativity, valuing, spirit" (p. 4). He states that the three modes function interdependently while still being able to remain distinct. Best believes "[i]f a work of art is a coupling of imagining and crafting, so is its performance" (p. 5).

Composer, Aaron Copland states:

> In the art of music, creation and interpretation are indissolubly linked. … Both these activities…demand an imaginative mind….Both bring into play creative energies that are sometimes alike, sometimes dissimilar. (p. 40)

Central to success in any undertaking is to have the "urge [or spirit] to succeed, to achieve, to grow" (Mattews, 1988, p. 191). Jaime Escalante describes this as the "ganas" in each individual that is waiting to be illuminated. It is by illuminating the ganas in each student that they may reach their own best creative potential.

The prevailing thought appears to be that the creative approach begins with the idea that nothing is as it appears. Also, creativity does not demand absolute originality, instead it may take the form of a traditional process being viewed or approached differently. Creativity offers the hope of new solutions to old problems. Given this view of creativity and what it means to be creative I suggest a paradigm shift in the rehearsal procedures for large ensembles.

Teaching and Learning in the Large Ensemble

Educational research suggests that individuals are better able to make meaning of information when the process is student-centered. For those of us involved in teaching/ conducting large ensembles the student-centered approach requires a major "shift in focus" in the process of teaching and learning. As music educators we must help our students come to know the music they perform. It is imperative that students grasp the "essence" of the composer's intent and conjoin in the experience of music making, thus going beyond mere skill and technical development. I believe that there are two main perspectives on Teaching and Learning. Perspective I is teacher-centered, while Perspective II is student-centered. The norm in our large ensemble classes is Perspective I where the students become mere receptacles, non-thinking vessels for our words of wisdom —such an approach stifles creativity" (King, 2000, p. 10). In 1929, Alfred North Whitehead wrote:

> In training a child to activity of thought, above all things we must beware of what I call 'inert ideas' — that is to say, ideas that are merely received into the mind without being utilized, or thrown into fresh-combinations. Education with inert ideas is not only useless: it is, above all things, harmful. (p. 1)

John Dewey in *Experience and Education* (1938) states that "everything depends on the quality of the experience [and] every experience lives on in further experiences" (p. 27). He believes that "if an experience arouses curiosity, strengthens initiative and sets up desires and purposes" (p. 38) then it is worthy.

We have made much progress in education; however, we must continually guard ourselves from falling into the "trap" of inert pedagogical practice.

Cycles of Teaching and Learning: Two Perspectives

Historically, Perspective I teaching and learning has been and continues to be the most common form of teaching and learning in the large ensemble performance classroom.

Table 1. Perspective I—Linear

Teacher Centred

TEACHER --->Student

one way communication leading to dependence

- The teacher provides the stimulus and the student is expected to respond without question.
- The teacher must re-teach both general concepts and specifics throughout every class.
- The student is an "empty vessel" — the teacher is a giver of information and possesses all of the answers.
- The student is not required to think on multiple levels; hence, the student is not often engaged. The student dependent on the teacher.
- The teacher has the power and is in control.
- Student learning is minimal.
- Student creativity is stifled.

A paradigm shift to a Perspective II approach to teaching and learning is essential if we are to guide each individual to reach their own best creative potential.

Table 2. Perspective II—Cyclical

Student Centred

Teaching

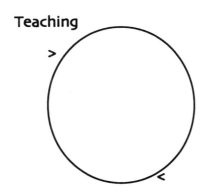

Learning

two way communication leading to interdependence

- The student is central to the teaching and learning process.
- The student contributes—questions are valued by the teacher.
- The teacher is a facilitator—a guide.
- The teacher works to "inspire" students to learn.

- The teaching/learning process becomes "Interdependent."
- Every students becomes a teacher and every teacher becomes a student [the essence of life-long learning].
- Students and their opinions, suggestions and questions are valued.
- Students are considered able and responsible.
- The teaching/learning process becomes more cognitive and less behaviorist oriented.
- Students take ownership for their learning —they are more able to reach their own best creative potential —they become self-actualized —the "ganas" within is unleashed.
- The cyclical approach encourages the development of the "interrogative mind" of every student; thus helping students to better understand the course content, and the importance and connection of the mind, body and spirit.

Score Study: A Foundation for a Mindful Pedagogy

Score study is best thought of as a process of analyzing, synthesizing, reflecting and expanding. The journey is one of discovery whereby the many layers of a piece of music, a composer, and a culture are studied which in turn helps one arrive at a thoughtful, often more authentic interpretation. The process of probing the many layers is similar to the metaphor of "peeling an onion" (Hanley & King, 1995) whereby all the layers are important in making up the onion as a whole. Score study when viewed as a study of layers is a way of approaching knowing—a way of illuminating puzzling connections and awakening consciousness of the unrecognized (Berthoff, p. xi). It is important that as educators we guide our students to go beyond the obvious. The essence of score study is to become the composer's advocate (Leinsdorf, 1981). In order to accomplish this daunting task we must come to know the composer and the composition on many different levels. Individual and collaborative problem-centered creative activities whereby the "score is the nucleus for teaching and learning" (Garafalo, 19 76, p. 2) allow all opinions and ideas to be considered. At this point the teaching/learning processes become cyclical and conjoined resulting in a Mindful Pedagogy whereby the creative potential of all individuals is unleashed. (King, 1994)

It is important to remember that through the score study process we must go beyond the intellectual approach and consider how our new discoveries influence our feelings about the music. Studying a piece of music in depth should awaken new thoughts and feelings about the music—we must remind ourselves of the importance in considering our feelings. Corporon (2000) believes that:

> To develop an environment that fosters and promotes creativity, we must come to understand not only what we think but, most importantly, how we feel. We must inject the thinking and feeling aspects of our-selves into the music throughout the course of the musical process. We must feel the music before we can become advocates for the music. To remain crea-tive, we must be willing to live 'forever in the ques-tion' and not become content with finding one—and only one—answer. (pg. 82)

We must continually ask, what do you think, feel, hear and see, and what are the relationships between these findings (Hanley & King, 1995).

I believe that detailed score study is a strong foundation for developing a Mindful Pedagogy to assist in unleashing the "ganas " in our students so that they might reach their own best creative potential. It has been my experience that skill development and technique are embraced when young mu-sicians have a desire to perform a work to the best of their ability given their deeper understanding of the piece of mu-sic being studied. The following best summarizes the crea-tive nature of the score study process.

The creative process is generally agreed upon by researchers as consisting of stages 1) preparation: time to play with the ideas, 2) incubation: letting things develop by having time away from the task, 3) illumination: the "aha" moment when solutions present themselves, and 4) verification: time to work in structured ways with the product (Webster, 1990, pg. 24: Balkin, 1990, pg. 31). Cskszentmi-halyi (1996) includes evaluation, which occurs after illumina-tion. (cited in Blanchard, 1999, pg. 20)

The Process

The study of theoretical and historical issues is not necessarily creative by itself; however, what is very unique in the large ensemble rehearsal process is to have musicians contribute their ideas based on their own independent research in order for the ensemble to arrive at a collective interpretation. As the teacher/leader we must provide a format that details the teaching/learning process, the responsibilities of each participant, the requirements to be completed, and assessment. Prior to this it is necessary that the teacher's philosophical position on teaching and learning be clearly defined. My personal philosophical position is that, "every conductor/teacher must be a humanistic leader who empowers each individual and ensemble to reach their own best creative potential." The teaching and learning process then must support this position. I suggest it is time to focus on Perspective II — a cyclical, Socratic approach to teaching and learning.

The score provides all the necessary information for the theoretical material. However, in order to gain a holistic view of the piece we must research historical information about the composer, the time period the work was written, as well as cultural specific information. Score study is usually done by the conductor in a solitary state—once the conductor has studied the score the conductor then shares his/her interpretation and understanding with the ensemble (Perspective I). I have used a collaborative score study process (Perspective II) for almost twenty years while teaching junior/senior high school and now at the university. The basis of discovery is the use of questions with the possibilities of many answers. Score study is effortful and is never complete, yet the more we study and ingest intellectually and emotionally the more authenticity we are able bring to the interpretation.

The following are some guidelines, activities and assignments associated with the collaborative score study.

> • Select a significant piece of choral, wind, or orchestral literature that is at the appropriate level for the students in the class. A conductor's full score must be supplied for each student.

212

• Designate a feature wall(s) in the music room for posting student research. Research relating to the composer, the historical time period, the compositional structure of the piece, recordings, other works by the composer, other composers from the same historic period, concert critiques, as well as student questions, reflections, and feelings are to be included. The research should be both collective and independent. Students should be encouraged to be creative in showcasing their findings using visual art, poetry, charts, tables, etc. The possibilities are endless.

• General headings for the study of theoretical materials in the piece would include melody, phrasing, harmony, rhythm-meter, texture, dynamics, articulations, orchestration and terminology. The teacher is to guide students through ways to explore the musical elements in the composition. Prior study and organization by the teacher is necessary if students are to feel comfortable and be successful with the process. Each element is to be studied independently with different assignments given to encourage students to explore in depth how the elements contribute to the piece. In addition to written assignments, performance and composition assignments are to be generated. For example, performance warm-up exercises and individual short compositions can be developed from the research findings of students. Students could be asked to identify the most common interval, the most common dynamic, the most common articulation and then suggest how these elements might be included in their personal/ ensemble warm-up and composition. As well, exercises focusing on the orchestration of specific sections of the piece may be considered so that students begin to hear the different colors possible by altering the orchestration.

Other possibilities include the exploration of key centers, chord types, phrase lengths, melodic contours and ways the composer creates tension and release. The depth of exploration will depend on the level of the class and assignments should reflect the needs of the individuals within the class. Student generated warm-up exercises and compositions should be performed and recorded—reflection and discussion should follow.

• Listening assignments are an integral component of the study. Numerous recordings (if possible) of the work being studied, as well as other works by the composer should be listened to, questioned, and discussed. Students should be asked what they hear and feel when listening to recordings or live performances and then discuss the similarities and differences of performances . Students are encouraged to express what they hear and feel through written critiques, drawings, collages, etc.

• During the score study process students should be encouraged to suggest ideas related to the interpretation of the piece. The interpretive ideas should be based on their findings of the composer and the work as their musical understanding evolves. A performance or performances of the work should occur with students providing pre-performance presentations showcasing the variety of ways they have come to know, appreciate and better understand the composer and the composition. Kratus (1990, pg. 34) believes that, "musical products are the improvisations, compositions, and performances that result when creative musicians engage in creative musical thought."

Due to the length of time and effort required to complete a collaborative score study I believe it reasonable to complete one or two studies of significant (choral, wind, orchestral) literature during the year.

Assessment

Traditionally, assessment in large ensembles focuses on individual skill and technical acquisition. Collaborative score study and the related activities not only suggest, but demand a more comprehensive approach to assessing individual student achievement. In addition to the evaluation of skill and technique the assessment process must evaluate each student's "reflective practice" (Schon, 1983) in coming to know the music. Assessment must recognise the growth of the student's research ability; their micro and macro knowledge of the music and composer; their individual and collaborative processes of discovery; and, their creativity in presentation of their new found knowledge encompassing the disciplines of theory, history, composition, and performance.

Throughout the study of the piece each student should keep a process-folio. Process-folios were developed by Arts PRO-PEL researchers to help document growth and provide a means for authentic assessment (Gardner, 1989). All student work should be maintained in the process-folio; including compositions, tapes of personal performances, listening critiques, reflections, feelings, questions, and final synthesis of the piece and composer being studied. The score study process and assessment process result in each student producing a rich product, that is, a collective body of new found knowledge.

Coda

On a recent trip to Chicago I had the opportunity to speak with Cliff Colnot, principal conductor for the Chicago Symphony Orchestra's MusicNOW series. Dr. Colnot stated that for years the brass players in the orchestra have done personal score studies of the repertoire they are performing, striving to better understand the relationship of their part to the entire piece so that they can perform to the highest possible level. Why should this approach be reserved for the professional world? I strongly believe that it is crucial for the longevity of large ensemble performance classes in the school system that we explore more in depth ways to teach music through performance.

In order for a significant change to occur in the classroom the teacher must consciously employ a "shift in focus." I believe that the teacher's philosophical position on teaching and learning must become congruent with a student-centered approach. We must consider our students as able, capable, valuable and responsible (Purkey and Novak, 1984). We must allow students to contribute to the teaching/ learning process by giving students permission to make decisions, to openly question and discuss issues that are important to them. As teachers we must make questions the

portant to them. As teachers we must make questions the
center of our teaching. Answers we provide are often for-
gotten quickly and little learning takes place. Questions,
primarily student questions engage the mind (Dillon, 1988).

As teachers, all of our thoughts and actions must be guided
by pedagogical purpose. Pedagogy is a planned behavior
that is adjusted in the process of enacting it. The approach I
have presented is not a panacea; however, it is a way to illuminate the creative potential in our students. "Creativity is
an illusive concept that defies definition; it does, however,
reveal itself through observation and evaluation"
(Corporon, 2000, pg. 82).

I believe that the development of a Mindful Pedagogy based
on the philosophical principle that the "teacher/conductor
must be a humanistic leader who guides each individual and
ensemble to reach their own best creative potential" is a
way to unleash the "ganas" or "spirit" in our students in
hope that they soar, thus empowering each student to be in
charge of their own learning.

References

Balkin, A. (1990). What is Creativity? What is it Not?
    Music Educators Journal, 76(9), 29-32.

Berthoff, A. (1990). *The sense of Learning.* Portsmouth, NH:
    Boynton/Cook.

Best, H. M. (2000). Arts, Words, Intellect, Emotion Part 2: Toward
    Artistic Mindedness. *Arts Education Policy Review,
    102(1)*, 3-10.

Blanchard, C. (1999). *Teaching for Understanding—Expressiveness in
    Instrumental Music Performance.* University of Victoria,
    Unpublished Masters Project.

Corporan, E. M. (2000). Fervor, Focus, Flow, and Feeling: "Making an
    emotionalConnection." In R. Miles, (Ed), *Teaching Music
    Through Performance in Band: Volume 3*
    (pp.81-101).Chicago, IL: GIA Publications.

Copland, A. (1979). *Music and Imagination.* Cambridge, MASS:
    Harvard University Press.

Csikszentmihalyi, M., & Robinson, R. E. (1990). *The art of Seeing;
    An interpretation of the Aesthetic Encounter.* Malibu, CA: J.

Dewey, J. (1938). *Experience and Education.* New York, NY: Collier Books.

Dillon, J. T. (1988). *Questioning and Teaching: A Manual of Practice.* New York, NY: Teachers College Press.

Garafalo, R. (1976). *Blueprint for Band.* Ft. Lauderdale, FL: Meredith Music Publications.

Gardner, H. (1989b). Zero-based Arts Education: An introduction to Arts PROPEL. *Studies in Art Education, 30*(2), 71-83.

Hanley, B. & King, G. (Fall, 1995). Peeling the Onion: Arts PROPEL in the University Classroom. *Journal of Music Teacher Education, 5*(1), 15-29.

King, G. (Summer 1994). Mindful Teaching and Learning in the Concert Band. *Saskatchewan Band Association Journal,* 10-13.

King, G. (September 2000). *The Mind is like a Parachute.* GlenLyon-Norfolk School, Victoria, British Columbia. Unpublished Keynote Address.

Kratus, J. (1990). Structuring the Music Curriculum for Creative Learning. *Music Educators Journal, 76*(9), 33-37.

Langer, E. (1989). *Mindfulness.* Reading, MASS: Addison-Wesley.

Leinsdorf, E. (1981). *The Composer's Advocate: A Radical Orthodoxy for Musicians.* New Haven, CT: Yale University Press.

Matthews, J. (1988). *Escalante: The Best Teacher in America.* New York, NY: Henry Holt.

Purkey, W. & Novak, J. (1984). *Inviting School Success: A Self-concept Approach to Teaching and Learning.* Belmont, CA: Wadsworth.

Schon, D. (1983). *The Reflective Practioner: How Professionals Think in action,* NewYork, NY: Basic Books.

Webster, P. (1990). Creativity as creative thinking.*Music Educators Journal, 76*(9), 22-27.

Chapter 16

Musical Creativity: A Teacher Training Perspective

Veronika Cohen

VERONIKA COHEN is Dean of the Faculty of Composition, Conducting,Theory and Music Education at the Jerusalem Academy of Music and Dance.

Dr. Cohen has a master's degree from Yale University in composition and Ph.D. in music education from the University of Illinois .

Her research and teaching interests focus on the development of musical cognitive processes, with special emphasis on musical creativity. She has developed an approach for intuitive reflection through the use of kinaesthetic analogues or "musical mirrors". She is pedagogic and musical director of a project which puts preparation for encounters with live musical performances at the center of the general music curriculum.

Her work has been presented at international conferences and published in various journals.

Before moving to Israel in 1979, she taught in Canada and the United States.

Wanted: Teacher to bring out the maximum musical creative potential of her students.

The successful candidate needs to:

> • have a solid understanding of the musical creative process; have excellent skills of observation;

> • have the ability to encourage the unique creative leanings of each pupil;

- provide the skills and knowledge the pupil needs to actualize his or her creative potential;

- be able to suggest musical problems that will challenge the pupil to engage in creative activities;

- be supportive and give helpful evaluation and suggestions and avoid imposing her/his own taste or musical values on the pupil;

- create an emotional climate which allows experimentation without fear of failure and yet instills a striving for excellence:

- be personally involved in some creative activities.

This may look like a tall order. However, one does not need a cloned combination of Mozart, Pestalozzi, and a whole collection of researchers in musical creativity to reach this ideal. A well developed pre-service or in-service course for music teachers should do the job.

In the article which follows, I will outline a course of study which has proven helpful to students of music education in providing them not only with the knowledge but also the pedagogic skills to become a capable guide through the creative process.

The course is comprised of several components:

A) Study of the creative process in general and the musical creative process in particular.

B) Analysis of the process of supporting creative development

C) Peer teaching

D) Student teaching: a series of one-on-one meetings to promote creative growth of the pupil

E) Planning of curriculum for improvisation/composition

F) Experiences in improvisation and composition, and

G) Acquaintance with available literature to support creative work.

My acquaintance with similar courses have shown that aspects of practice teaching (points C, D, and E above) are generally ignored.

Students tend to experience creative work from the vantage point of the student, i.e. they carry out a series of creative projects. However, they have little or no experience learning how to support this process in their students. Over the years, it has become clear to me that this lack in their preparation is what has prompted many teachers to do little or no creative work with their students once they begin teaching.

This chapter, therefore, emphasizes the difficulties teachers face in supporting creative work and the ways of overcoming these difficulties. I will point out the emotional barriers that teachers have to overcome in order to apply what they know in theory about the creative process to their teaching.

First I shall present a vignette of an actual, recent classroom experience that highlights some of these problems. Then I shall proceed to present ways of dealing with them in creativity-based teaching training.

The students in this vignette are third-year music education students taking my course on "Developing Children's Creativity" at the Rubin Academy of Music and Dance in Jerusalem.

For the exercise about to begin we need a volunteer to be the pupil (acting as himself, not as if he were a child). The whole class acts as the "teacher" -- to guide and support the pupil's creative explorations. I explain that I might want to take over the role of teacher if I think that is necessary.

In order to present the students with an intriguing sound source, I open the grand piano and sing into the strings, while holding down the pedal. The sound possibilities inside the piano are novel and, therefore, capable of arousing curiosity, a desire to explore. This is also a "safe" instrument to explore: there is no pressure to play "correctly," no worry about voice leading, harmonic progression etc. As always, this time too the echoes following my singing into the strings proves sufficiently attractive to prompt a number of students to volunteer to be the "pupil" exploring this instrument.

We are towards the end of an hour long session in which H has volunteered to be the "pupil.

She had just finished a long, intricate, emotionally charged improvisation on the low strings inside the piano and is flushed with pleasure, very pleased with what had just poured out from under her fingers.

She had explored the low strings. (Since she is a string player, she found playing on the strings natural, but the sounds of these low piano string were a novelty to her, as was the technique required for playing them.)

Several students had volunteered to function as her teacher, i.e., guide her exploration. At some point one of the students, `Y', said:" Why don't you leave these low sounds now and see what you could do with the high sounds?"

At that point I stepped in and took on the role of "teacher. I said to' Y' that I thought it was much too soon to go on to other sounds, there was so much more to be done with the low sounds. To show what I meant I began with H, working on mastering the sounds of the low strings ,then she took off and began improvising"

After she finished her improvisation, I asked H to comment on how she felt about various suggestions that had been made by her classmates and by me.

H is an exceptionally polite young woman. She responds carefully as I remind her of the various suggestions her "teachers" had made during the course of this activity: "That was a very helpful comment, thank you" or " I did not really know what to do with this suggestion, sorry" are typical responses.

"How did you feel when Y said `why don't you try working on high sounds now'?- "

" I wanted to punch her in the face" comes the reply, uncensored and uncontrolled, from somewhere deep inside her. No one is more shocked than H who immediately apologizes. After laughter and mutual apologies and reassurances that no harm was done, we address the very important question: What prompted such a strong response?

Y says she doesn't have a clue.

Other students volunteer the information that they made particular note of Y's suggestion as being exactly what they had wanted to suggest.

One student comments that she had noted that she could not understand why I had intervened at that point.

I ask if now, after they had heard H's very powerful improvisation on the low strings, someone can explain why Y's comment made H so angry and why I intervened?

Did Y and others who had agreed with her suggestion feel that H had exhausted all the possibilities of the low strings? **NO.**

Has she already acquired the best possible technique for playing on those strings? **NO.**

In fact, had she mastered them at all, at the moment the suggestion was made? **NO**

Had she had a chance to move from her explorations into creating a musical gesture, a piece, with those sounds? **NO.**

Did she seem bored? at a loss? in need of variety? **NO.**

Was she simply repeating herself- going around in circles? **NO.**

Then why interfere? *Why sidetrack her with a suggestion which, had she followed it, would have short circuited the process that ended in such a strong improvisation.*

Y is thinking out loud: **"It made me feel uncomfortable that no one was saying anything. Someone needed to function as** *a teacher and say something. Also, I was getting bored with what she was playing. I was not thinking about H's need at all."*

Another student adds thoughtfully: "Even as my own aesthetic choice, now that I think of it, asking her to move to a different set of sounds, it was very shallow. Instead of exploring all that can be done with the low sounds I just wanted to settle for whatever was most obvious and then go on to something else. No wonder H wanted to punch us in the face."

H adds; "I am beginning to understand what made me so mad; I was finding things I was so excited about and you were saying, in so many words, that what I was doing was worthless. As you admitted, you found it boring."

One of the students asks me: Didn't you feel at any time that some change or variety was needed?"

Another student answers instead of me: "She did. Didn't you notice that when H was improvising she joined in for a few seconds with some high sounds."

The student adds that he was surprised I stopped so soon.

I explained that I tried very gingerly to introduce a new idea but realized very quickly that it was inappropriate for H's piece, so I beat a fast retreat.

H confirms what I felt:" I was really glad you stopped. What you were playing bothered me. "

We try to draw conclusions from the mistakes of this session:

Curb the urge to teach.

Don't interfere if there is no need.

Unless there are signs to the contrary, assume the student is doing something that is worthwhile to him or her.

Treat the pupil's work with respect.

If you feel impatient work on your impatience or walk away.

Do not let suggestions for further work grow out of your impatience.

Do not impose your aesthetic values on the pupil. It is his piece.

Your job is to help him actualize what he wants to create.

If you hear a different piece in your head go create your own piece.

One might conclude from this vignette that the students were real beginners with as yet no clue as to the creative process. In fact, most of these students could have given a good lecture on the creative process and ways to nurture it. However, between what they understood intellectually and what they could actually put into practice, were enormous emotional barriers.

Study of the creative process in general and the musical creative process in particular

At the start of the course we studied various aspects of the creative process. We looked at it from the cognitive and psychoanalytic perspectives and in terms of personality traits.

Students went through some tests which measure fluency, flexibility and originality.(e.g. how many uses can you think of for plastic bottles.) In reflecting on their experience they concluded that being overly critical is harmful at an early stage and inhibits fluency. Whereas at a later stage in the process, flexibility and originality benefited from being self-critical, from striving for excellence. We discussed the various stages of the process, as described by Wallace and Vaughn: preparation, incubation, illumination, and working out process (see Hargreaves).

Students reflected on their own process for creating a short composition and read some of the accounts of the creative process as reported by Beethoven, Mozart, Einstein (see

Ghisellin).

We also viewed and discussed·my videotapes of kindergarten children's free, unstructured play, as well as videotapes
of older children engaged in musical creative activities. I
also presented my theory that children , and in fact, older
students as well, tend to engage in activities which can be
classified as:

> Exploration,
>> Mastery, and
>>> Gesture production.

We observed these processes on video with children. We
analyzed various segments to learn to observe and analyze
creative behaviors.

Students learn that "exploration " and "mastery" are part of
the "preparation and incubation process. With adults the
process can take the form of improvisatory play or an internal mental process. With young children, however, the process is acted out, making it available for study by the sensitive observer. After discussing the stages of creative behavior, students watch and analyze a video-taped segment
of children in the music center:

*A child in the kindergarten is seen playing a motive on the
piano over and over. As she plays her motive, she
sometimes varies it slightly. She is staring out into the
classroom with a somewhat glazed look, while doggedly repeating her pattern, prompting one student to exclaim:
"She is incubating like crazy", then the whole class exclaims
with amazement "Illumination!" "Gesture production!," as
the motive suddenly flows into a well shaped melodic
phrase.*

In discussing personality traits, we note that creative behavior is not necessarily synonymous with being nice. In the
act of creation (but not necessarily at other times) ego cen-
tered, domineering behavior tend to be typical.

We discuss how there are teachers who tend to be uncomfortable with creative children. Often students relate their
negative childhood personal experiences with unsympathet-
ic teachers.

Next we discussed the pedagogic implications of what we have learned about the creative process. These center around a number of questions:

Analysis of the process of supporting creative development:

How can we support exploration?
How can we encourage mastery?
How can we pose interesting musical problems that will serve as a framework for improvisations/ compositions?
How can we give helpful feedback?
How can we create "space" for the creative child to function in the school setting?
How can we build a sequenced curriculum for crea tive development?

Once the student starts exploring, we should be alert to see when he might need our help to keep his interest high, to keep his exploration focused. When appropriate, we can focus his attention on aural aspects of his exploration ("Can you figure out, with your eyes closed, how I made this sound?). We can expand his aural imagination by asking him to imagine what would go well with a sound he likes. What would sound very different from his sound? Which two sounds he discovered would go well together?

We can help him take stock of his discoveries by categorizing what he found in any way that makes sense to him, e.g. connecting tactile and aural experience by making clear how manipulating the instrument affects sound production. All this, however, only when there is a need for intervention, when the pupil appears to be unfocused, asking by word or action for intervention.

When the child finds something interesting, we should make sure he gains some technical mastery over the material. Otherwise, his creative options would be very limited and frustrating. Can he control the dynamics? Can he produce rapid sounds? Can he predict how the sound he produces will sound? Is he satisfied with it?

Once he begins creating musical gestures, the most helpful

intervention is to play " musical conversations" with him. In such a situation the teacher plays in the style of the pupil, makes use of the same types of sounds, the same level of technical mastery as that possessed by the student. At the same time, the teacher models some organizational principle, some compositional device, that has not been employed by the pupil, one that the teacher feels the pupil might adopt if he were exposed to the idea.

In regard to setting interesting musical problems, possible ideas relate either to musical or extra-musical sources. Extra-musical sources may be: movement, drama, graphic design, or text (poetry). Musical ideas are nearly limitless and include all compositional devices appropriate to the pupil's level of musical knowledge. A variety of excellent books (see Paynter, Shaeffer, Biasini, Self) can be consulted for specific ideas.

When a teacher wants to give constructive feedback, the essential principle is to describe, rather than evaluate, what was heard. A " very nice, thank you" response is meaningless. Worse, it may transmit to the pupil the feeling of polite indifference. But if the teacher describes to the pupil what she heard, this shows that she listened with concentration. This also helps the student understand what he had, most likely intuitively, created.

After describing in detail what was heard, it is appropriate (and necessary) to express personal opinions, e.g.: " You really grabbed my attention with that surprising change in rhythm in the maracas." Or:" I expected to hear that lovely melody from the beginning again. When you have such interesting material, the listener would usually like to hear it again. Did you have a particular reason for not returning to it again?" or " There were so many different ideas in your piece, I found it difficult to follow it. I would have preferred to hear fewer ideas and would have liked to hear some of the ideas developed."

Peer teaching

Having reviewed our tasks and our options, we are ready to start putting into practice what we have learned.

The first attempt involved the whole class, as in the vignette described above.

Next we move to group work:

The class is divided into small groups. In each group there is a pupil, a teacher, and several "researchers" conducting observational studies on what is going on between the teacher and the pupil.

One group gets the grand piano; other groups get interesting percussion instruments from the percussion room at the Academy.

At the end of the session, all are asked to evaluate, step by step, what was helpful, what was not, and what, if anything, was destructive. When we meet again as a class, we will listen to the reaction of all participants; first the observers, then the teacher, and last and most important, the pupil.

In this way students learn from their own shortcomings, and those of their fellow students; they learn by being on the receiving end of teaching which is often not very sensitive. As a consequence, intensive, self-critical reflection and analysis gradually help students gain the skill of being supportive and sensitive to what is happening to the pupil.

We begin evaluating what happened in each groups' session. It seems that, despite all the summaries of mistakes to be avoided, in most groups **the teacher still found it very difficult not to impose her own aesthetics, her values on the pupil.**

In this group, only one teacher really functioned in a sensitive way throughout most of the session:

Her pupil was very slow in making discoveries. Eventually the "teacher" suggested that they do a musical conversation; she modeled all sorts of interesting ideas to her pupil who picked up on many of the ideas. Interestingly, neither the pupil nor the observers had any criticism of this teacher, only she herself did: "Having gotten her going, at some point I should have stopped and let her play alone again. I gave her good ideas, but I also created the impression that she could only create if I was at her side."

One "teacher" concluded that the safest thing is to do nothing. The pupil challenged her by asking whether she did not think there is a middle ground between dominating and abandoning one's pupil.

"At times I was getting bored and there were times when I was really frustrated and you did nothing". The pupil complained. I was bored too", the teacher confided/"Well, you had no business being bored. You were supposed to concentrate on finding a way to get me excited about playing again."

One teacher functioned very well most of the time but then suddenly interrupted the pupil's improvisation. It took them a long time to get back on track, but they succeeded in restoring the pleasant and purposeful work relationship they had established earlier.

One group ran into serious difficulties. The teacher was constantly interfering with the pupil's exploration.

At one point the pupil played a short melody on the piano strings. The teacher asked him to figure out a way to mark the strings so he could repeat the melody.

The "teacher" and the "observers" got into a heated discussion: would it be better to suggest a way to mark the strings and let him get on with the improvisation, or should he be left to discover ways of marking the strings? I asked if the pupil wanted to remember the tune?

The pupil is bursting to have a turn to say his piece, but it is too early for that.

The "teacher" and the "observers" are surprised by the question. It had not occurred to them that he might not be interested in their suggestions. The "teacher" blurts out:" after all this aimless exploration he finally played a real tune. How could he not be interested in preserving this?"

D, the pupil finally gets his turn to speak. "Please don't take this personally, but what you just said explains and justifies my feelings of anger. I was irritated with you for going on and on about how I could remember the little tune. It came out accidentally and had no particular significance to me. I did not care about the specific pitches. I was delighted with what I was discovering and I was working in a very con-centrated fashion to learn to control the sounds I liked.

I thought it was ridiculous for me to feel angry at you, after all you were trying to help, but now I understand that my anger was justified: you were saying in affect that what I was doing , with such intensity and pleasure, was in fact nonsense, only the silly little tune mattered."

The "teacher" asks: "So what should I have done?" D an-swers her:"You could have asked me if I wanted to repeat the tune and if I needed help figuring out ways to locate exact pitches. It would have been nice if you would have been a little more enthusiastic when I discovered an amaz-ing new sound."

We discussed again the daunting problem of how to refrain from imposing our personal agenda on the pupil.

Someone remarks: "It feels like a Zen challenge: to be all there for the pupil but erase your personal will, want noth-ing for yourself only what the pupil wants."

We discuss how many ways there are to discredit, invalidate a pupil's effort. While no teacher, I hope, would verbally declare pupils' work meaningless, there are many other, seemingly harmless, ways to do this (like helping someone remember a tune he does not care about or asking him to leave low strings alone and go on to playing on the high strings).

D, who has been teaching for many years, wonders out loud:" I shudder to think how many times I have done ex-actly the same thing to children."

We discuss the **effect of the various non-helpful interven-tions on children**: some might give up on creative work, others might declare the teacher "mean" or "dumb." Some might throw a temper tantrum while others might con-clude that the teacher's comments are irrelevant and the best thing to do is to ignore it.

We discuss the difficult task of trying to intuit what the pupil needs. A lot of sensitivity, good observational skills are a must; a bit of humility helps too. Don't be afraid to ask the pupil, no matter how young, after you make a suggestion: "I don't know if this is helpful to you; if not, skip it."

To end the lesson, the "pupils" from each group are asked to improvise together. It is essential to end their explorations with some music making.

The percussion instruments are arranged around the piano.

Since D has discovered an amazing sound inside the piano. I ask him to start off the group improvisation with this sound. After that they are on their own. I turn off the light to make them less self-conscious and the improvisation begins.

At first all the players continue their explorations hardly listening to each other. Then slowly they begin to listen, to play together. Ideas get thrown back and forth, climaxes built together. Gradually, and wordlessly A takes over. She begins to conduct the others, motions to them to change, to repeat; then gradually begins to play on their instruments in addition to her own. The others accept her control easily. Several times the piece moves towards what feels like closure, but each time one of the players introduces just then a new idea and the piece keeps going. This goes on for more than fifteen minutes, when someone says in a loud stage whisper: " Soon we will have to go to our next lecture." This brings the players out of their trance and they conclude the piece.

I ask each "teacher" to say something to their respective pupils about their part in the improvisation. Most find it difficult to say anything. D's teacher says she was shocked by the way A " took over" and dominated. She could not understand why D let her do it. D responds that it was the most natural thing to do- it felt wonderful to grasp what A wanted and play along with her. A's teacher is also shocked: She says she could not recognize nice, quiet A in this controlling role. I ask the students to recall personality traits characteristic of people during a creative act. Wasn't her behavior really a textbook demonstration of some of the traits we read about?

I also ask if someone could describe the music we heard. **It transpires that most of the "teachers" were not really listening.** Under such circumstances it is not surprising that they threw themselves into discussions about peripheral matters- like who controlled whom. I ask the "teachers" to describe what were they focusing on during the improvisation? They said they wondered how long the improvisation was going to go on; how will the players figure out how to end it; how did they manage to get completely wrapped up in what they were doing and be obviously oblivious of the " audience".

I asked the" teachers" to reflect on why they were not really listening to the music. Were they bored? Not used to concentrated listening to a piece on first hearing or did it simply not occur to them that when their pupils play they ought to listen?

In this particular group only the "teacher" who functioned so well during the group session actually listened to her pupil. She described how she heard her use some of the patterns she discovered during their session together; she said she was impressed to hear how the pupil developed these ideas further during the improvisation, and gave a demonstration, on the pupil's instrument, of what she meant.

Concentrated listening with a view towards descriptive feed back at the end of the improvisation is another habit that has to be cultivated . Students gradually acquire the tools for concentrated listening that enables them to make meaningful, factual remarks at the end of an improvisation.

These are skills that are slowly and painstakingly acquired. The exercises described here are repeated a number of times. It is not enough to understand intellectually what the challenge is or how one needs to proceed. New habits of interaction with pupils have to be slowly, painstakingly acquired.

Two weeks after Y made H so angry that she wanted to punch her in the face. H is given the role of "teacher." Her "pupil" is the student who had dealt with D's explorations in such an insensitive manner. The pupil is blissfully exploring, playing fast tremolo sounds.

232

As I walk by, I hear H saying" Music is not only fast sounds, you know. I would like you to now try some slow deliberate sounds."

"The pupil looks hurt. "I am just beginning to get the hang of these sounds, which are really neat so why do I have to do something different?"

I ask H if she remembers how she felt when Y told her to move on to the high strings?

She does indeed remember. It takes her a few seconds to understand why I brought this up. Then she bursts into laughter." Oh no! I just made the same mistake, didn't I."

Student teaching: a series of one-on-one meetings to promote creative growth of the pupil

The next stage of the course is to begin **working with a real pupil**. Each student meets with his pupil four times. The objective of these meetings is to help the pupil discover and develop his creative potential to the maximum possible level. Students may choose anyone as their pupil. Many choose their children or spouses or private instrumental students (not instead of the lesson but in addition).

Each meeting is tape recorded. The student is asked to evaluate his interventions after each meeting and to plan out in general terms the strategies for the next meeting. After the four meetings, he summarizes and evaluates the entire set of interactions.

Tape recordings of sessions are brought to class and we problem solve together:

How do I get my pupil to loosen up? How do I get him to be more focused?

We figure out together appropriate frameworks for creating pieces for various pupils.

Sometimes students come to class in a panic: "I need help, I have no idea how to go on." Students discover, to their and

my relief, that though they might feel helpless about planning their next session, they are able to give excellent advice
to a class mate. Students discover that something that was
terribly wrong for their pupil is exactly right for someone
else's pupil. We listen to musical conversations and give the
student feedback on it: often there is a tendency to dazzle
the pupil with the teacher's technical proficiency; the student than might be puzzled as to why his pupil gave up after
the teacher has swooped up and down the piano at a dizzy-
ing speed.: "What were you trying to model for your
pupil?" is the obvious question, yet apparently it was not
obvious to the teacher, who at the time was trying to im-
press his pupil. At the other extreme, students simply mim-
ic their pupil without enriching them, thus missing the
whole purpose of the musical conversation.

It also turns out that it is often easier to get excited about
someone else's pupil's piece than about of piece by your
own pupil. This enthusiasm of his classmates often helps
the student to see his pupil in a much more favorable light.

The problem of not imposing the teacher's aesthetic preferences comes up again and again. It can't be helped, it just
happens every year that teachers who were hoping to discover another John Cage end up with a pupil whose fondest
wish is to make up a simple folksong with tonic dominant
chords, while the student who hates contemporary music
gets the pupil who wants to use tone clusters, etc.

By the end of the fourth session, most students decide to
carry on with creative work at the request of the pupil.
Most students continue from this project onwards to include creative work in their instrumental teaching. With
parents and their children such creativity often becomes an
ongoing form of interaction.

Experiences in improvisation and composition

Concurrently with solving these problems, we work on im-
proving specific skills such as musical conversations and
giving feedback to pupils on their improvisation. We continue with class improvisations. After pupils feel more relaxed
and open with improvising on percussion instruments and
inside the piano, we gradually move to improvising on the

students' own major instruments. We also carry out projects described in various books, e.g. Paynter's Sound and Silence and Sound and Structure, Murray Schafer's books, etc.

Planning of curriculum for improvisation/composition

Finally we discuss ways of implementing creative work in the school setting.

First we must distinguish between creative work as an end in itself versus creative work as a means for teaching some skill or concept. Both are important and valid parts of the curriculum. Creative work as a pedagogic tool for teaching concepts and practicing skills is much more commonly found in the curriculum than are opportunities for creative work as an end in it self.

Creative work as an end in its self requires individualized or small group settings. This can be realized in the framework of a music center, workstations or classroom situations where students work on individual projects. The teacher's input is, of necessity, less intense than what is possible in a one-to-one setting. Nevertheless, what was learned through the work with one pupil is equally applicable to the school setting.

Groups of children can explore alone or in small groups, with the teacher offering help as he/she interacts with different children, each in his/her turn, as well as through "work cards." Work cards for "Exploration of Instruments," "Mastery," "Getting started" (generating short musical gestures), "Ideas for Pieces" (divided into musical and extra-musical sections) can fill in for or complement the actual interaction with the teacher. Students learn to create such work cards, based on their experience of creative work with one pupil. Work cards are tried out on children, and improved in response to shortcomings that were discovered during such trials.

Many students get a chance to do a semester project of teaching music through improvisation as the primary activity. Skill training (ear training exercises in some parameter, such as rhythm, melody, harmony, and formal structure) precedes free improvisations. Compositional devices are presented, practiced, and identified in listening to musical works which serve as models exemplifying various compositional devices studied.

Students are then free to pursue their own creative projects. Whether they wish to incorporate new elements learned or not is their choice. What we often find is that new ideas of compositional devices show up in children's work several weeks after they have been presented with an idea. This is not surprising: a period of incubation during which new ideas become internalized, incorporated into the pupil's musical thinking, is natural.

The course presented above has indicated how student teachers can be helped to foster creativity and overcome common problems in this area. With ample opportunity to practice the skills described the task can be accomplished.

References

Biasini, A., Thomas, R., & Pogonowski, L. (1971) *MMCP Interaction* (2nd ed.), Bardonia, N.Y., Media Materials

Csikszentmihalyi, M. (1988) "Society, Culture, and Person: A System View of Creativity" in R. Sternberg, ed., *The Nature of Creativity*, New York, Cambridge University Press

Ghiselin B., (ed.)(1952) *The Creative Process.* Cambridge, Cambridge University Press

Hargreaves, David J. (1986) *The Developmental Psychology of Music,*Cambridge , Cambridge University Press

Paynter, John and Aston, Peter (1970) *Sound and Silence: Classroom Projects in Creative Music,* Cambridge, Cambridge University Press

Paynter, John (1992) *Sound and Structure,* Cambridge, Cambridge University Press

Schafer, R. Murray (1976) *Creative Music Education: A Handbook for the Modern Music Teacher,* New York, Schirmer Books, Macmillan Publishing

Self, George,(1968) *New Sounds in the Class,* London: Universal Edition

Sloboda, J. A. (1985). *The Musical Mind; the Cognitive Psychology of Music*,Oxford, Oxford University Press

Sudnov,David (1979) *Talk's Body*, New York, Alfred A. Knopf191919

Torrance, E. Paul (1963) *Education and the Creative Potential,* Minneapolis ,University of Minnesota Press

Vaughan, M.(1977) Musical Creativity: Its Cultivation and Measurement. *Bulletin of the Council for Research in Music Education* 50,72-77

A Creative Postlude

Peter Wiegold   *Thus Far, No Further...?*
Formal Learning-
Creative Learning

Chapter 17

Thus Far, No Further...?
Formal Learning-Creative Learning

Peter Wiegold

PETER WIEGOLD a composer, teaches in the Skills Department of the Guildhall School of Music and Drama in Great Britain. He is the creator of *Changing Arts Practices*, a program designed for professional musicians to develop a new way of thinking about creating and performing. He has presented CAP workshops regularly in Canada, often for "Orchestras Canada' and recently also in Italy, Spain, Norway, Finland, Holland, Belgium, Austria, Japan and Australia.

Since the 1960's there has been an ongoing debate about the teaching of English. The explosive ideas of that decade opened new doors and, especially, encouraged an emphasis on personal choice and imagination, and questioned received wisdom.

It was proposed that English be learnt experientially, and discovered or even invented according to need and interest. This was, and still is, sharply opposed by traditionalists who maintain that the only method of learning is that rules must be taught and practised - correct grammar, spelling and so on.

The two sides have fought vociferously, and each maintained that the other was the cause of failing students, poor achievement (and loss of moral value in society). One is child-centred, the other is authority-centred.

Yet, it would seem common sense that both approaches to learning are useful and important.

A synthesis of the formal and the imaginative, the received and the invented, will surely produce the strongest performer in any subject. This synthesis may well involve a struggle, but that very tension will help forge greater ability and confidence.

Let us take a moment and note the potential downsides of each of the opposing approaches. The traditional formal method of teaching provides clear materials and methods, but tends to exclude rather than include. By definition, failure is common, because wrong is wrong, instead of some kind of discovery.

It creates hierarchies of achievement, and underlines power and control, the reaction to which encourages rebels, who use the rejection of the "the system" as their fuel. Rebellion might not always be bad, but it can be a waste of energy.

Above all, formal teaching can lead to a sense of alienation, of being outside what is real and important, rather than feeling oneself a constructive part inside. And it can take away one of the most natural ways of learning - *messing about until a solution or invention is found.*

Despite its apparent affirmative and delightful qualities, the creative approach is not without problems. A typical down-side is the isolation of individual discovery. A discovery can be genuinely magical - but sometimes so magical it is im-possible to repeat. If it is individual and idiosyncratic, it can be hard to relate to the work of others. This can prevent students locking in to a constructive growth with common bench marks, and shared discovery. Individually conceived creative work can lack long term form and development that embraces contrasted, even contradictory, strands.

And, except in the most motivated of individuals, it can lack the form or the drive to suffer the dull, repetitive, numbing aspects of learning that in many circumstances are necessary fuel for technique or literacy.

There can even be a kind of tyranny of possession. A defen-sive possessiveness that conveniently prevents dialogue with others or the teacher (or the world).

While self-teaching can be rewarding and valuable, none of us see outside of ourselves very easily. Mentors, and real teachers who dare to trip us up and turn us over, shattering our self-delusions are vital. Someone who has the commitment and passion to say "stay with it," over and over again, rather than allowing us off the hook.

Music is both simple and spontaneous, and a very rich complex and exacting art. One of the constant struggles, (and joys), of music-making is the attempt to embrace the most technical and formal along with the natural and spontaneous. There are, for example, few things human beings attempt as challenging in both precision and motivation as playing the violin.

All music requires rigour of rhythm and tuning. A composer, even if not a performer, understands and works with these rigours. Even something as direct in purpose as "being in tune" has profound technical, emotional and spiritual challenges.

It is important, then, that music education, at all levels, embraces these extremes. The need for precise repetition, and the need for spontaneous choice. The need for a good degree of literacy in an increasingly plural world, with the need to discover a sound that is all your own.

There are many approaches to this challenge, a challenge that is at the heart of all learning. And many of them will be pragmatic - right for a particular person at a particular time. But I would like to suggest a simple model. And give some examples.

First of all a thought about musical language.

An Elemental Approach

Most musical languages are complex, and many very highly refined, like classical harmony for example, or Indian classical music.

It can be helpful and clarifying, then, to step back and look at musical language in an "elemental" way. Take a look at key aspects, in their most elemental form, then return to see how they apply, and differ, in sophisticated forms.

An element might be drone . A constant, stable pitch, or pitches, around which other pitches move. This will be found most obviously in music such as Scottish bagpipe music, Indian classical music and much folk music. Then one extends the concept to pedal points in Bach, pedal points in Miles Davis, or still, cycling pitches in contemporary composer Luciano Berio's beautiful "O King."

So, begin with an essential, simple definition, then look at very different examples and applications of it.

Another core element is pulse. While it is a universal aspect of music is function varies enormously: consider for example African drumming, Steve Reich, Bach's motor rhythms, Stravinsky, a Strauss Waltz.

But pulse can also be very simple. Just a pulse on a pair of claves.

If you ask a group of individuals to play, in turn, a simple pulse, each will be very different. Each will have a tempo, a sound, a feeling.

Some will sound alert, some dull. Some magical, embracing, others challenging, provocative. Each will have an implication, a suggestion of where it wants to go. There is something to discover within the pulse.

Played well, even something this simple will have a music. Of that time, of that place. And when that is felt and present, a dialogue begins - between the music of that pulse in that room, and the music of Bach, or the music of the latest club sounds.

Having worked simply with pulse, a second level might be accentuation , just accentuation, free of metre. What patterns are interesting in what way? (Remember the accentuation patterns in "The Augers of Spring" in the *Rite of the Spring*)

Or, explore regular accentuation - 2 x 4 or 3+3+2.

I once spent a whole term with a particular University class on punctuation. Looking at it in Korean music, in classical music, in Stravinsky, in the way that music can punctuate theatre.

Thinking elementally allows you to look for an essence, and then look through a simple keyhole at complexes. Look at

Stravinsky only in terms of "pulse." Then start to make connections. What kind of harmony does this approach to pulse naturally go with, what kind of instrumentation, what kind of form?

A Basic Ground

Here is suggestion of a basic ground of learning: Take a simple element, understand it fully. Place it in a simple form. Do it well . Begin to invent with it, or recolour it, within the form. Relate this learning to more sophisticated examples of the same thing. Return to the essence, expand on it, with another level of concept and with expanded materials, then repeat the learning cycle.

There is a "formal" progress then, an increasing awareness of form and function of pulse, at each turn discovering something afresh, partly through experiment, partly through key levels added by the teacher.

To do things well at all times is absolutely vital. To play that first pulse with complete commitment, complete feeling. So that at each stage of learning things are real and felt, not just concepts. When something is real and experienced, critical questions will naturally arise - was it too long, too forceful, unfocussed, incomplete? What does it call for next?

As this spiral-like process develops It is important to build in stages of completeness, a piece, a performance that brings a moment of wholeness and finality.

An Example Learning Process

This is a typical sequence from the post-graduate "Performance and Communication Skills" course I used to run at the Guildhall School of Music and Drama in London. It mixes skill learning, creative learning with the development of group awareness

The "element" was "cross-rhythm" and we were working on this cross rhythm in 5's.

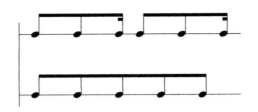

Eighteen students were lined up on two sides of nine drums, with me sitting at head. (How you set out a space is very important - this example has an element of theatre to it)

First preparation, learning to feel the weight and colour of the drums. A steady pulse was played together, aiming at playing easily with a good sound.

Straight away focussing challenges were introduced - get a different sound, edgy/soft, fast slow. Start to flex the ears, and muscles. Play hard, light, warm, cold. Always play well.

Then the given rhythm was learnt, initially by one side playing the top part and the other the bottom. Eventually everybody played both parts. Perhaps a set number of times, 1,2 3... always stopping positively together.

All alternate just top and just bottom, then the sides alternate just top just bottom between them. Keep shifting the challenge. Back to everyone playing both parts - alternate one person doing it alone with whole group. Cue just before this happens so the students have to stay alert. Then they begin to cue one another.

Now everybody plays both parts, reversing which hand plays upper and which lower parts, changing every 4 bars then every 2, then every one. (People always find one way round easier)

Play rhythm three times, rest for one time. Fill the rest with improvised solos, around the group or alternating two players. Gradually increase speed, keep them on edge. Sometimes break regularity of solos by allowing someone to solo openly for a few cycles.

A second improviser might join the first right at the end of their solo adding a short lead up to the return of the whole.

Invent a new closing cadential rhythm for everyone to be played on (visual or aural) cue. Allow"free" new parts to be invented as complementary secondary parts. Vary length of empty bar.

These are, of course, just the beginning of countless variations and extensions. A 5 might become a 7. A 1-bar solo, a 16 bar solo. The central point is that the rhythm has now been learnt technically, explored in several aspects and each person has had the focus on them, to lead or add their own contribution.

The important thing, I feel, throughout the entire process is to *keep a strong yoke!* Keep bringing new challenges that work the fine balance of responding to their responses while maintaining a bigger purpose.

Which could be, over the term, to cover 3's, 5's and 7's , relate the patterns to instruments as well as drums, look at repertoire, and then include something in a performance.

Exploring Triads

Two examples of music where triads are central are Bach chorales, and recent pop music. So, the element is the triad. First hear them, boldly, plainly, for themselves. Try them in major and minor form. Stretch the ears right from the beginning - are they different if placed right at top or bottom of piano?

Repeat a single triad in a simple pulse or arpeggiation, and change to another (Not necessarily conventionally related). Discuss the effect of different changes. Each person finds a favourite pair. me of these will be conventional, some surprising.

The purpose of this kind of process is to create a sense of permission. That it is OK for things to be familiar - and it is OK for them to be unique. new. This is an inclusive process - everything is usable, everything is workable. C major to G major is strong and familiar, Eb minor to A major is fascinating and might be extraordinary and just right at a certain time.

It is important to to break habitual patterns. To acknowledge convention while also allowing a fresh approach to it.
Isn't it fascinating how Bach does this, how Stravinsky does
that, pop does that?

The key is always keep the technical focus, the technical
understanding, absolutely clear . A triad is this. You are
working with this.

(You can see the wood for the trees!)

The next step might be to create a triad sequence with no
rhythm or articulation, just pure chords. Or make 4-bar cycles with a simple given template:

Having composed this, then begin to think about articulation - repetition, arpeggio,"vamping," perhaps separately
think about bass-line. When does it go with the given,
when against? This might be worked out on paper, or
practically. Alone or in a group. A directed group or a cooperative group.

What one is trying to achieve is to bring fresh individual
feeling and hearing to a key musical element. Templates are
given, but then they are interpreted openly and idiosyncrat-
ically , rather than imitating a specific style.

Templates create common grounds, common frame, demonstrate a typical kind of shaping but allow completely different colouring - faster slower, richer, thinner, odd,
straight. And then very useful comparisons.

Invite students to write new templates, share them around
- perhaps get them to write them especially for another
person - or conversely put them all in a hat, and allow
chance to decide who gets what.

Keep hold of the rope! Just when things are getting safe and predictable move to 5/4, or a 5 bar structure. or introduce a pause at a key point....

Keep moving the goal posts! Keep the students stretched and reaching beyond - beyond their technical abilities beyond their creative habits.

Have in mind always an evolving long-term structure.

Inversions, 2-note chords, 4 note chords, 11 note chords........

When does the concept of "chord" break down?

Encourage lateral thinking - what if instead of end to end you superimpose triads - what does Bb maj sound like over C maj or C min over F min?

The Middle Way

I hope it is clear overall that I am advocating a process that is placed somewhere between free creative work, and formal exercise. This is an approach which allows key, simple things to be common, while others can be entirely personal. The common draws in crucial debate and comparison and grounded development. The person allows flexibility for true response to the situation and the student.

Critical Form

I have written about an evolving process. The processes above work more in a spiral form rather than a straight line. Keep returning to, and remembering, the essence, but each time round go deeper.

It might be useful to also write a little about long-term form within a composition, something every composer struggles with. Because, while it is relatively easy to write something short, it can be very hard to make a piece of music coherent over 15 or 20 minutes. When do you hold, when move forward, when turn everything upside down?

Every piece of material has a size, a shape, a weight, a colour, proportions. A melody has a range, harmony an average density of notes, a rhythm a number of components and so on.

These in any particular piece will have "natural" dimensions. There might be a 4 note melody in a particular folk song, chords made from 3 or 4 notes in Bach, the total chromatic in Schoenberg, between 3 -6 durations in a typical "clave" rhythm in Latin music.

When beginning the journey with the key materials, three formal concepts might be kept in mind: establishment, consistency and critical change.

The first concept is quite straightforward, the need to state essential key ideas near the beginning. To create a sense of place, character, pace and timing.

Consistency is the need to respect and stay close to these essential ideas. Pieces lose their power and concentration if they make what seem to be random or frivolous changes.

But then, when does something in the music become critical? When after a period with only 4 pitches do they call for a fifth? In that one moment where Bach has a 5 note chord, what precedes and follows this?

At what point do tone clusters pounding at the bottom of the piano, quite naturally transform to quiet sounds at the very top?

All ideas need to be "tested," almost on a scientific bench, pushed, pulled, stretched , compressed, heated, cooled, fragmented, melded, pushed to their limits, then at a certain point they will want to change substance. Just as at a certain point boiling water will leave the pot and become steam.

This is not to suggest every piece needs to head towards a big climax. But virtually all music (consider Indian classical sitar music, African drumming or modernist Stockhausen) has power from sustained working of its material, concentrated commitment to every last piece of potential in it. And then critical moments of change or transformation.

Critical change has a thousand forms. Sometimes just

stretching the melody by one note, sometimes doing something slightly different at the end of 4 bars to bring back the repetition of the first, sometimes a point of no return, a real transition. The change may represent a return, a transition to another level, a complete transcendence, or simply an end.

But the maintenance of the tension between working material within a frame, then expanding or breaking that frame at a critical point is one of the most important aspects of long (and short) term form.

Music that is "all things to all people" will not be interesting.

Music that sustains its character with pride, while also testing itself to the limits, will be invigorating and rewarding.

Happy Composing!